AF576955

TROUPING

RY GOODS

TROUPING

HOW THE SHOW CAME TO TOWN

By PHILIP C. LEWIS

HARPER & ROW, PUBLISHERS
New York
Evanston
San Francisco
London

Picture credits:

Nebraska State Historical Society: title page and 113.

The Walter Hampden Memorial Library at The Players: pages 58, 129, 138.

Museum of the City of New York: pages xii, 59, 175, 184.

The Theatre Collection of the New York Public Library: pages 36, 41, 46, 47, 88, 96, 97, 101, 161, 170, 171, 189, 199, 200, 201.

Grateful acknowledgment is hereby made for permission to reprint excerpts from the following: *The Cowells in America* by M. W. Disher, published by Oxford University Press. *America's Music* by Gilbert Chase. Copyright © 1955 by Gilbert Chase. Used with permission of McGraw-Hill Book Company. *Prince of Players* by Eleanor Ruggles, reprinted by permission of W. W. Norton & Company, Inc.

 For information address Harper & Row, Publishers, Inc., 10 East 53rd Street, New York, N.Y. 10022. Published simultaneously in Canada by Fitzhenry & Whiteside Limited, Toronto.

FIRST EDITION

Designed by Sidney Feinberg

Library of Congress Cataloging in Publication Data
Lewis, Philip C.
Trouping; how the show came to town.
1. Performing arts—United States—History.
I. Title.
PN1582.U6L4 790.2'0973 73-4103
ISBN 0-06-012602-7

For

ELISABETH,

who came in

from the road

Contents

Illustrations

TROUPING

DUSTIN FARNUM in *The Virginian*. Holyoke, Massachusetts, was thrilled.

☛ 1

Tonight: All's Well

It was to be some time—years, in fact—before actors and actresses became as ordinary as people, so the company gathering in Grand Central Station had attention. In a time when the majority rarely went anywhere, a railroad platform made a dramatic stage for the players. It reminded the locals that part of the romance of the theatre business was traveling from hither to yon, to so many yons and so fast the actors were often not sure whether tonight's stand was in Ohio, Indiana or Tennessee.

They were unique, they looked it, and they enjoyed it, and this is why the common people were turning to stare. They were struck by the worldly look of the men actors and impressed by the fashionable appearance of the women. The flair of the ladies' voluminously feminine clothes, the grace of their gestures, and the enhanced blush of cheek proclaimed them to be from the stage, and this September morning in New York's main depot, the players were enjoying their effect as they would when they repeated this performance in Terre Haute, Denver, Sacramento and Savannah.

For the women it was a pleasure that lifted their bosoms as it confirmed that they and their professional sisters were the most interesting and attractive females of the day. Although the society women tried to compete and sometimes shared the newspapers, the actresses had the advantage, for their images were tacked to fences, pasted on walls and hung in windows. Not that the society women could really compare—most of them had the shape of Grover Cleveland and wore their raiment like squaws in fresh blankets.

The leading lady, aware, peripherally, that the women in the crowd were observing the details of her outfit, cleverly moved to let them see. She was especially pleased with her present regalia for it had been described in Theatre Magazine:

> The handsome coat is of pale mauve cloth, handsomely trimmed with castro. The coat is sleeveless, having a cape à la militaire with a jabot of Irish point lace laid in pleats for a depth of some six inches and flaring flouncelike to the waist. The skirt of the coat is finished with a heavy band of the castro about twelve inches in depth.

Now a younger woman, the ingenue, arrived and was complimented on her "Syrian scarf, quite the style this season." After which, all dutifully admired the character woman's hat, a sort of vivid idealization of an eagle's nest, although only a velvet canary was spread on the upturned brim.

The men of the company looked smart, too, with their high pinched-collars attached to white shirts, their watch-chained vests and bare faces (the fashion for beards was passing), but they were drab compared to such feminine details as "moire astrakhan with edging of ermine . . . cut like a kimono jacket . . . lined with exquisite Chinese embroidery . . . and fastened with military frogs." The men could only play support as the spectators gawked at the show-women. The watching females might be noting gores and gussets, but the male appraisal was confined to the manner in which the tight-waisted corset, currently de rigueur, gave to each of the women the effect of a tipped pelvis, putting her tail jauntily up and remindful of a receptive filly. Of course it was said the old notion that actresses were "loose" was unfounded and foolish; still the ogling males were enjoying the illusion of smelling smoke.

The distinction, the difference, that impressed the observers most was the manner of the company, men and women both, their carefree air. They smiled so easily, the sexes conversed so equally, they looked so full of assurance. It was this show of cheerfulness, this apparent lack of concern about some stormy day, this apparent confidence in perpetual prosperity, that provoked the silent applause of the crowd. As Americans, the onlookers believed, wanted to believe, that now was the time for all good men to have faith in the wealth of the country, and they liked the way the actors let themselves dress so smartly and were taking their share of the American reward. The people watching knew that the actors, too, had once been poor, and it was fine the way they were showing how to enjoy the triumph and success of democracy—which is to say, the U.S.A.

Now the players brightened even more as they saw the last of their company approaching, and the onlookers turned to see, striding through the station, a man of imposing physique, with a godlike head, handsome enough to please a sculptor of outsize men. That is if they were American, for the man coming toward them had that tall wholesome masculinity, that clean, healthy and virtuous sandy look, which all German- Hungarian- Polish- Irish- Greek- Italian- Chinese- and Litvak-Americans recognized as so typically American.

A man in the audience exclaimed, "Say! you know who that is? That's Dustin Farnum! I saw his show—The Virginian. He's the star, Dustin Farnum, that's him! He looks just like he does in the show!"

Now they watched as the company greeted its leader with pleasant laughter, congratulating him for being right on time for the conductor was opening the gate, and with the savoir-faire (a popular new expression) of seasoned travelers, still chatting, amusing one another, the troupers made their exit and passed from view toward their car in the train.

Their confident good cheer was real. Along with 310 other troupes leaving New York that September, they were anticipating audiences waiting eagerly from Portland to Portland and from Phoenix to Key West. There would be night after night of affectionate applause, often cheers, and there would be at *least* thirty-eight weeks of salary—*minus blizzards. Never had things been so good for the actors as now in this perfect American year—1905.*

THERE had never been a year so good for *all* Americans, with the exception, perhaps, of the farmers. But theirs had been a doleful occupation since the first man tried to manage nature, so there was no urge to lament their condition when everything else looked so bright. The nation's young President, Roosevelt, affectionately called "Teddy," with his ebullience, his bellows of *Bully!*, his inexhaustible confidence, embodied the spirit of the day. And, incidentally, there was a young actor now playing small parts in New York and about to bounce to stardom who would match Roosevelt's energy and his ingratiating, flashing smile. Douglas Fairbanks would also represent this hyperthyroid era.

The United States of America was optimistic and everybody could explain why. And did. Claiming how you could now expect *any*thing from this people who had conquered a continent of wilderness, plains and mountains, and had tied the whole thing down with railroads. It was *only the start!* Could anyone doubt but what there'd soon be a train stopping at every place in the land with a letter to mail? And speaking of that, they also liked to remind one another of how folks—the privileged ones—were now shouting over a wire from New York clear to Chicago and hearing crackling voices in response! Could there be any question about the telephone's going on to Frisco? Give it time!

Everything seemed just about perfectly perfected. If you counted Deere's plow, McCormick's reaper and Edison's electric lights, you could about say that every essential invention had been made. Thus it was only a matter of improvements and extension. So they were positive, because of plain logic, that even better times must come, especially now that the country was secure and didn't have to fear *any*body outside!

For, as they also liked to say, especially on the Fourth, it was a great triumphant distance from the insignificant nation fearfully holding to life along the Atlantic shore to this present forty-five-state country reaching to the Pacific. Back then, when it began, you might succeed in throwing off history's greatest empire, but who knew if you could make it stick? Now, through the history books at school, young Americans were reminded also of those suspenseful days of 1812 and then the Civil War. Those years were tense, the students learned, because of the fear that hated Britain or deceitful France or both might take advantage and end the dream. But no need to worry now—there wasn't a nation that wouldn't hesitate before trying to annoy Uncle Sam today! Not after the world had seen the quick one-two way America had disposed of the latest threat. Ask Spain about that!

This was the United States, 1905: confident, cocky and full of applause for what had happened and how. They recognized the cues, they had had intensive training in the heroics of melodrama and they knew a good line when they heard it, and there never was a better one than that spoken by our hero, the calm, stage-center Admiral Dewey. It sounded like William Gillette in his imperturbable character of Sherlock Holmes:

ADMIRAL DEWEY: You may fire when ready, Gridley.
[*Offstage, the guns are heard. "Boo-o-o-o-o-o-mm!" Then cheers*]

CURTAIN

Now if anyone else wanted to try us, the country knew that "Teddy" himself would lead us up their hill, wherever it was. He could speak a good hero's line, too. At San Juan: "*If you're not going up, get out of the way, for I am!*"

Not only did the country feel sure of itself and just and tough and Christian—things everybody had to respect—it felt rich and getting richer—something everyone ought to admire. And every American could share the returns; all you needed to do was work! *Any*body! Look at Rockefeller and all those other poor boys: Russell Sage, Armour, Jay Cooke, Wanamaker, Carnegie, Marshall Field. The country had read, was reading, would read, 200 million copies of Horatio Alger—*Struggling Upward, Strive* *and Succeed* and similar—that gave the formula: be alert, respectful to power and *ambitious*, and you, too, can ascend. Now, looking about and seeing the great new well-fed middle class, Alger's lesson appeared to be confirmed, so who could say what's the limit?

The actors settling into their seats in the train accepted this faith in more-and-bigger without a thought. Anyone who had been in their business even ten years had seen new towns with new opera houses springing up along every new railroad, and that was proof enough for showfolks. All had listened to the character man (in every company) telling about the crudities of Omaha twenty years ago as experienced when playing there with Edwin Booth in *Hamlet* (if you listened to all who said they had played with Booth, you would think he always carried two hundred in support), and then the difference when they stopped at Omaha last season to give them *No Mother to Guide Her*. No comparison—now the hotel has hot and cold water in every room and a bath on every floor. Yes, if anyone had seen the country prosper, it was the troupers.

The newspapers gave evidence of this national well-being every day. You could read how the swells were living. They could afford parties almost as lavish as old Rome, without the unmentionable immorality. It was true that the bill for one ball staged by an insurance tycoon precipitated a bankruptcy wounding several thousand policyholders, but that was an exception; there were others who could pay the piper without strain on anybody, so people thought, and the dancing never stopped. More and more you could *see* the rich in their elegant equipages—some were even raising the dust in carriages without horses, called "horseless carriages."

It cheered the common heart to watch it; the common folks had no complaint for now almost every man, woman and child (except the "shiftless" poor) had a bicycle. They called it "the craze" and made jokes, sang about Daisy going to her wedding on a vehicle built for two—*and,* you were urged to remember, the point was this: these benefactions were because the American people had *worked* and earned God's smile. See how He had placed the incredible rich lode where Comstock was looking because Comstock *was looking!* See how He had helped Edison create because Edison *worked* for it, eighteen hours a day! See how the mills were expanding because the God-fearing owners had the energy never to be satisfied with the returns!

In the "opera houses" and the places where they were frankly called theatres, in Fall River, Massachusetts—Columbus, Ohio—Vallejo, California—Paris, Texas—Eufaula, Alabama—and the thousands of others between and beyond, the box offices were open. Except in homes that disapproved of diversion such as scratching yourself on Sunday, there was talk of the coming season. Even in the one-night towns, there could be as many as 228 different shows through the winter and it was difficult and exciting to decide which you wanted to see.

The very fact that you could see *any*—that the country had become free-minded enough to permit it and that people had the means to indulge—was more evidence of the luxurious advance in America. To many, the theatre symbolized the new release from drudgery, from the toil that formerly sent folks from work to bed to work. There was less need now of the stump-grubbing struggle to gain land, there were more machines in the mill to relieve human brawn, there were even shorter hours for the few but increasing number in the new unions. It made a mood for celebration and, in 1905, the theatre was the place—usually the only one.

So what would it be: the show they'd seen and loved before, now returning for the second or seventh or eleventh time? a big star in Shakespeare? a favorite comedian? a famous foreign luminary the whole world wanted to say they'd seen, like *Mme.* Bernhardt? or a good story of courage, honor and the thrilling defense of Fort Maidenhead? In Springfield (two nights), Holyoke (one), New Britain (one) and Hartford (two), where *The Virginian* would be week after this, customers were getting their tickets. "Direct from New York" was the clincher. Who could afford to miss it?

Now the train was slowing for New Rochelle, New York, the first stand on the tour. Glancing out the window to see if there was anything they might remember from times before, the actors were provoked to standard reminiscence.

"I played here with Joe Jefferson."

"I was here two seasons ago with *The Light That Lies in Woman's Eyes.*"

"With Harned? I played with her ten years ago at Palmer's."

Since the company knew the play forward and back (actually they had already played their first week out of New York—across the river in Brooklyn), the most important thing in New Rochelle was the tryout of their trunks. Actors knew there had to be order, system—they would be opening and shutting these trunks hundreds of times in the coming weeks with no time to hunt; everything must have a place and be there.

After New Rochelle had given them a refreshing start the train was arriving at Bridgeport.

"Did the conductor say this is Bridgeport? I was here season before last in *Business Is Business.*"

"I'll always remember Bridgeport because I was here with Barrett in *Macbeth* and he had a terrible cold, could hardly talk, and he said to me, 'If I don't feel any better by tonight, you're going to be Macbeth.' But he was a trouper, he got better."

It was an excellent audience in Bridgeport, sharp, appreciative, five curtains. Next day, as they were on their way to Waterbury, someone passed around a copy of the New York *Dramatic Mirror* in which Fred Niblo, "The American Comedian," had an ad saying, "Well, what do you think of that? In Chicago two days and not robbed yet." The whole company smiled. Ah, Chicago! But the folks out there were responsive when they liked you. And everyone told of their success in Chicago.

Until a lull and they noticed Mr. Farnum was reading a script. Something for next season? they wondered; anything in it for them? Not that any of them worried, there would be something somewhere. They were established in their profession and there had never been more demand. These days, the actor's life was good, steady and, except for that occasional longing to stop and briefly stay put like those people outside the window . . . But as anyone could tell you, "If that's the way you feel then you've got no business being in the business."

This *was* the business, touring. Shows were then produced in New York for one purpose, to play the land. The road was where the money was, New York was just another stand. A manager who had the product could be sure of his dates from the end of August to the end of May and, with a good title or a good star or, better, both, he only needed to worry about the integrity of the bank where he put his take.

It could be big business. Everyone talked about how one producer alone, Charles Frohman, had ten thousand employees and an annual payroll of $35 million. There was still room for others. Not only were there 311 shows beginning the season out of New York in 1905; there were Chicago producers, too. The latter offered some 100 to 200 cheaper attractions that, having a high content of the sensational, gave total satisfaction to a cheaper audience and were profitable at cheaper prices. In addition, there were certain stars in hits that didn't need to be produced anywhere; they existed and simply resumed season after season.

Since there were some three thousand theatres in America with over a thousand adequate for first-class touring productions, this large supply was needed. Sometimes theatre managers advertised for shows:

> FIRST CLASS HOUSE to open about April 25th, 1905. Good mining and pottery town. Monthly pay roll of $60,000. Pay days, 10th and 25th of each month. Crooksville, Ohio, is located on the C. & M. V. RR. 14 miles west of Zanesville, Ohio, 30 miles from Lancaster. Ohio. Wanted a *NO. 1 ATTRACTION TO OPEN HOUSE. Will guarantee or buy.* Also good attractions for balance of season 1905–1906. Write or wire CROOKSVILLE OPERA CO., CROOKSVILLE, OHIO. Drawing population 10,000.
>
> EMMETT E. BRANNAU, Mgr.
>
> Also on Z. & W. RR.

That was the business of the theatre manager, to get his house booked. If the house was attractive, meaning lucrative, he could choose from a vast menu of attractions for the producers were equally anxious to get good houses for their shows. (To the producers, the houses were best when they were in towns reasonably adjacent—Kalamazoo/Battle Creek—so profits would not be wasted on long jumps.) A producer could pick up *Julius Cahn's Official Theatrical Guide* and thumb through its 954 pages checking out the 1,746 theatres or stands listed therein. Each one gave its specifications:

> AMERICUS [Ga.]—Pop. 10,000. Glover's Opera House. Geo. H. Fields, Mgr. S.c., 800. Prices, 25¢ to $1. Illum., gas and elec. Chas. Lingo, stage carp. Width prosc. opening, 26 ft. Curtain line to footlights, 3 ft. Dist. bet. side walls, 56 ft. Bet. fly girders, 34 ft. Grooves from stage, 13 ft. Stage rigging to loft, 26 ft., 4 grooves. Depth under stage, 4 ft. 2 traps, front and back. C. Schneider, orches. leader. Orches., one pianist. Printing required, 7 stands, 20 3-sheets, 150 1-sheets. Dates read, Glover's Opera House.
> NEWSPAPERS—"Times Recorder," daily and Thurs.; "Herald," daily and Fri.
> RAILROADS—C. of Ga., J. M. Fagan. G. & A., E. B. Everette. Transfer Co., Steve Worten.
> PUBLISHER OF PROGRAM—R. E. Guerry.

[Interpretation:

S.c.: seating capacity.

A *groove* was a wooden channel to receive a sliding flat, especially in a wing setting.

Orches., one pianist: Presumably, anything the visiting show wanted for music beyond the house pianist must be brought or hired. But why wouldn't the show's orchestra have a pianist? And a conductor? A riddle.

Printing required means, send in advance the specified paper for posting. In other words, don't expect to play without advertising. A *stand* is a 24-sheet poster.

The newspapers' *daily and Thurs., daily and Fri.* perhaps meant, as Bernard Simon suggests, that special entertainment sections were printed on those days.]

The booker, depending on the type of show, had his choice of an eight-hundred-seat house like the one in Americus or larger, up to:

> BRIDGEPORT [Conn.]—Pop. 82,000. Smith's Theatre. S.c. 2,210, standing room for 900.

Thus the producer could work his way through *Cahn's Guide* and compile a route. Often those showmen with tawdry shows or wanting a margin of finance and reputation would book only a week or so in advance. They would be looking for "open dates" when a theatre lacked an attraction or had suffered a cancellation and might be amenable to a deal to avoid a dark house. This was called wildcatting, and since the phone was still not in general use (not a theatre in *Cahn's Guide*, 1905, gave a phone number), this kind of negotiation would have to be done by letter, telegram or an advance man scouring the land.

Practically every town or village was sure to have a theatre as *Cahn's* indicated. And most of these theatres wanted an attraction every night of the week, Monday–Saturday, in season, and the range could be from the best *Hamlet* of the time to such titles as *A Trip to Coontown* or *A Turkish Bath*. At a time when the national population was 76 million, here were the number of stands (places with one or more theatres) per state with representative towns indicated:

ALABAMA (including Talladega, Selma)—17
ARIZONA (Tombstone)—6
ARKANSAS (El Dorado)—15
CALIFORNIA (Needles, Eureka)—50
COLORADO (Cripple Creek, Greeley)—20
CONNECTICUT (Jewett City, Putnam)—29
DELAWARE—2
FLORIDA (Apalachicola, Key West—but no Miami)—16
GEORGIA (Atlanta, Madison)—30
IDAHO (Moscow)—6
ILLINOIS (Anna, Barry)—88
INDIANA (Bourbon, Lawrenceburg)—81
INDIAN TERRITORY (Ardmore, Krebs, Lehigh, Muskogee, Purcell)—5
IOWA (Davenport, Lisbon ["Pop. 1,200 and Mt. Vernon, 1 mi. west, sidewalk bet. two towns. Mt. Vernon has Cornell College with close to 800 students. Also drawing from Martelle and Solar—no opera houses. Drawing population 3,500"])—84
KANSAS (Cawker, Hiawatha, Hutchinson ["Pop. 12,000. Home Theatre. The only amusement place in the city."])—53

Kentucky (Midway, Paris)—25
Louisiana (Houma, Napoleonville)—14
Maine (Togus, Saco)—31
Maryland (Bel Air)—15
Massachusetts (Athol, Springfield)—60
Michigan (Romeo, Cadillac ["Fire. No opera house at present"])—76
Minnesota (Le Sueur, Detroit City)—39
Mississippi (Sardis, Holly Springs)—18
Missouri (Mexico, Nevada)—66
Montana (Bozeman, Hamilton)—11
Nebraska (Weeping Water, Red Cloud)—42
Nevada (Virginia)—4
New Hampshire (Exeter, Dover ["A special theatre train is run from surrounding towns"])—19
New Jersey (Clinton, Keyport)—26
New Mexico (Raton, East Las Vegas)—7
New York (Albany [5 theatres], Sodus)—158
North Carolina (Hickory, Henderson)—20
North Dakota (Devil's Lake)—11
Ohio (Piqua, Tippecanoe City)—118
Oklahoma (Kingfisher)—6
Oregon (Portland)—12
Pennsylvania (Beaver Meadow, North East)—121
Rhode Island (Hope Valley)—8
South Carolina (Columbia ["Opera House destroyed by fire"])—19
South Dakota (Lead, Deadwood)—17
Tennessee (Memphis, Nashville)—22
Texas (Plano, Hico)—76
Utah (Salt Lake City)—11
Vermont (Bennington ["Pop. 10,000. Electric road to Hoosick Falls, N.Y., just completed, adding at least 10,000 more to draw from"])—14
Virginia (Culpeper, Orange)—29
Washington (Puyallup, Pullman)—16
West Virginia (Elk Garden, Keyser)—19
Wisconsin (Oconomowoc, Kaukauna)—61
Wyoming (Cheyenne, Sheridan)—6

[Total: 1,726. Many others did not subscribe to the *Guide*.]

The most customary procedure for booking shows and houses was, or had been, for theatre managers to come to New York in the booking season and bargain with the producers. They would take office space in the dramatic agencies located in the heart of the theatre district, then Union Square, or they would use brokers to book for them. A fault of this system was that no one, on either side, trusted most of those they dickered with, usually for good reason. Because if later, after the signatures and handshakes, a showman got a chance at what he considered a better date than the town of Speck, say, he might forget his contract with Speck, leaving the opera house there without an attraction and a blank or open date. On the other hand, if the theatre man in Speck got an offer from a better show than *A Step-Mother's Tears*, say, he might book the favored production, obliging the manager of *Step-Mother* to scout for a date somewhere else or declare a night off. (Since the producer was not likely to pay nonworking actors, it was not the disaster it might have been—for the producer.) The party who had been bilked was usually out of luck. Since the show of necessity moved on, who sued?

In 1905, this chicanerous confusion was being rapidly resolved. A small self-selected group of New York producers, including the mighty Frohman and a couple of despised characters named Klaw and Erlanger, were in the business of producing order with a formula based on what Americans like to call "plain business common sense." They were signing up the theatre owners with the argument: Let us book your house (exclusively) and it will save you all your present headaches and uncertainty, because we will send you a regular supply of our first-class productions, either our own or those contracted for (exclusively) from other producers. As simple as that. It will be good for you and good for us; we'll know *where* we're going to play, you'll know *what* you're going to play.

This obliging organization was called The Syndicate, and almost immediately, according to the testimony in court of David Belasco, a producer who declined to be included or excluded, the Syndicate had signed up a thousand choice theatres. It also had a formula which pleased the public: potent stars in happy-ending plays. As Frohman explained to a reporter in London: "The Americans are a health-minded people."

Belasco and friends were shouting "Trust!," a dirty word in the time of Roosevelt I. And trust it was, but inasmuch as the theatre owners and the public and most of the stars were satisfied, and since America had great respect for efficiency and profits, there was small prospect of curtailing the Syndicate with its formula for making millions. Such profits were due in part to the sharp terms dictated to the independent producers for access to those thousand-plus theatres. One valiant person, Mrs. Fiske, "The First Lady of the Stage," who was her own producer, refused to submit and spent the succeeding seasons playing what theatres the Syndicate had not cornered or did not want because of their poor address or condition. She received great approval from the liberal press but eventually retired to Staten Island without much money.

The train with the "Virginians" slowed for Middletown. The conductor told them there was talk of still another new theatre being built in Middletown and this added to the actors' content. The new efficiency and the appetite for entertainment and culture—it was as if all had been brought to pass for their benefit, as compensation. Once the actors had been rejected and despised; now the businessmen, architects and craftsmen were building temples for them in places like

> SISTERSVILLE [W.Va.]—New Auditorium. Neighboring cities and towns make a drawing population of 20,000.
> E. J. THOMPSON, Mgr.

The ad noted that the illumination was electricity.

What changes and improvements since that night when the special trains took people across the river from New York to Menlo Park, New Jersey, to be awed by Edison's electric lights strung on wires between the trees. Three thousand had come to partake of history, knowing they would have this to talk about until they left this miraculous world. And as soon as the lamps, switches, fuses and transformers could be perfected, the theatres adapted to the new odorless electricity so their customers could come and see how different this was from oil and gas. In 1905, the theatres in *Cahn's Guide* showed how extensive the transition already was when they reported their illumination:

931 with electricity
543 with gas and electricity
103 with gas
46 with oil
9 with gasoline
4 with oil and electricity
3 with acetylyn
1 with acetylyn and oil
1 with acetylyn and electricity
1 with oil and gas
1 with patent lights

The voltage varied: Canton, Missouri: *52*. Holdrege, Nebraska: *90*. Hamilton, Montana: *100*. Hamilton, Ohio: *104* and *110*. Columbus, Nebraska: *112*. Rochester, New York: *115*. Evanston, Nebraska: *124*. Corinth, Mississippi: *1,500*.

The systems varied: Brunswick, Missouri: *Edison* system. Fremont, Nebraska: *Westinghouse*. Hudson, New York: *Houston*. Cambridge, Ohio: *Fort Wayne*. Sycamore, Ohio: *Wood*. In choosing their systems, the buyers were placing their bets knowing they might lose, knowing that in America time standardizes all things. Only two theatres described their equipment: the City Opera House, Saint Ansgar, Iowa, spoke of its dimmer, and the Fort Collins Opera House, Fort Collins, Colorado, said it had three borders: white, red and blue.

As the train with *The Virginian* company went from Middletown to New Haven, the actors talked of plays, actors and the gossip of the new season. Someone referred to that old indestructible, *Camille*, and it was agreed again that the only part in *Camille* was Camille. The men despised it. There was a sorrowful moment as they spoke of Joe Jefferson, dead this year—there'd be no *Rip Van Winkle* without Jefferson, *the* Jefferson

—*Rip* without Jefferson, what would you have? There was talk of the new play Frohman had for Maude Adams, about to open, called *Peter Pan.* The word was that she was going to play the part of a boy. The women were interested in the reports of the elaborate wardrobe brought from Paris by the French actress, Mme. Réjane.

Mr. Farnum was reading another script. It was true that the theatre had never been so exciting, actors had never been in such demand, but it didn't lessen the worries of a star. Where was the next play? How to maintain the status, how sustain the fame? *The Virginian* had been good for him and he for it.

> The leading actor, Dustin Farnum, won a personal triumph, being obliged again and again to come forward in acknowledgement of sincere and genuine applause.

How could he repeat this and hold attention?

The theatre was full of magic but with no genie to tell Dustin Farnum what was to happen to Dustin Farnum. If informed, could he have believed it? Even Thomas Edison would have been skeptical. When they asked him if he wanted to obtain foreign patents on the "toy," as he called it, the moving picture machine he had invented, he asked how much would it cost. They told him $200. He snorted and said it wasn't worth it.

•

The train was slowing, they were coming to Brockton and this would be the end of the first week out. In towns across the country, North and South, the season had begun. The reports would be coming into New York to be published in The Dramatic Mirror:

Peoria [*Ill.*]—*Grand.* Walker Whiteside *in* David Garrick's Love, *fine company and production, swell house.*

Lexington [*Ky.*]—*Opera House.* Little Johnny Jones *to capacity; special matinee; George Cohan absent from cast; William Seymour essayed title-role very creditably.*

Bloomington [*Ind.*]—*Grand Opera House.* Dockstader's Minstrels *to very large house.*

St. Paul [Minn.]—Metropolitan. Ethel Barrymore in Sunday, with a company of strength, is playing to capacity. Three nights.

Las Vegas [N.M.]—Duncan Opera House. The season was opened by Rose Ivy in her song recital and feats of strength. Miss Ivy has a fine voice; pleased and mystified fair houses.

Nome [Alaska]—Margaret Longacre, soprano, will return to organize a company to produce Mikado, Martha, Pirates of Penzance, and The Geisha. The buildings recently destroyed by fire are being rebuilt.

It seems astonishing that even towns as small as 1,500 and 2,000 could afford the feast, yet the records prove it. But not all was SRO, the public was fickle as it always would be; even some attractions that the stringers called "strong companies" were reported to have "very poor houses," but the opera house stayed lighted. And this was entertainment live, these talented and beautiful people (for the most part) were staying at the local hotel, and tonight they would be churning laughter with farce, or commanding attention to Shakespeare; they would be exploiting the mood of this special instant, this particular audience, lifting it, riding it, making it behave, to enjoy and cheer!

How grand it was to have September leading into the whole winter filled with wonder down at the theatre. It made life brighter in Calumet, Michigan, and Opelika, Alabama—for three hours each evening you could forget your rut, your town, just as people attending the theatre could forget the city turmoil in New York, Boston, Philadelphia. What a glorious thing, folks thought, to be an actor and please so many so much—what an ideal life. Usually the actors agreed, although after a few seasons there wasn't an actor who didn't marvel at his survival. They endured because they were troupers, because in spite of hell, high water, diarrhea or pregnancy, the show must go on! They believed it.

The train stopped at Brockton. The actors straightened, set their faces in smiling charm, as if making an entrance. It was an entrance. When they came down the steps of the coach, people would stare, nudge, whisper to one another, be excited to see them, and the actors would play to the welcome.

In 1880, there had been fewer than 5,000 actors in the United States. Now the government census said there were more than 21,000. Professionals, experienced, blooded, of the tradition that dated back five centuries before Christ. So how could they suspect, looking forward to another season, a season more triumphant than any before, that 1905–6 was the beginning of the end of their world?

☛ 2

A Difficult Illegitimate Birth

The Virginian company changed trains in Boston. It had played there last season.

Boston was sophisticated and it liked the actors, and the goodhearted players returned the appreciation, which was gracious of them for they had a long reason for grievance. It was here that their thespian ancestors had been called harsh names and invited to absent themselves forever from the capital of Puritania. The Boston city fathers in 1750 had passed an ordinance:

> To prevent and avoid the many mischiefs, which arise from public stage plays, interludes, and other theatrical entertainments, which not only occasion great and unnecessary expense, and discourage industry and frugality, but likewise tend greatly to increase impiety and contempt for religion.

There were some would-be playgoers who protested, but with caution, for who wanted to be misunderstood in the defense of persons charged with subversive licentiousness? It was something like pleading for the right to hear a naked homosexual Communist some two centuries later. The public revulsion being what it was, freedom seemed a tenuous issue.

Had this virtuous prudery confined itself to Boston, the effect would have been mild, and the rest of the country could have had its pleasure. But the influence of the clergy was op-

pressively profound throughout the land, and, with some exception in the wicked cities, those resident moral authorities, the parsons, promulgated the bias of the theocrats in New England, who, even before the nation was secured, accepted the full responsibility for keeping it out of hell. Otherwise persons like the liberal Catholics (cf. Maryland and points south) might attempt another Merry Mount, wherever it so pleased them.

The actors, then, were charged with being the carriers of contagious sin, and the public exercise of their beguiling witchcraft was suppressed or severely inhibited for a long time. This not only made it difficult for those stubborn enough to want to perform plays, holding such infidels in disgrace and penury; it was also hard on those who did not find sufficient entertainment in sermons and amateur hymn-singing, who did not feel wicked for laughing, and who would have liked some of the wonder and release of imagination in the playhouse. If only this audience and the players could get together.

A hundred and fifty-five years later, Boston had relaxed, mellowed, enough to have charm, and the susceptible actors responded. All thirteen of Boston's theatres were aglow and it was pleasant and cheerful for the actors to walk to work across the Public Gardens. Seeing their names in front of the show shops did not offer any occasion for bitterness. Besides, Boston was usually only a one-week town and there wasn't time to spit old resentments.

IF New Englanders could have trusted their emotions as did Virginians and could have had people like George Washington, the theatre in America would have avoided its sense of shame and might have flourished a hundred years earlier than it did. George loved to go to the show. This weakness bothered the Puritans, and it was only because he achieved deification during the Revolution and as First President that they were able to hold their tongues and accept this flaw of vice in their beloved leader.

When the players were in town, George was known to attend their performances three and four times a week, which indicates either unusual intellectual courage or a helpless passion, for it is hard to think of any other American in public life at that time who would have risked opprobrium by playgoing, if he cared to keep his reputation. There is some evidence that John and Abigail Adams were more discreet. They had lived in France and knew that attendance at the theatre could be quite naturally enjoyable without a scar on the soul. Still, back home in the States, it appears they did not choose to be seen at the play except in the company of, and thus under the protection of, Washington, in whom all was forgiven. Abigail wrote to her daughter:

> I have been to one play, and here again we have been treated with politeness. The actors came and informed us that a box was prepared for us. The Vice-President thanked them for their civility and told them we would attend whenever the President did. And last Wednesday we were all there. The house is equal to most of the theatres we met with out of France. It is very neatly and prettily fitted up; the actors did their best; *The School for Scandal* was the play [which] on the whole was very well performed.

If Washington had remained a Virginian only, his profligacy would have been expected by the people in the North for they considered the people down there notoriously self-indulgent. The Southerners spent time at concerts, entertained themselves with cockfights and, it is said, erected the first theatre on this side of the Atlantic where the Puritans hoped the world was to be beyond such sin.

We know that the first professional troupe in the colonies came to Williamsburg in Virginia in 1752. Washington, though only twenty, was the District Adjutant, and had business at the capital, especially when the House of Burgesses was in session, as it was when the visiting Hallams presented their first offering. It is likely that this was when Washington's addiction began. The play was *The Merchant of Venice*, and Washington, said to be an "intensely ambitious" young man, may have received inspiration.

I hold the world but as the world, Gratiano;
A stage, where every man must play a part.

The Hallams were a stage family in London and, in the not unusual manner of their trade, they had suffered reverses. They were in fact bankrupt, which was fortunate for American theatrical history since it is doubtful that they would otherwise have felt the necessity to barnstorm the colonies. We can believe they found their reception encouraging for the burgesses of Virginia heartily approved of their talent. In fact, after the Hallams had stayed eleven months and exhausted their repertoire—*The Merchant*, *Richard III*, *Hamlet*, *Othello*, Marlowe's *Tamburlaine*, *The Beaux' Stratagem* and *The Recruiting Officer* by Farquhar, Cibber's *The Careless Husband*, Steele's *The Conscious Lovers* and *The Mock Doctor* (from Molière?)—and were departing to look for further audiences northward, Governor Dinwiddie presented them with a certificate signed in council, recommending their company as comedians, and testifying to the propriety of their behavior as men.

Did the Hallams leave this relaxed gentlemen's climate in innocence? They must surely have known the past attitude of the Puritans in the Mother Country. They had padlocked all theatres when they gained power for a time in 1642, and they were still bitter that these "dens of iniquity" had been permitted to resume and thrive. Now in America, as the Hallams advanced, not only the Puritans but the Quakers and Lutherans resisted. Well they knew that the devil lived and that even in New England there were persons who would give the actors welcome if permitted.

The Hallams and the other actors who came later found themselves barred wherever they turned. Newport was tried, but there were laws against "plays, games, lotteries, music and dancing." And Boston, of course, had a standing interdiction against "painted vanities" and anything else that might be attempted in "the devil's chapel," and also—to make it ecumenical—in "the devil's synagogue."

There was a century of virulent opposition. There were those who supported the actors, who did not believe the colonies or the nation should belong to the Puritans and who thought the theatre could be not only harmless but instructive and sensibly inspiring. However, the political edge was maintained by the anti-joy faction, who had the strength of sincerity in their fear of hellfire, and many a time they felt vindicated, as when the plague came to Philadelphia.

In Philadelphia, the people who wanted amusement, who wished to see Shakespeare off the page and living, finally persuaded the Legislature to license a playhouse. With that accomplished, they wanted the largest and the finest to be had and as quickly as possible. They persuaded the carpenters to work even on the Sabbath. When it was completed, there were fathers who paid handsomely and took their wives and innocent children to see the performances within. The place, said the newspapers, was mobbed.

Small wonder, then, said the ones who wouldn't be caught dead in such a place, that the fever erupted and seized the sinners, carrying them off in multitudes. (If any of the virtuous also expired, it was never explained.) So who, attending all those funerals of dear ones, could scoff at the holy warning? Descended from generations who had heard sin explicitly defined by the preachers, who now could be certain that the Jeremiahs were wrong? Would that the actors had never arrived to bring temptation!

And still the players would not accept the charge. Steeped in their own bible as composed primarily by Shakespeare, they thought of themselves as purveyors of the excitement of beauty and truth. Contrary to the opinions of their clerical opponents, they were certain that never had there been an actor with a tail or cloven hoof and if only the devout would be tolerant enough to *enjoy*, all would be happier and, being happier, less mean and sinful. The argument was called heretical, leaving the actors to wonder where in this benighted place they might find an audience, perform, be paid and survive.

A remarkable subterfuge was conceived and attempted. An audacious troupe headed by Hallam's successor, David Douglass, invaded New England offering "A Series of Moral Dialogues." They arrived in Newport, and if what the public wanted was a sermon, and if that could be accepted, they would get it. In a playbill announcing that the text of their discourse was the subject "Of Jealousy," we see where they found their material. What could be more didactic than:

> MORAL DIALOGUES,
> IN FIVE PARTS,
>
> Depicting the Evil Effects of Jealousy and other Bad Passions, and Proving that Happiness can only Spring from the Pursuit of Virtue.

The theme was to be demonstrated by several persons. First:

> MR. DOUGLASS will represent a noble and magnanimous Moor named Othello, who loves a young lady named Desdemona, and after he has married her, harbors (as in too many cases) the dreadful passion of Jealousy.
>
> *Of jealousy, our being's bane,*
> *Mark the small cause and the most dreadful pain.*

The preachment would be illustrated by way of a bit of story involving conflict, plot:

> MR. ALLYN will depict the character of a specious villain, in the regiment of Othello, who is so base as to hate his commander on mere suspicion, and to impose on his best friend. Of such characters, it is to be feared, there are thousands in this world, and the one in question may present to us a salutary warning:
>
> *The man that wrongs his master and his friend,*
> *What can he come to but a shameful end?*

There would be a lesson for the young, something always pleasing to the old:

> MR. HALLAM will delineate a young and thoughtless officer, who is traduced by Mr. ALLYN, and, getting drunk, loses his

situation, and his general's esteem. All young men, whatsoever, take example from Cassio:

The ill effects of drinking would you see,
Be warned and keep from evil company.

And now for a component which made this exhortation different from any provided by the pulpit Puritans: there would be the assistance of the feminine sex:

MRS. MORRIS will represent a young and virtuous wife, who, being wrongfully suspected, gets smothered (in an adjoining room) by her husband.

Reader, attend; and ere thou goest hence
Let fall a tear to hapless innocence.

MR. MORRIS will represent an old gentleman, the father of Desdemona, who is not cruel or covetous, but is foolish enough to dislike the noble Moor, his son-in-law, because his face is not white, forgetting that we all spring from one root. Such prejudices are very numerous and very wrong.

Fathers, beware what sense and love ye lack,
'Tis crime, not color, makes the being black.

One wonders about this last. Even abolitionists, if they then existed, would not, never did, favor miscegenation. But perhaps the players could not bring themselves to the presumption of correcting Shakespeare or they may have felt the urge to express their repugnance at the existence of Colonial slavery.

Anyhow, the "dialogues" worked, the audiences were enthusiastic. Which must have been superb training in that essential part of the actor's craft: maintaining a straight face while the stomach is boiling with laughter.

Douglass felt so encouraged he proceeded to Providence and hastened to build a theatre. When he sensed that the opposition there was more intense than in Newport, he exercised his guile and said he was building a "schoolhouse." It didn't work. The Rhode Islanders insisted it was nothing but a House of Satan, their term for playhouse, and the Rhode Island Assembly passed an act "forbidding further building of playhouses under the severest penalties" and the act was ordered "to be proclaimed through the streets of Providence by the beating of a drum."

Another defeat for the cause occurred when a different company had the gall to try the Moral Dialogues gambit at the wellhead of Puritanism, in Boston itself. It is said they got away with *Othello*, but when they changed the bill, someone began to suspect it was a play. They were trying to present *The School for Scandal* and the authorities swooped. This literary acuteness may have been the beginning of Boston's self-esteem as a cultural Athens.

Though outskirmished, the actors kept trying because they could see the audience was there. The petitions that were now signed protesting the suppression of the drama proved how many were eager to attend. Then, too, when performances were attempted, the audience would often risk as much as the players. It was the usual prohibition situation of clandestine demand and supply, but for a long time the authorities, prodded by the church, lopped the "weeds" of plays, interludes, extravaganzas, dancing, etc.

There was little the actors could do in direct confrontation with their persecutors. Offstage they had no standing—it would be a couple of centuries before they became accepted as senators and governors and then only if they identified with the conservative status quo. Also, the artist is usually inept in practical politics; his focus is narrow, on his art, and, however blessed, his knowledge can be so limited as to make him seem ridiculous to his adversaries. To take an example of how gifted and limited an actor can be, there was John Hodgkinson, the first star in America.

John Hodgkinson arrived in 1792 and for years afterward dominated the American stage. He came, as the surviving scuttlebutt states, because he had amorous inclinations that often complicated his career. He had eloped with the wife of his manager, making it advisable for them to leave London and dub themselves Mr. and Mrs. Hodgkinson. His name had been

Meadowcroft, and now at age twenty-six, with his bogus name and spouse, he crossed the ocean.

Even in that Puritan climate, he developed a loyal following that thrilled to his gift for making an audience suspend disbelief. You gain some understanding of the force of his appeal when you read a contemporary appraisal:

> Hodgkinson was a wonder. In the whole range of the living drama, there was no variety of character he could not perceive and embody. . . . He was also a singer, and could charm you in a burletta, after thrilling you in a play; so that through every form of drama he was qualified to pass, and it might be said he "exhausted worlds" if he could not "invent new." I doubt if such a number and such greatness of requisites were ever before united in one mortal man.

Put Hodgkinson on stage and he "was a wonder." Once he stepped off, he would have been helpless in a fight against cold-eyed clerics, armed with exegesis and screaming damnation ("To indulge a taste for playgoing means nothing more nor less than the loss of the most valuable treasure, the immortal soul" —Reverend Timothy Dwight, president of Yale), and Hodgkinson would have been as ineffectual as breath against berg. Here is how Hodgkinson appeared to be when he was not enthralling as Hamlet or warbler:

> His ignorance of all beyond theatrical limits was profound. . . . At a time when he was the delight of the town, the companion of most of the wits, and the soul of our musical societies, he—having made out a programme for poetical recitations—was sportively asked by Judge Cozine, "Who's this Anon you've got down on the bill among the poets?" To the judge's astonishment, he answered in serious earnest, "Oh, he is one of our first poets, Sir."

The case for the abused mummers and their art would need the help of friends to confute the sanctimonious who saw the theatre as a harlot threatening their buttons. Against such fearful opposition, deliverance was a slow process—what could be said? Years later, on different occasions, actors did use their opportunity to one-up the opposition. America's greatest tragedian and greatest comedian, though both were gentle men, said the stern right word on behalf of the profession when they got the chance.

Edwin Booth had built a palatial theatre and was staging magnificent productions of Shakespeare, and a clergyman wrote to inquire if there could not be some way for him to attend without the risk of discovery by his congregation. Booth replied, "There is no door in my theatre through which God cannot see."

Joseph Jefferson was also propositioned by a minister. This one asked if Jefferson could perform *Rip Van Winkle* in a church; the divine would like to see it, but it was not possible for him to enter a theatre. The reply was succinct. Said Jefferson, "Since I never enter a church, I don't see how we can get together."

•

The urge for theatre, to make it, to enjoy it, slowly surmounted the wrath of the dealers in damnation. Fortunately the country was too large for the Puritans to watch all of it, and there were areas—in the big cities and on the frontier—where the people were impervious to the old hell-warnings. Eventually, far away in time and mood from sin-bitten Salem (where Hawthorne had cursed his ancestors as "those miserable wretches"), and far from the rest of the only-one-salvation realm, the theatre flourished.

Edwin Booth
Dec. 23, 1886
Utica — Othello — $2,100 — (1 performance)
Dec. 25, 1887
Dallas — Hamlet — $2,654 — (1 performance)
May 5, 1887
Indianapolis — Hamlet — $4,470 — (1 performance)

Edwin Booth			
Dec. 23, 1886			
Utica	Othello	$2,100	(1 performance)
Dec. 25, 1887			
Dallas	Hamlet	$2,654	(1 performance)
May 5, 1887			
Indianapolis	Hamlet	$4,470	(1 performance)

Albany, N.Y.
Harmanas Bleecker Hall. The House of Mystery, a sensational melodrama in 4 acts by Langdon McCormick, had its initial presentation on any stage here and scored a pronounced success, drawing large and enthusiastic audiences. It tells a story of New

> York life and the author has centered the interest about a secret order, The Black Five. Faith Worthing, a young and pretty shop girl, is abducted. . . .

Dustin Farnum in The Virginian finished the one-nighters of the first two weeks, and moved on to the next two stands, Philadelphia and Washington.

You Should Have Been Here in the Old Days

The week of October 8, 1905, the Sothern and Marlowe company playing Romeo and Juliet for one night, arrived at Sacramento, California, on the Southern Pacific Railroad. The Child Wife company, playing Salem, New Jersey, was due in at 4:38 P.M. on the West Jersey Railroad. The Woman Hater company was only thirty-two minutes late when it arrived at Selma, Alabama, via the Western of Alabama Railroad. Thanks to the C.R.I. & P. Railroad, the Leah Kleschna company reached Cedar Rapids, Iowa, on time, and many of the admirers of Mrs. Fiske were at the depot to see her arrive.

In 1905, the U.S. railroad service had improved, was improving remarkably. In some places, the stations were achieving grandeur and the trains were getting electric lights while the service was getting elegant. The conductor was often magisterial in his responsibility, and there was a new breed of public servants the likes of which most had never seen until they "rode the cars."

These were Negro porters and waiters who seemed to be watching for the chance to bow, who smiled you aboard and brightly responded, made profound your most casual remark ("Yes, SIR, that a fact, yes-s-s, SIR!"), who brushed you off as *if a speck of dust were an offense to your splendid person—not subservient, exactly, but with the pleasant familiarity, efficiency and acceptance of class distinction of your personal valet. Even if most passengers didn't know how to pronounce "valet," they enjoyed the attention, and it would not be until the railroads were running on rust that the customers would begin to realize that those submerged Americans were simply desperate to hold their jobs, get the tips, without actually getting down to make some indecent obeisance. But it did make travel much pleasanter for the passengers than it had been.*

In the year 1838 the new town of Chicago had just turned from an Indian village into a thriving little place, and my uncle had written to my father urging him to join in the management of the new theatre which was being built there.

This was Joseph Jefferson speaking, a fourth-generation actor and third of the name, and undoubtedly the most beloved performer America has had.

My father . . . had scarcely finished the letter when he declared that our fortunes were made, so we turned our faces toward the setting sun. . . . We travelled part of the way in a fast-sailing packet-boat on the Erie Canal. The boat resembled a Noah's ark with a flat roof, and my father, like the patriarch of old, took his family on board, with this difference, however,—he was required to pay his passage, it being understood between him and the captain that we should stop a night in Utica and one in Syracuse, give a theatrical entertainment in each place, and hand over the receipts in payment of our fare.

As you read Jefferson, recalling all this at the end of his life, you feel not even a voyage with Long John Silver could have been more adventurous and satisfying to a boy of nine.

In Buffalo, we waited for the steamer. . . . In a few days we steamed up the beautiful lakes of Erie, Huron and Michigan. The boat would stop sometimes at one of the stations to take in wood, or a stray passenger, and then Indians would paddle out to us in their canoes offering their beadwork and moccasins for sale. . . . What a lovely trip as I remember it!

Any adult worries such as what might or might not be in the western world of Chicago did not affect the lad, nor does it seem to have bothered him when the "season" there was brief, necessitating their pressing on to a place called Galena,

traveling in open wagons over the prairie. Our seats were the trunks that contained the wardrobe—those old-fashioned hair trunks of a mottled and spotted character made from the skins of defunct circus horses; "To what base uses we may return!"

Occasionally the actors had to relieve the horses by pushing or walking, and we get some insight into the source of Jefferson's charm, which audiences were to love for fifty years:

Often I have seen my father trudging along ahead of the wagon, now and then looking back with his light blue eyes, giving my mother a cheerful nod which plainly said: "I'm all right. This is splendid; nothing could be finer." If it rained, he was glad it was not snowing; if it snowed, he was thankful it was not raining. This contented nature was his only inheritance; but it was better than a fortune made in Galena or anywhere else, for nothing could rob him of it.

Any mode of transportation then existing was used. As Galena was good for only a night or two, they went on.

We traveled from Galena to Dubuque on the frozen river in a sleigh. A warm spell had set in. We would sometimes hear the ice crack under our horses' feet: now a long-drawn breath of relief as we passed some dangerous spot, then a convulsive grasping of our nearest companion as it groaned and shook beneath us.

Well, the passengers arrived safe, but, horror to relate, the sleigh containing the baggage . . . the scenery and properties . . . broke through the ice and tumbled into the Mississippi. My mother was in tears, but my father was in high spirits at his good luck, as he called it—because there was a sand bar where the sleigh went in! The opening had to be delayed in order to dry the wardrobe and smooth the scenery. . . . Mildew filled the air. Armor hung wet and dejected from the lines. . . .

After a short season at Dubuque, we traveled along the river to the different towns just springing up in the West—Burlington, Quincy, Peoria, Pekin, and Springfield.

This was 1838, and for sixty-two years this had been the far, far West of the United States. For a generation, Americans had been living here, many born here, and the Atlantic seemed far, far to the east of them. Most had never seen a metropolis with as many as a thousand souls, and, needless to say, the majority had seen few shows or none.

One of the best statements of what it was like to bring entertainment to these outposts is Sol Smith's book, entitled:

THEATRICAL MANAGEMENT
IN THE WEST AND SOUTH
FOR THIRTY YEARS
INTERSPERSED WITH
ANECDOTAL SKETCHES:
autobiographically given
By SOL. SMITH,
Retired Actor.
With Fifteen Illustrations
And A Portrait Of The Author.

Sol was one of ten sons. The family couldn't afford him, and at the age of eight he was "put out," meaning it was decided he was old enough to earn his own livelihood, so was "put out" to a Mr. Eli Wildman, a neighbor six miles off through the woods. They told him which way to go to get there, to "the new home where I was to remain four years, and learn the trade, mystery, and calling of a Farmer." Which, he states, he might have been if two of his brothers had not opened stores in Albany, New York, and he got employment there, becoming, it is assumed, a gofer for the two stores.

He says he learned quite a bit about business, and that might have been it, too, except that "my leisure time was mostly spent in reading Shakespeare's plays, with which I became familiar long before I ever saw a play." When a troupe opened up in Albany and he bought a ticket, that determined his fate beyond correction. "My head was full of acting from that time forward; my duties at the store became irksome to me; in brief, I became, as thousands had become before me, and thousands will become after me—stage mad!"

The brothers, not wishing to have a lunatic sibling and employee, refused him permission to attend the theatre. He got down from his bedroom at night by means of a sheets-and-blanket rope and soon had persuaded the manager to let him be a super, thus saving the costs of admission. Which was fine until the company ran out of business and dispersed. Eventually he left Albany, too, looking for more experience on the stage, in the course of which he acquired a wife and got to New York, where he was told he was not needed, a fact that could not amuse him until long after, when he was there as a New York star.

He did get an eight-dollar-a-week engagement with a company playing towns in western New York State, and when their luck ran out, he decided to get his own company—"a few people"—and go west, where, the rumors said, there could be luck.

> At Warren [we] embarked on board two large skiffs, built for the purpose, and floated down the beautiful Allegheny. The skiff containing the young men of the company was considerably in advance of us, with the understanding that if they came to a town worth "taking," they were to leave a flag flying on the bank of the river as a signal that the town was taken or, in other words, they had made arrangements to perform there.

One day they did see a handkerchief tied to a pole but seeing no evidence of anything human, they were passing it by when a native appeared and hallooed them. "Pull ashore; this is the town you are to stop at; your actors are up at my house waiting for you!" This, they were told, was Lewiston, New York.

> He had a conveyance (a one-horse wagon) for the women, and Francisco and myself walked up the hill in search of Lewiston but no town could we see.
>
> "Oh, you are looking for the houses! Bless ye, they are not *built* yet; but we *shall* have some splendid buildings shortly. Here's Broadway; Wall Street runs down in that direction; and do you see the blazed tree yonder? There is *to be* our court-house."

The theatre turned out to be a room, twelve by sixteen, in a cabin in a clearing. Sol could not imagine where the patrons would come from in this wilderness but

Dinner over . . . the audience began to assemble from every direction —the men and women all coming on horseback. An unexpected difficulty now presented itself—*there was not a candle in the town*—that is, in the house! Night was coming on; we could not act in the dark.

The landlord hit upon an expedient. He tore up some linen, of which he made wicks, and, rolling them in tallow, soon made six decent candles. He thereupon took half a dozen large potatoes, and, boring holes in them, converted them into candlesticks, placing them on the floor in front of the curtain for *foot-lights!* He next called his neighbors and proclaimed the *box-office* was open. In ten minutes they were all supplied with tickets (mostly on credit) and . . . when our audience was seated, he announced the fact. . . .

The benches being all occupied, he squatted himself down by the potato footlights, and, at intervals, amused himself by snuffing the candles. At length, one by one, the lights began to give out, and we were in danger of being left in total darkness! Observing the state of affairs, I thought it time to bring the farce to a close, which I did by cutting *Lovers' Quarrels* rather short, reconciling the parties in the middle of the piece, and speaking the "tag." Down came the curtain, and out went the last candle!

In a few minutes, the auditors [were] making their way down stairs the best way they could, highly delighted with their entertainment.

The Smith company floated on down the river. The flag was out at a few more towns, but at Pittsburgh Smith found it practical to give the players "letters of recommendation" and he and his wife (and child), *en famille*, again started drifting, clinging to midstream because of fear of the wolves along the bank. "I shall not attempt to describe the tedious journey of 326 miles, performed in the heat of summer, on the Ohio River. . . . Early in October, 1826, we arrived at Cincinnati—without a dollar in my pocket."

This was the discouraging beginning of one of the most adventurous and successful careers in the theatre. Alone and with various other managers, Smith sparked the birth of theatre throughout the South and the West. Often they played in rooms little better than their "theatre" in Lewiston and, except perhaps in New Orleans, the playhouses were makeshift affairs so rickety

Sol Smith. An actor on horseback, he brought hilarity to Natchez when it was mud.

and such tinder, half the suspense of attending must have been the risk of a collapse or fire.

The dollars came hard. It was a time when pence were squeezed hot and to earn them, to make profit, actors and managers had to sweat. Once, when Smith was playing Natchez it was obvious the engagement could not break even. It occurred to him that he might do better by splitting the company between Natchez and Port Gibson, giving performances on alternate nights and appearing himself in both places (he was becoming a star: "The Comedian of the West"). That way he might improve the receipts. What this required of him was revealed in his diary:

Wednesday: Rose at break of day. Horse at the door. Swallowed a cup of coffee while the boy was tying on leggins [*sic*]. Reached Washington at 8. Changed horses at 9—again at 10—and at 11. At 12 arrived at Port Gibson. Attended rehearsal—settled business with stage manager. Dined at 4. Laid down and endeavored to sleep at 5. Up again at 6. Acted *Three Shingles* and *Slash*. To bed at 11-½.

Thursday: Rose and breakfasted at 9. At 10 attended rehearsals for the pieces of next day. At 1, leggins tied on, and braved the mud for a fifty mile ride. Rain falling all the way. Arrived at Natchez at half past 6. Rubbed down and took supper. Acted *Ezekiel Homespun* and *Delph* to a poor house. To bed (stiff as steelyards) at 12.

Friday: Cast pieces—counted tickets—attended rehearsal until 1 P.M. To horse again for Port Gibson—arrived at 7. No time to eat dinner or supper! Acted in *The Magpie and Maid*, and *No Song No Supper*, in which latter piece I managed to get a few mouthfuls of cold roasted mutton and some dry bread, they being the first food tasted this day! etc., etc., etc. *But I paid my debts!*

All barnstorming troupes in that time faced a competitor they avoided whenever possible. This was the camp meeting. They dodged day-and-dating with these gatherings because it was traditionally sensible not to buck anything with religious bias and because these spiritual extravaganzas were too good a show, too uneven a match.

The camp meetings had become a well-established business.

Usually sponsored by Methodists, they provided excitement and release from the drabness and repression of frontier life, times for the "lonesick" to meet old friends and make new ones. Led by "sons of thunder" ministers, speaking in the vernacular, skilled in raising hysteria in crowds by invoking guilt and describing punishments everlasting—"sarpints of hell will raise thar tails roun' thar naiks, chokin' clost, poke thar tungs up thar noses, an' hist intu thar years"—they could induce crowd emotion with such orgasmic reactions that many would enjoy the ecstasy of fits and fainting.

There was this appeal to the devout, and for others there could be equally exciting and more tangible reasons to be a camp-meeting follower. In the darkness at the edge of the flickering bonfire light, as the multitude was coming to Jesus, the wolves learned that many a lamb could be separated from the flock, willing to give her soul and everything with it. Said one observer who did not approve, "There are probably more debauches by night within one mile of a camp meeting . . . than occurred in the whole nation of Israel at the feasts of the tabernacle."

The camp-meeting business, exercising customary religious tyranny, would permit no competition, however small. The Joseph Jefferson family and company, approaching Springfield, Illinois, led by the innocent, cheerful father, were unaware they were to meet the holy enemy. Only by a humorous miracle would they be spared a rout.

> Springfield being the capital of Illinois, it was determined to devote the entire season to the entertainment of the legislature. . . . [But] a heavy blow fell upon us. A religious revival was in progress at the time, and the fathers of the church not only launched forth against us in their sermons, but by some political manoeuver got the city to pass a new law enjoining a heavy license against our "unholy" calling; I forget the amount, but it was large enough to be prohibitory.
>
> Here was a terrible condition of affairs; the legislature in session, the town full of people, and we by a heavy license denied the privilege of opening!
>
> In the midst of their trouble a young lawyer called on the managers. He had heard of the injustice, and offered, if they would place

the matter in his hands, to have the license taken off, declaring that he only desired to see fair play, and he would accept no fee whether he failed or succeeded.

The case was brought up before council. The young lawyer began to harangue. He handled the subject with tact, skill, and humor, tracing the history of the drama from the time when Thespis acted in a cart to the stage of to-day. He illustrated his speech with a number of anecdotes, and kept the council in a roar of laughter; his good-humor prevailed, and the exorbitant tax was taken off.

This young lawyer was very popular in Springfield, and was honored and beloved by all who knew him, and after the time of which I write he held rather an important position in the Government of the United States. He now lies buried in Springfield, under a monument commemorating his greatness and his virtues—his name was Abraham Lincoln.

Soon the pioneer managers had created a circuit of theatres in the expanding territory to the west, but the going remained rough. Few today would want to risk their spleen riding in a stagecoach over the roads as they were then or hazard the risks of boiler explosions on the river steamboats. Even to arrive in one piece might be a dubious achievement, for some of the theatres were in such miasmic cities as Mobile and New Orleans where yellow fever could reduce the attendance.

So it seems surprising that so many stars ventured that way except that, for stars especially, it could be profitable if they could take it. As you study the list of actors famous then, and whose names continue to be known, you notice Junius Brutus Booth season after season playing the better frontier stands and making a profound impression in the diaries of playgoers and in reviews.

Booth was another English player with wife trouble in London, and he persuaded a pretty flower girl in Bow Street to come away from his marital woes to America. His talent was such that he was an instant favorite, and he placed his Mary Ann on a farm in Maryland where she raised their ten children as they came while he toured to support them.

Actors who played with him sometimes considered his behavior odd enough to suggest insanity—he chose to play one whole performance on tiptoe—but the force of his acting, the fire in his eyes, were so overpowering that people were reluctant to make such judgment aloud, especially when he had a rapier in hand. And considering the strain of trouping then, every man must have needed a touch of madness to keep him sane.

Tyrone Power, an actor of a line that continued down to his great-grandson, the Hollywood star, includes in his *Impressions of America* vivid accounts of the ordeal of touring, even in the East, which had railroads. Train wrecks produced an intimidating death rate; since practically everything back of the boiler was made of wood, a trip could be a ride to disaster.

> [We were] anticipating a quick and pleasant ride to Bordentown. For a time all went well: various surmises were made as to our rate; some calculated it at 20 miles an hour; [some] were disputing the point when an alarm was given from the rear: loud cries of "stop the engine." . . .
>
> On the halt being accomplished, the carriages were deserted in a moment: for it was discovered that one of those in the rear had been overturned in consequence of the axle breaking. . . .
>
> I was soon on the spot, and what a scene was here to witness! Out of twenty-four persons only one had escaped unhurt. One man was dead, another dying, and five others had fractures, more or less serious; a couple of ladies (sisters) were dreadfully wounded; the children of one of them, two little girls, with broken limbs, [all] exposed to the glare of a hot sun without the possibility of procuring them shelter; for we were some miles from the nearest village when the accident occurred.

Mr. Power, as did all who traveled America in the 1830's, risked not only fracture by train wreck but crushed vertebrae in the stagecoaches. It should have been a relief when he made one jump on the Erie Canal, that much romanticized ditch which offered a gliding ride at "a cent-and-a-half a mile, a mile-and a-half an hour." Mr. Power, though, did not find it relaxing.

> The boat was exceedingly clean, not over-crowded; and . . . for a few hours went on merrily; the eternal forest closed about us, and the sound of our horses' feet [towing the boat] alone broke upon its

Tyrone Power. He might have thought of Hannibal as he endured the hazards of Hannibal, Missouri, for one night only.

silence. Towards evening the heat became great, and . . . increased as the night closed in. . . .

All [next] day the air absolutely stood still. . . . At Lockport we found business nearly at a stand-still; the thermometer was at 110 degrees of Fahrenheit. We passed several horses dead upon the banks of the canal, and were compelled to leave one or two of our own in a dying state. . . . This night I . . . resolved not to sleep within the den below, which exhibited a scene of suffocation and its consequences that defies description.

I got my cloak up, filled my hat with cigars, and, planting myself about the center of the deck, here resolved, *malgré* dews and moschetoes, to weather it through the night.

"What is the name of this country we are now passing?" I inquired of one of the boatmen who joined me about the first hour of morning.

"Why, sir, this is called the Cedar Swamp," answered the man, to whom I handed a cigar, in order to retain his society and create more smoke, weak as was the defence against the hungry swarms surrounding us on all sides.

"We have not much more of this Cedar Swamp to get through, I hope?"

"About fifty miles more, I guess," was the reply. . . .

"Thank Heaven!" I involuntarily exclaimed, drawing my cloak closer about me, although the heat was killing; "we shall after that escape in some sort, I hope, from these legions of moschetoes?"

"I guess not quite," replied the man; "they are as thick, if not thicker, in the Long Swamp."

"The Long Swamp!" I repeated: "what a horrible name for a country! Does the canal run far through it?"

"No, not so very far, only about eighty miles." . . .

"And is the next swamp as much infested with these infernal insects as are the Cedar and Long Swamps?"

"I guess *that* is *the* place above all for moschetoes," replied the man, grinning. "Thim's the real gallinippers, emigrating north for the summer all the way from the Balize and Red River. . . . They're strong enough to lift the boat out of the canal, if they could only get underneath her." . . .

I closed my eyes in absolute fear, and forebore farther enquiry.

Here I remained through the whole night, dozing a little between whiles, but never foregoing my cigar for a minute. Towards day-light the dew descended like rain, but brought with it no coolness to earth or man: it felt exactly as though it had been boiled the day before, and had not been left long enough to get cool.

Power was popular enough from New York to Chicago and to New Orleans and had sufficient fortitude to return for two more visits. It seems unjust that when returning to England from his third visit, his ship sank and he was drowned.

Despite the still strong feeling in the States against the British, Americans never questioned their cultural superiority. The adolescent nation was full of boom and boast, but with respect to the arts, its sense of inferiority provoked impotence. It was their assumption, that *should* greatness ever come to some American actor or dramatist, sufficient to be comparable to the English, it would naturally occur in the capital of English-American culture, in New York City.

However, in keeping with the nature of drama there was a twist and the unexpected happened in the person of Edwin Forrest, who learned his craft and acquired his patriotic assurance out yonder in the inferior theatre of the frontier. He had been born in the East, in Philadelphia poverty, a frail child who built up his physique with determination and circus acrobatics, then took himself west looking for his chance. One of the first unsteady jobs he got was in Cincinnati, where Sol Smith was experimenting with newspaper publishing until failure gave him the courage to stick to the theatre. It was as publisher that Smith spotted Forrest when

> Late in the winter of 1823, Messers Colins and Jones again opened the Cincinnati Theatre. . . . The opening play was *The Soldier's Daughter*, the part of young Malfort by Mr. Edwin Forrest. Being editor of a paper, I was, of course, an ex-officio judge of theatrical matters; but when I gave a very favorable opinion of Forrest's acting, my brother editors laughed at me—and they set me down as little less than a madman. They said I would "spoil the lad"—he *was* a clever boy, certainly, but plugging would ruin him.

Smith's praise did not relieve Forrest of the ordeals of the beginning actor. He continued to hunt for work and once was so discouraged that he joined a circus. Smith says it was he who persuaded Forrest that if he would persist he could be much more than an acrobat, and Forrest then joined a group of players that got as far as Dayton without profit and had to turn its wagons back to Cincinnati. On another occasion, there was a forty-mile jump which Forrest took on foot after leaving his trunk with his costumes, the tools of his trade, in the hands of a sheriff collecting a boardinghouse bill.

These years of failure were about ten, if we accept the record that he played his first part in Philadelphia at age eight, because before he left his teens he was a star in the West. The system then had resident companies in the different towns and the star was the visiting attraction, which meant continued training in getting to one's dates by stagecoach, river craft or horseback.

Forrest's best engagement and most valuable experience was in New Orleans. The city had much to teach and Forrest's tutors included Jim Bowie, inventor of the lethal Bowie knife, while another and more important friend he acquired was Chief Pushmataha of the Choctaw tribe. Forrest was inducted into that tribe with considerable consequence to American cultural history.

Forrest was twenty-one when he arrived in New York. Soon he was the nation's first and favorite *American* star, to remain so for a lifetime. Perhaps the best word to describe his appearance and talent is *formidable.* He had a magnificent body and a magnificent voice, the body looking as if chopped out of marble and the voice sounding like the full scale of thunder. Playgoers had never seen or heard anything like it. A visiting English star who saw him in *Metamora* wrote:

> I never heard any thing on the stage so tremendous in its sustained crescendo swell, and crashing force of utterance, as his defiance of the Council, in that play. His voice surged and roared like the angry sea, lashed into fury by a storm; till, as it reached its boiling, seething climax, in which the serpent hiss of hate was heard, at intervals, amidst its louder, deeper, hoarser tones, it was like the falls of Niagara, in its tremendous down-sweeping cadence: it was a whirlwind, a tornado, a cataract of illimitable rage!

"He could sigh like a zephyr or roar like a hurricane," says another, adding that he could command tears as easily as terror, and when he went off in *Virginius* after denouncing Appius, his exit would excite the wildest huzzas, the men in the pit standing with their hats in their uplifted hands, and the women in the boxes waving their handkerchiefs. Walt Whitman thought he was phenomenal. America was his, and for the next forty years the towns and cities everywhere were always waiting to huzza him over and over again.

At approximately the same time that Forrest was becoming a national star, Emerson was giving a Phi Beta Kappa address at Harvard and stating that Americans had "listened too long to the courtly muses of Europe" and that they must learn to speak their own minds. Forrest thought so, too, and, with Jacksonian spirit, decided he would like material for his career that was not made in England.

There was a question: would Americans accept the American-made? A few native dramatists had attempted to offer plays in the native voice and had been humiliated by the public's prejudiced indifference, and they were seldom if ever paid for the effort. One such writer named Baker related that when his play *Marmion* was put on, it was announced as "an English play by Thomas Morton, Esq.," and further that it had been "received with unbounded applause in London." After running several nights with success, its American authorship was revealed, and the receipts immediately fell off.

Forrest announced he would give a five-hundred-dollar prize plus half of the third night's receipts for an American play he could use. The winner was the actor, John Augustus Stone, the play was the Indian drama, *Metamora*, and this remained in Forrest's repertoire to the end. It was his lifesaver whenever his career threatened to sag. William Alger in his *Life of Edwin Forrest* (1877) helps us attend a performance of *Metamora* and to sense what the honorary Choctaw had absorbed from his mentor, Chief Pushmataha. Now, if we listen, we can hear how Forrest played the lines of the climax on his throat-organ.

With a slow and heavy step, he is approaching his wigwam, where his wife, Nahmeokee, waits to receive him. He has seen that the too

Edwin Forrest. Audiences in Dayton, Ohio, didn't appreciate him when he was young and handsome.

The same audiences thought Forrest was amazing every time he returned in *Metamora.*

unequal struggle of his countrymen is hopeless, and he appears sad and gloomy. He says, "Bring me thy little one, that I may press him to my burning heart to quiet the tumult."

Without his knowledge, the child has been killed by the white men a few hours previous. Metamora looks at the child, at the mother, stoops, and, with rapid motions, feels the little face, arms, and legs. Suppressing the start of horror and the cry of grief a white man would have given, he sinks his chin slowly upon his breast and then utters the simple words, "Dead! Cold!"

Having lifted the dead child and fondled it in his bosom, he says, in a soft voice quivering with the tears not suffered to mount to his eyes, "Well, is he not happy? Better that he should die by the stranger's hand than live to be a slave. Thou wilt see him again in the happy land of the spirits; and he will look smilingly as—as—as I do now."

Drawing Nahmeokee closer with his left arm, and lowering his eyes, he whispers, "Hark! In the distant wood I faintly hear the tread of the white men. They are upon us!" [To protect her from capture] he strikes the blow, and in an instant she is dead in his arms. He then shudders, exclaiming, "She knew no bondage to the white men. Pure as snow she lived, free as the air, she died!"

At this moment the hills are covered with white men, pointing their rifles at his heart. "Hah!" he cries. Their leader shouts, "Metamora is our prisoner!" "No," he proudly responds, "I live, the last of my race, to defy you still, though numbers and treachery overpower me."

The order is given to fire upon him; and he replies, "Do so. I am weary of the world; for ye are dwellers in it. I would not turn my heel to save my life."

They shoot and he staggers, but in his dying agonies launches on them his awful malediction: "My curses on ye, white men! May the Great Spirit curse ye when he speaks in his war-voice from the clouds! May the words be like the forked lightnings, to blast and desolate! May the loud winds and the fierce red flames be opposed in vengeance upon ye, tigers! May the angry Spirit of the Waters in his wrath sweep over your dwellings! May your graves and the graves of your children be in the path where the red man shall tread, and may the wolf and the panther howl over your fleshless bones! I go. My fathers beckon from the green lakes and the broad hills. The Great Spirit calls me. I go—but the curses of Metamora stay with the white men! I die—my wife, my queen—my Nahmeokee!"

Metamora loosed a flood of Indian plays. For years (at least until *The Squaw Man,* 1905), American playgoers reveled in heroic, noble redskins, of the breed that until recently had been declared no good 'cept dead. They found it a satisfying restitution, particularly as it did not include the sacrifice of even an acre of Indian land. And also gratifying was the fact that *Metamora* was an *American* play—would a Britisher know how to write about our Indians? To some there was a question whether Americans knew how to write about them. It was Mark Twain who observed of James Fenimore Cooper's Indians, "They belonged to an extinct tribe which never existed."

Forrest also played Shakespeare, as did all actors, but the $500-plus-benefit *Metamora* (given today's standard royalty, the author might have made a million even then) and *Spartacus* and *The Gladiator* were the plays most identified with this greatest exponent of what might be called the oratorical school of acting. Though *Spartacus* and *The Gladiator* lacked an American setting, the audiences considered their themes American because they spoke for freedom and against tyranny, a concept the Americans believed they had patented and to which they responded with money at the box office, huzzas and handkerchiefs waving.

The American pride in Forrest's talent made him an idol, and when he went to London and it was reported he had been abused by the audiences and critics, it was considered an affront to the nation. In the resultant sullen mood, there was an incident that led to blood. There was an English actor, Macready, with a different, more genteel style, yet the American public matched him and Forrest as rivals. Forrest contributed to the bad feeling when, in Edinburgh, he attended a performance by Macready of Hamlet. Taking exception to a piece of business by Macready, he hissed, which, considering the consequence, was a hiss of death. For when Macready came to America, there was trouble.

It should have been anticipated, the temper of Forrest's partisans being conspicuously hot. A letter published by one of the newspapers was indicative:

ELEGANT THEATRICAL CRITICISM.
THIS CHOICE EPISTLE
CAME TO US
THROUGH THE POST OFFICE:

Mr. James Gordon Bennett.

You say in your paper of yesterday that Forrest, Hamblin, Hill, Hackett, & Rice all went to England & that Rice succeeded best. You are a God damned liar! And if I ever catch you, you God Damned Scotch son of a bitch, I'll mash that God Damned Scotch face of yours by Jesus Christ! You have once or twice intimated in your paper that Mr. Forrest's conduct while in England, manifested a lack of regard for the land of his birth. This is also a God damned lie, & you know it, God damn your Scotch soul! You have only one eye now, & if I ever come across you in the vicinity of the Park Theatre, I'll knock out the other. By Christ! Beware.

BUSKIN.

Forrest's critics and Macready's critics met at Astor Place the night Macready opened there at the Opera House, May 10, 1849. When the count was made the next morning, twenty-two had been killed and the wounded numbered hundreds.

Forrest played on into his old age. By then, styles had changed, he was ill, and only by playing smaller and smaller towns could he find audiences and more money to go with his money. Most people who had known him offstage had never been able to like his niggardly arrogance—William Winter, the critic, said that he was "a vast animal, bewildered by a grain of genius," and many had been revolted by the harsh, crude way he had divorced his wife—and there was not much professional sympathy as he played out his last scenes. Whenever he acted in *Damon and Pythias*, he was concerned about the climax, where he would leap onto the scaffold. Each performance, before the curtain, he would try the jump. Once it had been a thrilling three feet. Finally, one night, suffering the humiliation of stagehands watching, the platform was lowered until it was three inches. He tried it, nodded that that would do, and turned away in tears. Later, shivering in the wings of a small-town opera house, he was heard to mutter, "I am worth three hundred thousand pounds sterling, and I can't purchase five cents' worth of heat for my body."

•

In 1905, weeks of November 21 and 28, the actors were on the road performing more than three hundred plays. Thanks in no small part to Forrest, most of these were American plays and playwriting was becoming a lucrative and occasionally a respectable business. There were such U.S. products as:

A Royal Slave: *Weston, W. Va., Nov. 21; Shinnston, Nov. 22, Monongah, Nov. 23; Grafton, Nov. 24; Martinsburg, Nov. 25; Piedmont, Nov. 27; Frostburg, Md., Nov. 28.*

Peck's Bad Boy: *Columbiana, Ohio, Nov. 22; Salem, Nov. 23; Dennison, Nov. 24; Steubenville, Nov. 25; Newcomerstown, Nov. 28; Scottdale, Pa., Dec. 1; Mt. Pleasant, Dec. 4.*

Hearts of Gold: *Toledo, Ohio, Nov. 18–22; Dayton, Nov. 23–25; Cleveland, Dec. 2.*

On the Bridge at Midnight: *Fresno, Calif., Nov. 21; Oakland, Nov. 23–24; Napa, Nov. 25; Stockton, Nov. 26; Sacramento, Nov. 27.*

Josh Spruceby: *Troy, N.Y., Nov. 29; Saratoga, Nov. 30; Gloversville, Dec. 1; Utica, Dec. 2.*

Here and there were English titles, too:

Hamlet: *Bellefontaine, Ohio, Nov. 22; Winchester, Ind., Nov. 25; Greenville, Nov. 27; Eaton, Nov. 29; Lebanon, Nov. 30; Circleville, Dec. 2.*

And the popular imported melodrama:

The Mummy and the Hummingbird: *Uniontown, Pa., Nov. 22; Steubenville, Ohio, Nov. 23; Franklin, Nov. 24; Sharon, Nov. 25; Erie, Pa., Nov. 27; Niagara Falls, N.Y., Nov. 28; Oil City, Pa., Nov. 29.*

☛ 4

The Saints Enter the House of Satan

By the eighth week on the road, often a troupe had played some forty towns—at six one-nighters per week with, perhaps, an occasional two-night stand. The places were becoming a blur, with the common name "Tonight." In the state of "Only."

In the weeks to follow, opening trunks, closing trunks, they found their way through limbo asking three questions: Which way to the hotel/boardinghouse? Where is the theatre? How do we get to the station?

At the season's end, a few scenes might linger in mind for various and often peculiar reasons that rarely described the locale. Niagara Falls, New York. *We could hear the roar but we didn't have time to see them, but I remember the hotel had beautiful new carpets.* Erie, Pennsylvania. *The audience sat there as if they were frozen dead! We found out later they were mostly Poles and Russians who didn't understand half we said.* Springfield, Missouri. *Those two boys trying to peek in the dressing room and there I was in my corset!* Klamath Falls, Oregon. *That hag of a landlady, always watching us; what did she think we were going to steal, the lumps in the mattress?* Traverse City, Michigan. *Never saw so much venison in my whole life.* Vicksburg, Mississippi. *Such a lovely place. The mayor came backstage.* Jackson, Tennessee. *That man trying to kill that colored man, beating him with a club. He must have done something wrong.* New Brunswick, New Jersey. *I'll be glad if I never see that place again; there's some kind of college there and those boys spoiled the whole show.*

THE men who laid out the towns may have thought each was unique, but to the actors passing through half a century later they were all uninspired copies of one another. If you didn't know Ed Kimball, what did it matter if the drugstore was his or if it was William Lake's or George Russell's in Newton, Wisconsin; Newton, Georgia; or Newton, Kansas—they all looked the same. And so it was down the length of Main Street: the buildings, the towns and the inhabitants, about as distinctive as dried apples.

If the founders dreamed of a grateful future, they were wrong again because the dullness of village life, in appearance and spirit, began to set in with the second or third generation. By that time the thrill of pioneering was over: that sense of discovery, the feeling that the only being ahead of you in this solid forest, in the air on this peak, in the stillness on this crater lake, was God himself. Now nature was a mass of scars: clearings hacked out of woods, hillsides timbered off, ruts of oozing mud in what had been the firm delicious earth of leaf-mold or needles or the webbed roots of prairie grass.

By the time the settlers' kids were grown to live here raising their kids, the buildings were weathered and out of plumb, and the people, slowing down from the grind of daily survival, were beginning to wonder where had the awe and the excitement gone? They were almost wishing they were back with the risk of panthers and Indians—it was more interesting even if the ordeal of breaking nature broke half the people who tried it. By comparison, there was now leisure and that was becoming the problem.

The town's specified workday with evenings and Sundays free was a great change from the constant day-and-night struggle and taut alertness of the time before. Was this, then, the reward: toil plus nothing to do? It took a long time for Americans to learn to play. The Puritans had taught America the gospel of work. Confronted as they had been by a wilderness and their ignorance, they could not conceive of a day when there might not be the need for incessant toil—on behalf of survival, God and their righteous posterity. Now, however, with enough soil cleared for crops, with the mills on the race, with trade established, there were people wishing for a distraction and a pleasure more inspiring than callusing your hands or chasing money twelve hours per day.

The towns had no beauty to cheer anyone; they were drab, makeshift, their streets mostly mud or dust with a high content of horse-age manure. The men and women were locked in monotonous customs and habits, their only satisfaction a mindless virtue. Increasingly, it was not enough. This was due in part to the coming of the railroads and newspapers, which brought awareness of a different way of life, of interesting diversions in the cities. Couldn't there be fun, laughter, something pretty, stimulating, here too, before it was your turn to supply the event of a funeral?

Even the people who cared about salvation were beginning to doubt you would see hell if you touched a deck of cards, or perhaps jigged a little, or even maybe attended a show. But the old morality was as difficult to discredit and disregard as the superstitions folks still lived by—"That's what they say, you take the child to the barn and let him breathe the cow's breath and the whooping cough goes away. You ought to try it"—and why take a chance being different, why offend those who still believed, why make them talk—remember your reputation—it's a small place, we all have to live here together.

Dead center. Sitting around the stove—spitting tobacco—bragging—louts drinking—

Hail, Columbia, happy land,
If you ain't drunk, I'll be damned

—bored boys putting turpentine on a cat's asshole to watch it scream and run—waiting for the mail, unexpecting—revival meeting—reading a chapter a day in The Book—picking water lilies—Fourth of July only on the fourth of July—getting married, a rare day of difference—trimming graves so someone will do it to yours. As late as 1878, Nathaniel Eggleston wrote: "As for amusements and recreation, there is next to none, at least that is worthy of the name. It has been said of the New England villagers that their only recreations are the funeral occasions. . . . There is little to break the monotony."

If the town got a theatre, it was rarely called a theatre. To relieve it of stigma, encourage acceptance, it was called an opera house, though no one ever expected it to house an opera. Even so, most folks were slow to attend, in part because the preachers still warned. A Reverend W. G. Elliot gave a "Lecture on Amusements":

> It is a fair objection to the theatre, that, as an amusement, it is too exciting. . . . To older persons it may not be so hurtful; but for the young man, I do not know of any habit . . . which is more injurious, or more fraught with serious danger, than that of theatregoing. It stimulates the imagination too strongly; it awakes dormant passions; overtasks the sensibilities, and generally makes more quiet and less exciting amusements seem flat and tasteless. . . . I feel justified in advising you strongly against it.

So those not wishing to stimulate dormant passions stayed away from the opera house.

The theatre was never going to be much of an institution, have a respectable audience and a firm economic base, until it gathered in those people other than the godless or those willing to disagree conspicuously with the "spiritual leaders." The opera house could not bring much to town just for the minority, and how could it get the majority when, as ever, the last thing the majority wanted was to be identified with the minority? But it happened. There is an old theatre saying that the thing that will always solve the theatre's problems is a *hit*. Now came a hit such as there had never been before nor has been since and it changed the theatre and changed America.

The theatre of that period was often a family business. As with farming, it helped the unit survive if even the toddler could play a role. It helped though it gave no assurance of success, as the Howard family was aware when it was desperately fighting to hold on in Troy, New York, in 1852.

Business at the box office had been terrible and Howard was desperate enough to try anything. Right now they were rehearsing a stage version of Dickens' *Oliver Twist.* Although Dickens' books were extremely popular, you could not be sure the Trojans would pay for an American interpretation by the Howards, and Howard wasn't even sure they could present it for they still had not been able to locate someone to play Little Dick, the sick pauper boy who bids a tearful farewell to Oliver when Oliver is running away from the poorhouse.

It was a very important scene, for the people of that time dearly enjoyed any form of sadness involving children. It made them weep with pleasure whenever they could listen to a good song of infantile misery:

When scarcely old enough to know
The meaning of a tale of woe,
'Twas then by mother we were told,
That father in his grave was cold!
For long we watched beside her bed,
Then sobb'd to see her lie there dead;
And now we wander hand in hand,
Two orphan boys of Switzerland!

Manager Howard knew what audiences liked and why it was essential to find a child to play Little Dick. It was suggested (by her doting mother, perhaps—Mrs. Howard?) that they use their own four-year-old daughter, Cordelia. Dress her in one of her brother's suits and make the lines simple and she might do. But we can believe that even if Mr. Howard was a loving father, he was even more the harassed manager facing ruin and he may have hesitated to trust their fate to a nonprofessional four-year-old of the wrong sex! However, desperation made the decision.

At the first rehearsal, it was astonishing how quickly Cordelia grasped her little part. Without suspecting it, the Howards appeared to have spawned a natural actress. They whitened her face to make her look consumptive and sat her on a pile of dirt, gave her a small spade and directed her to pretend she was digging little graves. Curtain!

Oliver entered and saw Dick digging.

OLIVER: I'm running away, Dick.
DICK [*Cordelia*]: Won't you come back any more?
OLIVER: I'll come back and see you some day.

At which point, instead of Cordelia delivering her simple line, "Goodbye, Oliver," she said, with a complete conception of the character and a sense of the dramatic that jolted the cast watching from the wings:

"It won't be any use, Olly dear. [*Sobbing*] When you come back, I won't be digging little graves, I'll be in a little grave myself."

A murmur of adoring sympathy swept the audience. And that was the story as it was to be told for a hundred years after. It doesn't matter if it was not precisely accurate (although from listening to plays, rehearsals and songs, the child could well have been aware of the public's fix on childhood death and could have learned how to incite that favorite grief)—what matters is that Cordelia had done something sensational to the audience, and that led to historic consequences.

Howard grasped at the straw. Quick, where could they get another play, more material, to exploit the child's gift? Instantly he must have seen the billing as it was to be: "LITTLE CORDELIA IN——." The circumstances forced them to brainstorm and someone wondered if something dramatic might be made from the book everyone seemed to be talking about, *Uncle Tom's Cabin.* There was a child in that story and also of the right sex, Little Eva.

CORDELIA HOWARD. The original Little Eva of *Uncle Tom's Cabin*. In 1933, eighty-one years after Miss Howard first appeared in her family's production, The Players Club staged an all-star revival with Otis Skinner as Tom. Miss Howard was invited to attend a performance and wrote about it to her family:

"Well, they did give me an ovation Monday eve. So many years since I have received the plaudits of an audience! And do you know I rather liked it! . . . Mr. Skinner made a speech and said the original little Eva was present and pointed to my box. The applause broke forth and I had to bow to the audience. Well, it was my swan song, that is the end. . . . I saw Mr. Skinner afterwards. He was very complimentary about my looks, the old flirt! But as he is a widower and I am a widow it was all right. . . .

The play follows our dramatization pretty closely. The auction scene was excellent. . . . It is a good thing to show the young people the conditions of those days. Mr. Skinner, of course, was a fine Uncle Tom. . . . Eva was charming—her voice childish and her movements natural and she is very pretty. Between ourselves, Topsey was awful! The first thing she did was to pick her nose! Disgusting . . . Not the innocent, childlike Topsey of our mother. Mr. St. Clair was rather old, I thought, and not very good-looking—not the handsome cultured gentleman that our father made it.

But on the whole the old play was well given and seemed to please the audience. They played Father's song, "I'se So Wicked." I told the children it was their grandfather's composition. . . .

The Players presented [me with] four dozen red roses. I placed some on our father and mother's grave in Mt. Auburn. I thought it was appropriate. . . .

Again with love.

Delie

EVA TO HER PAPA
as Sung by
LITTLE CORDELIA HOWARD
IN HER ORIGINAL CHARACTER OF "THE GENTLE EVA" IN
Little Cordelia Howard has no interest in the Sale of this Song.
UNCLE TOM'S CABIN
Words and Music written expressly for her by her Father
GEO. C. HOWARD,
& most affectionately dedicated
TO HER MOTHER.
NEW YORK.

LITTLE CORDELIA HOWARD AS LITTLE EVA!

George L. Aiken, a cousin-member of the company and a budding playwright, undertook the dramatization. Howard, being a manager, of course advised. The script was done in a week.

Copyright protection in those days was designed for piracy. They never troubled to consult Harriet Beecher Stowe, author of the novel. It would have made no difference—someone had already written to her suggesting there might be a play in her book and she, in a classic document of smug error, had replied discouraging the idea:

> I have considered your application and asked advice of my different friends. The general sentiment of those whom I have consulted so far agrees with my own, that it would not be advisable to make that use of my work that you propose. It is thought, with the present state of theatrical performances in this country, that any attempt on the part of Christians to identify themselves with them will be productive of danger to the individual character and the general cause.
>
> If the barrier which now keeps young people of Christian families from theatrical entertainments is once broken down by the introduction of respectable and moral plays, they will then be open to all the temptations of those which are not sure, and it will be, as the world now is, five bad plays to one good.
>
> However specious may be the idea of reforming dramatic amusements, I fear it is wholly impracticable. The world is not good enough yet for it to succeed.

(She had yet to learn just how bad the world could be. Her brother, Henry Ward, the most famous member of the clergy in America, was to be exposed for thoroughly servicing one of his married parishioners in a back parlor of his Brooklyn tabernacle.)

> I preserve a very pleasant recollection of your family . . . and it gives me great pleasure to number you among my friends.
>
> HARRIET BEECHER STOWE

Another writer who was left out of the take. In this instance, it was millions beyond calculation.

The Howards rehearsed and opened September 27, 1852. The play ran one hundred nights in Troy. It moved to New York, where it opened without fanfare because the manager of the New York house, Howard's brother-in-law, had been badgered into giving it a try against his judgment. He saw no reason to think that what excited Troy would impress New York.

Almost immediately, they added two afternoon performances to the weekly six at night, and almost immediately after that they were doing two by day and one by night—eighteen performances a week—and the actors were eating their meals in costume backstage.

Other, competing companies rushed in to stage *Tom* in other theatres. The public could not get enough. And it continued—companies took to the road until even the towns that had never seen or expected to see a show were seeing Uncle Tom and Little Eva. Wagon companies brought it to areas beyond the railroads, tents holding as many as two thousand were used where there were no theatres. According to one historian, it ran somewhere in America *continuously for ninety years!* This writer saw it in Saginaw, Michigan, in 1922, seventy years away from the opening night in Troy.

It meant, of course, that more than the previous clientele came to the box office. Although he had no empty seats, the brother-in-law manager, so as to assure any of the righteous who were hesitating, ran an ad quoting a reliable parson:

> "The question has been asked would it be improper for clergymen and church members to visit the National Theatre during the performances of this piece? Our answer would be, as there is no other theatrical representation given with it, there would be no impropriety in the religious portion of the community witnessing it. It is a moral, religious, and instructive illustration of the justly celebrated work of Mrs. Harriet Beecher Stowe and is most faithfully dramatized. The representation of Little Eva, by little Cordelia Howard, should be witnessed by every lady in the land. We are informed that the Manager has taken every precaution that no disorderly person be admitted to the Theatre during the performances of this great production."

The ad, except perhaps for the plug for Cordelia, was unnecessary—you could not keep the "religious portion" away. One writer observed, "Among the audience, we recognized many people who have been taught to look on the stage and all that belongs to it with horror and contempt; and, not the least conspicuous among the rare faces, was that of a Quaker gentleman whose drab, shad-belly coat and remarkable broad brimmed beaver, gave him a commanding aspect. . . . There were also recognized among the mass who occupied and crowded the theatre, Methodists, Baptists, Presbyterians, and Congregationalists whose creeds are not accounted absolutely orthodox."

One explanation, as suggested, was that this was what they had been waiting for, a reasonably conscience-justifying excuse to *enjoy*, to partake of the magic of theatre, and now it could be considered a *duty* to attend this sermon against slavery. But inasmuch as there was a plethora of abolitionist tracts and lectures and meetings, they were hardly compelled to enrich the managers of the Tom shows.

The truth was that it was an irresistible play and everything else was an excuse about as valid as saying you were going to a whorehouse to give the girls the benefit of a higher grade of custom. They went and were thrilled and they went again, and those that held back soon felt they had been abandoned by some mass exodus from traditional morality. So *they* went to find out why.

It did not matter that there was not a character on stage with any resemblance to life. Precocious Little Eva, saintly old Tom had never existed, and neither had villainous Simon Legree, even with a red neck. The characters in a play exist to the extent the audience *wants* them to, as, much later, they were to exist in *Our Town.* They wanted to believe every word of *Uncle Tom's Cabin* for the sake of the cause, but there was much more than the didactic dramatization of protest—there was love and grief and comedy and action, suspense! And scenery!

Instantly, Act I, Scene 1, we are plunged into a dreadful domestic situation involving George and Eliza. (Both are black, though they look as white as angels with a tan.) George tells Eliza he has heard he is to be sold and they are to be separated and he is going to have to go to the buyer's place and take a wife there.

ELIZA: But you were married to *me* by a minister, as much as if you had been a white man.

George says it makes no difference and becomes rather intellectually bitter.

GEORGE: Who made this man my master? What right has he to make a dray-horse of me?—to take me from things I can do better than he can, and put me to work that any horse can do? to take every chance he can to insult and torment me!

This is rather militant stuff, many people in the audience might not want to hear even a free hired man talk like this, but Eliza quickly identifies them with the right-thinking pious.

ELIZA: Well, I always thought that I must obey my master and mistress or I couldn't be a Christian.

George makes his decision, he's going to run for it, to Canada, and then he'll buy Eliza and Harry, their little boy. *Exeunt omnes.*

Enter, instantly, the master, Shelby, and a slave buyer, Haley. Mr. Shelby, financially embarrassed, is trying to sell a property called Tom.

SHELBY: The fact is, Haley, Tom is an uncommon fellow! He's capable, he's honest, and runs my plantation like a clock.
HALEY: You mean honest as niggers go. [*Drinks*]
SHELBY: No; I mean, really. Tom got religion at a camp-meeting, four years ago, and I believe he really *did* get it.

Haley is a hard bargainer and for the price Shelby asks, he wants Tom *plus* a boy he has seen, *Little Harry!*

SHELBY: What on earth do you want with the child?
HALEY: Why, I've got a friend that's going into this yer branch of the business—wants to buy up likely boys to raise for the market.
SHELBY: I'll have to talk with my wife.

End of Scene 1. Is anyone in doubt as to what they would like to see happen? to whom? But there is lots to come before we know how it all turns out—seven more scenes in Act I, eight scenes in Act II, seven scenes in Act III.

Next scene: Exterior of Uncle Tom's cabin. Eliza tells Tom of her terrible plight. He advises faith.

> TOM: Him dat save Daniel in de den o' lions an' brung de chillun outer de fiery furnace—Him dat walk on de sea an' tell dem winds dey got to be still—He's alive.

Next scene: A tavern by the river. Enter Eliza with Little Harry.

> ELIZA: Thank God—we have reached the river. Let it but roll between us and our pursuers, and we are safe! [*Goes to window*] Gracious! The river is choked with ice!

She withdraws, men enter, there is some comedy tavern dialogue involving a shyster lawyer, Marks—"I'm a lawyer and my name is Marks—have a card"—until Haley comes. He is after that kid he paid for who was then kidnaped by his mother; he has "tracked her to this very place!"

Marks gets an idea—why not catch the mother, too, take her to New Orleans, sell her and split the proceeds? Eliza, hiding, hears, screams, runs out.

"*Let's after her!*"

Next scene: Road to river. Snow landscape. Hurry-up music.

> ELIZA: They press upon my footsteps—the river is my only hope. Heaven grant me the strength to reach it, ere they overtake me! My child, *we will be free—or PERISH!*

Next scene: The entire depth of stage represents the Ohio River filled with floating ice. Eliza appears with Harry on a cake of ice and floats slowly across the scene. Hounds chase after her. Haley and Marks try to follow across after the hounds. *Eliza makes it to FREEDOM!*

Next scene: St. Clair's parlor. St. Clair arrives home with Eva.

> EVA: Oh, Mama! Mama! [*Throws her arms around Marie's neck and kisses her*]
>
> MARIE: That will do—take care, child—don't you make my head ache. [*Kisses Eva languidly*]

So, with a pain-in-the-head mother like that, there is instant audience sympathy for Eva, especially as she is so pretty, polite, loving and has such golden hair. St. Clair tells Marie he has bought her a new coachman.

ST. CLAIR: And a pretty price, too! Fourteen hundred dollars! The fellow was on the steamboat and this little minx [*Pinching Eva's cheek*] gave me no rest until I had paid down my good cash for him.

EVA: And oh, Mama, you'll never guess. Something terrible happened.

MARIE: Don't tell me! My nerves, my nerves!

ST. CLAIR: Oh, it turned out all right! But we had a fearful few moments. At the gangplank when we landed, there was a fearful jam and Little Eva was pushed off into the river.

MARIE: Gracious heavens!

ST. CLAIR: But she no more than struck the water before a man leaped over the rail and as she rose to the surface, grasped her in his arms.

MARIE: Oh! Oh! I can't bear it! [*Buries her face in her hands*]

ST. CLAIR: Now tell your mother—Eva—who was that man?

EVA: [*Running to the door and throwing it open*] Uncle Tom!

Enter dear old Tom. Eva kisses him. Introduction to the mistress, Marie, whom Tom charmingly is "painful glad to see."

EVA: Papa, may I show Uncle Tom the house?

ST. CLAIR: If you like.

EVA: [*Pulling him by the hand*] Come along, Uncle Tom!

TOM: Kin I go, massa?

ST. CLAIR: Of course! And remember, Tom, from now on she's your little mistress. Her word is your law.

TOM: Yassa, yassa, looks like it's gwine to be a very nice kind of law!

Next scene: St. Clair's garden. Tom is singing "Let My People Go." Eva is filling his buttonholes with flowers. They leave after St. Clair enters with Ophelia, his cousin from the North. Ophelia disapproves of the familiarity between Eva and Tom.

ST. CLAIR: You would think no harm in a child's caressing a big dog, but a black creature that can think, reason and feel, you shudder at. Confess it, Cousin! You shrink from this as you would from a toad; yet you are indignant at his wrong.

It is something for a Northern audience to chew on. The moral is pressed when Topsy enters and St. Clair informs Ophelia he is going to give her Topsy for her to educate. But the situation doesn't get somber because Topsy is so perverse and funny.

OPHELIA: Who was your mother?
TOPSY: [*Grinning*] Never had none.
OPHELIA: Never had any mother? What do you mean? Where were you born?
TOPSY: Never was born!
OPHELIA: You mustn't answer me that way. Tell me where you were born, and who your father and mother were.
TOPSY: Never was born, tell you; never had no father, nor mother, nor nothin'. I was raised by a speculator.

How the audience is amused by the comical old-maid Ophelia and the quick-witted Topsy, giggling and rolling her eyes. But not for long, for life must be sad, too. We learn that Eva is not well, in fact she says she knows she is dying. And:

EVA: Papa, isn't there a way to have slaves made free? If I should die, won't you think of me, and do it for my sake?
ST. CLAIR: Oh, child, don't talk to me so! You are all I have on earth!
EVA: Papa, those poor creatures love their children as much as you do me. [*Looks at Tom*] Tom loves *his* children. [*To St. Clair*] Oh, do something for them!
ST. CLAIR: There, there, darling; I will do everything you wish.

She asks him to free Tom. He promises. Now she is ready to die and all gather around to watch her go.

MARIE: My dearest! [*Kneels by the bed*]
ST. CLAIR: Do you know me, darling?
EVA: Dear, dear Papa! Mama, please kiss me!
[*Marie does so*]
Uncle Tom, now, I'm happy. [*She sighs*]
TOM: Look! Look! Massa, she can see things we can't see! [*Tom kneels reverently*]

EVA: [*Staring before her and smiling*] I see . . . I see . . . the crystal gates, wide—wide open—love—joy—peace—

[*Her head falls to one side, her eyes close. The Nurse puts her finger on the pulse. All look at her. She lays Eva's wrist down*]

NURSE: It is over!

ST. CLAIR: Eva! My darling!!

SLOW CURTAIN

In the next scene, St. Clair is distraught.

ST. CLAIR: Oh, Tom, my boy, I want to believe, but I cannot. And there is no more Eva—nothing!

TOM: Oh, yes, Massa St. Clair, there is. I knows it!

ST. CLAIR: How do you know there is? You never *saw* the Lord!

TOM: Well, Massa, you can't see pain, kin you? But you kin feel it—jes' so Ah feel de Lawd, in my soul, Massa St. Clair. When I was sold away from mah old woman an' mah children I was jus' mos' broke up. I said they ain't nothin' left—nothin' at all. Then the Lawd He stood by me and He say: "You cheer up, Tom, they ain't nothin' to be 'fraid of!" An' what He done fo' me, He do for Massa St. Clair!

ST. CLAIR: Singular! That the story of a man who lived and died eighteen hundred years ago can affect people still! [*Rises*] But I am forgetting why I sent for you. Tom, go pack your trunk and get ready. As I promised Eva, I'm going to make a free man of you!

TOM: [*Joyously*] Oh!! Bless de Lawd! Bless de Lawd!

Next scene and the next and the next: trouble. St. Clair has taken to dissipation, has lost his money and might have to sell his property. Tom, too? But he *promised!*

Next scene: an auction block. Marks is here and meets Simon Legree.

MARKS: I'm a lawyer and my name is Marks—have a card!

[*Legree shakes his hand, Marks winces*]

Hold on, hold on, hold on!

LEGREE: That's what I am doing.

MARKS: When I say hold on, I mean let go.

LEGREE: Well, why don't you say what you mean!

[*Swings Marks away*]

MARKS: My, my, that's a hard hand you've got.
LEGREE: Do you know how that hand became so hard?
MARKS: How did it?
LEGREE: By knocking down niggers. There's nothing soft about me!

Slaves are auctioned. Slaves, we learn, that belonged to the "late" Mr. St. Clair. They are auctioned like cattle, with cruel comments from the stonehearted Legree. Including Topsy! But she is *saved* by Ophelia's bid!

OPHELIA: Good heavens, what will people up in Vermont say when they find out I've bought a slave! You come with me, Topsy!

They exit. Uncle Tom, who has been sitting back to audience on a bale of cotton, now turns around. Bidders swarm about him.

LEGREE: Let's see your teeth, old man! [*Grabs him by jaw and opens mouth*] Where was you raised?
TOM: In old Kentucky, massa!
LEGREE: What did you do there?
TOM: Had charge of massa's plantation. Massa St. Clair.
LEGREE: Ha, that's a damn lie!
AUCTIONEER: It's quite true, Mr. Legree.

So the bidding starts and Legree gets him for twelve hundred dollars.

LEGREE: Now you belong to me. Come along!
TOM: May heaven have mercy on us!
LEGREE: Mercy, eh? Ha, ha! I'll give you mercy! [*Cracks whip*]

Act III. Things get worse than a Christian audience could ever expect. Tom has to watch as Legree makes an insinuating proposition to Emmeline, a young girl he has bought at the auction. He promises a lady's earrings if she will be a compliant "house girl."

EMMELINE: No, no, let me work in the fields; I don't want to be a lady!
LEGREE: Oh! You're going to be contrary, are you? I'll soon take all that out of you!

EMMELINE: Please! Please!
LEGREE: Tom, take that gal out and flog her.
[Tom stands aghast]
I told you I didn't buy you just for common work, I mean to make a driver of you. Ye may jest as well begin to get yer hand in. Take her out and flog her, do you *hear?*

Tom protests. That's something he "neber did." And then comes the scene that nobody could forget.

LEGREE: What! Ye black beast! Tell *me* ye don't think it right to do what I tell ye! What have any of you cussed cattle to do with thinking what's right? . . .
TOM: If you mean to kill me, kill me; but dis yere I can't do it— I'll die first!
LEGREE: Well, here's a pious dog—didn't you ever read out of your Bible, "Servants, obey your masters"? Ain't I your master? Didn't I pay twelve-hundred dollars for all there is inside your cussed old black hide? Ain't you mine, body and soul?
TOM: No, no, Massa, my body belongs to you, but my soul belongs to de Lawd, an' *you never can buy that!*

Any actor who didn't bring down a storm of applause with that speech was too incompetent to take tickets at a free performance.

LEGREE: We'll see, we'll see! Here, Sambo, Quimbo! Take this dog up to the whipping post, an' give him such a floggin' he'll remember it till the day he dies!
TOM: [*Going*] Oh Lawd, help me!
LEGREE: Well, now, let's see if He will! [*Starts to embrace Emmeline*]

CURTAIN

Through an abundance of fast fortuitous plot, we come to the end. Legree gets his when he is shot by Lawyer Marks. Tom dies, but that is not too bad because he lives in the tableau.

In analyzing the appeal of this masterpiece of everything, the tableau must be credited as the tremendously thrilling, uplifting, inspiring, beautiful and gloriously sad climax that it was.

Actually, it was an epilogue, fundamentally this:

Gorgeous clouds, tinted with sunlight. Eva, robed in white, is discovered on the back of a milk-white dove with extended wings, as if just soaring above. Her hands are extended in benediction over St. Clair and Uncle Tom who are kneeling and gazing up at her. Expressive music. Very slow curtain.

The expressive music would be a chorus singing a mellow, doleful spiritual, and after the patrons had been shaken by this glamour of dying, had absorbed its pathos and had cleared their noses, they would proceed to the lobby where Little Eva—"Oh, look at her; isn't she the sweetest thing!"—would be selling her pictures.

The script quoted here is one version. There were hundreds of others, for actors and producers would realign the plot and add their own lines and business that they found effective—plus what they chose to lift from others. This receptiveness of the story helped keep the play fresh and vital—it was a unique form of folk art adaptable to the varied genius of its interpreters and to changes in public attitude and style.

In the succeeding years, most of the greats of the theatre would list an appearance in *Uncle Tom* as part of their early training. Maude Adams, who was to be the original Peter Pan, played Eva as a child in Utah. But for the most part, *Uncle Tom* was played by specialists, "Tom actors," "Tommers," who rode this one vehicle as their life's career—they were born into and died in it. A girl would start as Little Eva. If it was a boy, they put a blond wig on him and who knew? A genuine female Eva graduated into Topsy. When her proportions grew wrong for Topsy, she could become Eliza or Mrs. St. Clair or Cousin Ophelia. As for the men, there were parts of all sizes and ages and ordinarily they doubled. If they lived the good life, they would be apotheosized and eventually play Tom.

A standard attraction of Tom shows was the parade down Main Street. You can be sure that in any town in the United States in which you now live, there was a day when a Tom-show parade came down the main street. Legree would walk by glowering, whip in hand. The bloodhounds—fortunately, most people didn't know what a bloodhound looked like so a variety of breeds and mongrels got this thespian chance—would snort past, Topsy would make faces and get laughs and finally, in front of the band (actors "doubling in brass"), would come dear old Uncle Tom riding by, smiling benignly, with dear Little Eva. If you hadn't bought your ticket, this was the nudge.

Eventually, after everyone had seen *Tom* enough times to memorize it, there began to be novelties to prolong the business. Productions became elaborate beyond reason, with casts large enough to swing an election, frequently with

2 UNCLE TOMS! 2 LITTLE EVAS!
2 SIMON LEGREES!

And, it is assumed, enough hounds to tree all the natives.

As we visit Gettysburg and similar battleground-cemeteries, we grasp some of the political effect of what began in Troy, New York. Lincoln is supposed to have said, on meeting Mrs. Stowe, "So this is the little lady who started the great war." Considering Mrs. Stowe's aloof attitude, if the President had in mind the play, he should have said this to Cordelia Howard, Little Cordelia.

It had other effects even more unfortunate. The nation of the North, genuinely loving freedom, disapproving slavery, conceived of the issue in terms of the characters provided by Mrs. Stowe and played by those broad-style actors. Legree became the symbol of the white male South. Helpless, swooning Mrs. St. Clair represented Southern womanhood, lacking the candid directness and stiff-spined integrity of the Northern Ophelia.

If it was thought that the novel and play treated Negroes well —and it was obviously so believed by Northern whites—then that made it difficult later for the whites to understand the Negroes' resentment, even hatred, toward the play. The whites could not see that they, with their money at the box office, had established a set of stereotypes that were to blind them to human reality; nor did they see how for a century this would keep the Negroes who did not choose to fit those stereotypes from approaching freedom and equality through acceptance.

To begin with, the most intelligent Negroes in the story, George and Eliza, were so white they had to explain that they were black. This subscribed to the whites' contention that intelligence came to that race through the infusion of whiteness, by a process no clean-minded white cared to discuss in the presence of women and children.

As for the true blacks, the millions of whites who accepted *Uncle Tom's Cabin* now let themselves believe that blacks were either saintly or comical—anything else was a deviance. This wish of the whites to believe the black-blacks were congenitally carefree and funny was demonstrated by Topsy. Blacks like her, rolling their eyeballs and with their watermelon grins, could not resist being amusing in *any* situation. Consider the scene when Topsy is at the auction:

SKEGGS [*Auctioneer*]: Topsy, take the stand!
TOPSY: I am standin' right now, ain't I?
SKEGGS: [*Exasperated*] Come, and stand up here on this block! Do you hear me?
[*Topsy goes on block*]
This yere gal, gentlemen, this yere gal has got talents!
LEGREE: You don't say so!
SKEGGS: I do say so! They tell me she's a right smart dancer! Topsy, show them what you do!
TOPSY: What I do?
SKEGGS: You heard me.
TOPSY: I do a lot of things.
LEGREE: Including stealing, I reckon!
SKEGGS: Not at all, not at all! Her record's first class. Come on, Topsy, shake your feet now!
TOPSY: My feet don't feel very shaky, boss!
SKEGGS: Well, they better!
TOPSY: I'm powerful sorry, boss, but I don't reckon they do!
SKEGGS: All right, then we'll sell you for a field hand, how will you like that?
TOPSY: Does that mean work?
SKEGGS: That's it!
TOPSY: Sweatin' in de sun?
SKEGGS: That's it!
TOPSY: Reckon I'se goin' to dance, boss!

You can hear the sure-fire laugh. As for Uncle Tom himself, he was cast in the white mind as the embodiment of all "good"

Negroes: gentle, kind, Bible-soaked, willing to give his life for good white folks and theirs.

Perhaps the most pernicious effect was due to the fact that these Negro characters were played by whites in blackface. If they had been actual Negroes, it might not have been so acceptable, it might have required the audience to make a saner adjustment. The whites accepted the whites pretending to be Negroes, but could they have accepted Negroes as Negroes? The true attitude of the whites was probably indicated by Eleanor Roosevelt, a white of rare honesty and possibly the person with the best will and most sensible kindness of any woman in this century; yet Eleanor Roosevelt had trouble in adjusting to people who were actually black. Her biographer, Joseph P. Lash, tells us:

> A personal experience with Mrs. [Mary McLeod] Bethune taught her how deeply inbred racial feelings were among whites. She liked to kiss people whom she knew well when greeting them and saying good-by, but it took some time and a conscious effort for Eleanor to give Mrs. Bethune a peck on the cheek, and it was not until she kissed Mrs. Bethune without thinking of it that she felt she had at last overcome the racial prejudice within herself.

There is a report of a 1905 production where Negroes did play some of the Negro parts in *Uncle Tom*:

> GRAND [New York City]—*Uncle Tom's Cabin*. Because of trouble with the Hebrew Actors' Protective Association, Jacob Adler was forced to give up the management of the Grand Street Theatre . . . [so he] hurried a production of *Uncle Tom's Cabin* for Sept. 15. The character parts were better than the straight roles, and the whites who were made up as blacks were far better than the blacks, who could not play themselves.

However talented the Negro actors, it would have been difficult for them to play Negroes as white actors in blackface played Negroes. By 1905, the stereotypes were so set that to play *Uncle Tom* Negroes straight would have been as unacceptable and "unrealistic" as doing Cyrano with no nose.

When, a century later, the romantic scrim was lifted and the blacks began to appear as they really were, there was a great white disappointment. Uncle Tom didn't actually love them—in fact, all the time he had been internally muttering his anger at his subjection. And George was still full of fury even though he had come north. And Topsy hated dancing. To many whites, it seemed hypocritical, disloyal, that they were not true to character, meaning their characters in *Uncle Tom.*

Uncle Tom's Cabin may have been hackwork, it may have had a cruel effect, but it was a godsend to the American theatre. Once that great public had enjoyed the show without loss of virtue, it could not resist, it would find further excuse to leave Humdrum and go to Elsinore and Verona and other dark and bright climes, to share the sorrow and joy of Juliet or the Moor or Katharine or Mrs. Wiggs or Rip, and feel in turn that its own emotions, dreams and regrets were understood.

So the opera house became profitable and every town built one, and the tribe of playwrights and actors increased to fill the demand, and theatre became part of the culture, bringing the gifts of talented mesmerists who, in precious moments, could make all those strangers out front feel that they were one.

•

1905—fifty-three years into the run and forty years after the war to make the Negro equal:

Under the heading "Record-Breaking Audience" the Peoria, Illinois, Journal says of Stetson's "Big Double Uncle Tom Company":

> *The Grand Opera House held the largest crowd that ever entered its doors yesterday afternoon at the matinee given by Stetson's* Uncle Tom's Cabin *company. 200 people were turned away, every seat in the house, including the galleries, being filled. In the evening the house was again crowded and Peoria theatregoers demonstrated the fact that they were not tired of* Uncle Tom's Cabin. *The performance given by the Stetson company was the best ever seen in Peoria. The details of the familiar old play were worked out admirably, and the acting and settings were consistent in every respect.*

☛ 5

Hits! Palpable Hits!

Any night of the week except Sunday, the U.S. Sabbath, between September 1, 1905, and May 30, 1906, the industrious actors were demonstrating the ingratitude of children (King Lear); more were advocating forgiveness for erring daughters (Her Only Sin); many were proving that the infidelity of wives doesn't pay (Wife in Name Only); while several troupes were declaring that a virtuous woman deserves respect though one-eighth of her red blood is black (The Octoroon).

In San Francisco genteel actors were showing how far a mother's love is apt to go to save a daughter's reputation (Lady Windermere's Fan), and in the same place, same time, others were telling (in A Winter's Tale) how a jealous husband can make life hell for everyone and still have a happy ending. "It is such a complete success that it has set people wondering why this masterpiece of the great playwright is not more often presented."

In New Orleans the thespians were revealing that a man may be a poet and expert fencer even if he is a freak with a hypertrophied proboscis (Cyrano de Bergerac), and in Kansas City they were telling the Missourians how the French enjoy being naughty (M'amselle Fifi), and in Alabama, Washington, New Hampshire and Arkansas and points between, they were saying that pure love is better than anything (Hearts of Gold).

While the actors took their bows, Charles Frohman, the great New York producer from whom many of these blessings came, was riding in his private Pullman built expressly for him, which, it was said, the railroads accorded "the same precedence of schedule that they did to the U. S. President's Special."

A very satisfactory business, the 1905 theatre, with every prospect of becoming bigger and greater. Why not?

THE Civil War ended with hate and grief. In the deluge of war plays that would come, there would be new characters for an ancient plot. Instead of Montagues forbidden to marry Capulets, or lower class denied access to upper, or contact barred between those of the true faith and those of the sane sect, now the daughters and sons of the ex-Grays were prohibited from having desire for the sons and daughters of the former-Blues.

There were graves in every village to be decorated with flags in May, family hopes buried, the hearts of mothers scarred. The only thing that relieved the bitterness was that business—in the North—had never been so good. Railroads were spreading almost as fast as the surveyors could lay them out, giving access to bonanzas of ore and oil, with the cars going in the opposite direction filled with goods for Main Street stores. Enough money was being made so even the dullards could feel smart.

All of which was good for the theatre, although there was still some soulful hesitancy on the part of the new customers. They were learning how much easier it had been to resist when they had less money to go. Now, though they were not ready for wanton indulgence, they wanted more of that uplifting pleasure at the playhouse. And it would be easier to attend, it might avoid criticism, the raised nose at church, if they could find a rationale such as they had when they were protesting slavery by applauding Uncle Tom.

Nothing was more eager to oblige than the theatre of the past, and it managed to fulfill this very need. Looking for a theme and a cause, it turned to that second great national blight: the demon rum. Today, despite education, there are some curious gaps in the average American's knowledge of his history; few seem to know, as an instance, just how besotted their country once was.

You could say the American taste for the spiritous stuff began at the beginning. The Pilgrims didn't make it to Virginia as planned but chose to stop farther north because "We could not now take time for further search or consideration, our victuals being much spent, especially our beer."

It was soon found there were a number of things that could make a stronger brew to keep a man warm of nights in this climate that made Old England seem balmy. There developed such a dependence on these fortifiers that William Penn started breweries to get people off likker and back to beer, but the weak stuff persuaded few. Then rum began to be made or imported, and there was enough demand to make it one of the issues in the tension between London and here. George Washington would fight to give every man his untaxed grog, but later he was much concerned about the effect; he referred to drink as the "source of evil and ruin of half the workmen in this country." It was even the custom to give spirits as part of wages. Grandmother Brown, who lived a hundred years in Ohio, could remember that "a man was considered very mean if he didn't keep whiskey for his help."

The swilling was so general it corrupted all classes and professions. Rum was considered the beverage for special occasions, and it was easy to make the occasion special, as one historian has observed: "No child was properly christened unless all present drank to the health and future prosperity of the infant. At weddings, the tankard passed from hand to hand. The time-honored practice of serving drinks to the mourners at a funeral was universally observed. Church, as well as home festivities, were made the merrier by reason of the 'good creature.' The blessing of a new edifice, the installation of new pews, and especially the ordination of a new minister were occasions when slight restraint was placed upon the appetite."

This may have made it more congenial for the ministers who officiated at these events, but in time it was too good for business. The Reverend Leonard Woods, a noted professor of theology at Andover Seminary, wrote: "I remember when I could reckon up among my acquaintances forty ministers, who were either drunkards, or so far addicted to drinking, that their reputation and usefulness were greatly impaired, if not utterly ruined."

(I got some insight into conditions as they were even much later when talking with my mother. She was born in a town of some three hundred souls, and I was born in the same place that still had the same head count. She spoke of the drunks the children used to watch from the school windows and said, "You see, in those days we had thirteen saloons"—a statement that jolted me not only because it seemed an overaccommodation for a population of three hundred but because, in my dry time, all a man could do was wait for the cider to turn hard and hope nobody heard about it. I did not understand how this could be until I learned how the distillers used to encourage and often finance any saloon or tavern outlet they could find or create. It was called the spirit of competition.)

So before the last divine lost his way completely and the last workman failed to show up for work and the last student at Harvard became a hopeless addict (something John and Abigail Adams worried about terribly—their son John Quincy got past the temptation but his brother didn't make it), before the country fulfilled Washington's dread, *Temperance came!* The protest against the Demon began to be heard, and whatever *Uncle Tom's Cabin* was for abolition two other plays were for Temperance.

The Drunkard, or The Fallen Saved was the first one. When it opened at the Boston Museum (another name for a theatre), it ran for 130 performances, breaking the custom of changing the bill each week. The other play was 10 *Nights in a Barroom,* and it would be difficult to say which was seen by the larger public. You could say both had more than they deserved unless you believe people should endure what they pay for.

These were plays the pious "should" support—so they thought, and all managers agreed, although some of the actors may have retched. These were plays you could take father to so he would be dissuaded from stopping off with the boys on the way home with the paycheck; or take junior to scare him from ever wondering what the stuff really tastes like; or take Uncle Jay to, the souse, to make him cry and feel ashamed of himself.

Fundamentally the two plays were alike. Both had abundance of plot and long staggering speeches, but *10 Nights* not only had the more memorable title, it had Little Mary. From this distance, it would seem as though Little Daughter Mary would have driven any father to drink, but this is to ignore the true misery from alcohol that existed in so many families of that time.

Yet, pertinent and instructive as *10 Nights* obviously was, there are lines in it—almost all—which logically should have emptied theatres and filled saloons. For example, when Little Mary, who was always tailing father, comes to the saloon to wheedle him home:

MARY: [*Outside*] Father! father! Where is my father? [*Enters*] O, I've found you, have I? Now won't you come home with me?

MORGAN (*Father*): Blessings on thee, my little one! Darkly shadowed is the sky that hangs gloomily over thy head.

MARY: Come, father, mother has been waiting a long time, and I left her crying sadly. Now do come home, and make us all so happy.

MORGAN: Yes, my child, I'll go. [*Kisses her, looks at Slade, the barkeeper (whom he apparently holds responsible for what he has drunk)*] You have robbed me of my last penny, Simon Slade, but this treasure remains. Farewell, *friend* Slade. Come, dear one, come. I'll go home! Come, come! I'll go, yes, I'll go.

That last speech was stretched to cover the business of getting his legs functioning to wobble him to the exit. The scene as given here is truncated. There was sure to be enough more so Mary's plight, nobility, sweetness, daughterly devotion could affect everyone in the audience. That is what they paid for, to be affected and to see how no drunkard could escape calamity, even if he had a Little Mary to fetch him home.

We jump to a dreadful turn of events in a later scene, again in the barroom. Slade, the proprietor, is greeting the customers:

SLADE: Good evening, gentlemen. I'm glad to see you all looking so sociable this evening.

[*Sees Morgan*]

Joe Morgan, what the devil brings you here, like an evil stain to mar our happiness?

MORGAN: O, yes; I know I am an unwelcome guest! My presence displeases the *landlord!* He has become ashamed of his old friend!

SLADE: Off with you, Joe Morgan! I won't put up with your insolence any longer! Leave my house and never show your face here again. If you can't keep decent, don't intrude yourself here.

MORGAN: You talk of decency!—a rumseller's decency! Poh! You was a decent man once, but that time is past and gone. Decency—poh! How like a fool you talk; as if it were any more decent to sell rum than to drink it!

SLADE: I've heard enough from you. [*Takes up glass*] Now, leave my house!

MORGAN: I won't!

SLADE: Won't you?—take that, then! [*Throws glass, it passes Morgan out R.1E (right, first entrance)—Mary screams—runs in R.1E, forehead bloody—falls c. (center)*]

MARY: Father! dear father! They've killed me!

MORGAN: Curse you, Simon Slade! Villain, your career of landlord shall be short; for here I swear, by the side of my murdered child, you shall die the death of a dog!

[MUSIC]

She was murdered but expired slow for there had to be the death scene. It would require a convocation of psychoanalysts and computerized theoreticians to explain why, in an era when death was so prevalent and early, people received so much benefit from mourning on stage and in song. Everyone seems to have been gratified by the lay that sang of the husband and child transporting the remains of mother.

While the train rolled onward,
A husband sat in tears,
Thinking of the happiness
Of just a few short years,
For baby's face brings pictures of
A cherished hope that's dead,
But baby's cries can't waken her,
In the baggage coach ahead.

To return to *10 Nights in a Barroom*. Next scene: Mary is dying. She becomes delirious.

MARY: Mother, I see him! There he is now!
MORGAN: Her mind wanders!
MARY: Remember, you have promised me, father. O don't!—go! —don't! There, he has gone! Well, I'll go after him again! I'll try and walk there! I can sit down and rest by the way! Oh dear, how tired I am! Father? father! oh, dear!
MORGAN: Here I am, my child. I have not gone and left you.
MARY: O, I know you, now! It is my father! Stoop down to me. I want to whisper something to you—not to mother. I don't want her to hear it—it will make her feel so bad.
MORGAN: What is it, my child?
MARY: I shall never get well, father; I am going to die. . . . There, mother; you go away—you've got trouble enough. I only told him, because he promised not to go to the tavern any more until I got well. O! Mr. Slade threw it so hard; but it didn't strike father, and I'm so glad! How it would have hurt him! But he'll never go there any more, and that will be so good, won't it, mother?

Now comes the BIG scene. Mary is gone, meaning dead, and Joe, almost overcome with remorse, after a struggle, gives in to the bottle to relieve his grief. Almost instantly, it precipitates a malady common in that time, delirium tremens! The actor playing Morgan must now scare hell out of everyone watching so they will swear off for life. It is said that a star named Watkins ruined his health because of his writhing, flopping, screaming through this scene. If any have doubt, let them push back the furniture and practice:

> My brain is on fire! . . .
> Oh! OH! . . .
> Hideous visions are before my eyes! . . .
> Look! LOOK! . . .
> What's this—what's there—in the corner! The CORNER! . . .
> [*Scream*]
> A snake! A SNAKE! . . .
> Oh, horror—take him off! . . .
> *TWO* snakes—and their eyes glaring at me! . . .
> Hor-*ror!* Quick! Take them *OFF!* . . .
> OH-H-H-H-H-h-h-h-h . . .

Rather than risk a gentle reader's mind, we forbear giving more of this exhausting speech. After a scene of recovery and when noble reform has been sworn—giving the empathizing spectators time to control their shakes—the play concludes with Joe Morgan speaking the tag to the audience:

> Restored once more to happiness, we pray that others may learn from our past experience, and that none will regret deducting from the calendar of their lives to 10 *Nights in a Barroom!*

Curtain and applause . . .

The play had one other feature that became historic. It was learned then, and relearned many times after, that if you have a musical theme identifying the attraction (vide "Limelight," "Around the World in 80 Days," "Lara's Theme"), it can be a valuable box-office assist as people recall and recommend. 10 *Nights* had one of the most famous ever, Little Mary's song:

> *Father, dear father, come home with me now!*
> *The clock in the steeple strikes one.*
> *You said you were coming right home from the shop,*
> *As soon as your day's work was done.*
> *Our fire has gone out, our house is all dark,*
> *And mother's been watching since tea,*

With poor brother Benny so sick in her arms,
And none to help her but me.
Come home, come home, come home!
Please, Father, dear Father, come home!

For years the local opera house had one or more guaranteed sellout engagements per season as the innumerable companies brought Slade, Morgan, Mary and the hallucinatory snakes to persuade the local inebriates to quit. Again.

The companies came because the theatre had reached the era of "combinations." Originally the local theatre had a stock company—so called because the actors had shares in the company and were paid accordingly. The number of shares an actor held would be determined by the manager, usually the leading player, an arrangement that was not conducive to contented employees —so we hear. Inasmuch as such a company might stage as many as sixty plays a season, an actor had to be able. Any applicant who was not up in at least fifty parts—including Shakespeare and the most popular contemporary comedies and melodramas—would be invited to go away and learn his business and then he could try again.

Even for veterans the strain of this life could be terrible. Rehearsing all morning, searching for wardrobe, sewing, patching costumes, memorizing, performing—"a sweatshop life," one actress called it, "the most sweatshop kind of work I ever heard of, and the most exhausting for the brain and body. Fifteen hours a day in the theatre, many towns played daily matinees and the middle West played seven days a week"—sometimes the weariness, tension, competition would cause these purveyors of emotion to lose control and pretense would become real. Once in Louisville, we are told by a diarist, the leading lady chased one of the actors offstage with a spear. When he tried to return, she renewed the attack with a screwdriver, dramatically screaming, "You son of a bitch, *die!*"

After this original stock company era there came the visiting-star phase. A luminary (such as Forrest, Junius Booth, *et al.*) would join the resident company for a special engagement.

Usually with one rehearsal—"I play it standing here and you stand there—no, don't cover me, to the left!—and when I finish '*Away, away, away!*' you say 'dah-dah' to '*have lost him too*' and then I say '*Had it pleas'd heaven*—dah-dah-dah' long speech moving to here, where I end '*look grim as hell!*' and then you give me my next cue"—the star would then give his performance, frequently with the rest of the cast tense to get out of the great one's way or often simply frozen, standing and staring at the famous wonder. Then the star would take the curtain and most of the receipts. Once when the play was *Lear* a member of the audience in Philadelphia gave his reaction to star and company. "I'm not much of a judge," he said, "but I should think the star was a damned fine actor for he played this piece all by himself."

Walt Whitman, who was a constant theatre buff, railed in the Brooklyn *Eagle* that "one of the curses of the Park, and indeed of nearly all theatres now, is the star system." Yet he praised so enthusiastically those stars he liked that, willy-nilly, he supported the very system he condemned. And that is why the star business, for all its imperfections, continued. Even in remote places, the people going to the opera houses were privileged to witness genius—again: Forrest, Booth and then their successors.

It was the visiting star, however, who would ultimately put the stock companies out of business. Since the public would come only when there was a star, the stars could and did charge more and more for their visits. To meet this cost, the managers cut the stock actors' salaries more and more until the quality of the support became absurd: automatons throwing cues.

The next phase was a considerable improvement. The stars began to bring their own companies, and this was called the combination or, in the trade, simply a combo. "*Twelfth Night* in a combo played here to capacity house." Again, it was the increase in railroads, the possibility of convenient, profitable jumps, the cheapness of this travel: twenty tickets (and every company needed twenty for cast, crew, manager and so forth) got you a coach for the company and a baggage car for your gear. There were no one-set plays with casts of three and four in those days; the public would never have accepted such small measure, and there was no need: actors were inexpensive.

As for the price of stagehands, although those who traveled had begun a union in 1886, and although producers and actors were soon calling them "arbitrary," it was some time before their wages were called "exorbitant." While so slow was the organization of local unions it was years before house managers had to pay union scale—if indeed they paid anything.

> ELYRIA [Ohio]—Opera House. The stage hands receive no regular salaries, but each year Manager Park allows them to secure an attraction for a benefit, giving them the house free. Joe Ott plays their benefit this year.
>
> —January 1905

A far cry from

> STAGEHANDS AT KENNEDY CENTER
> SAID TO EARN UP TO $1,500 A WEEK
>
> —*New York Times*
> February 2, 1972

Now that *Uncle Tom's Cabin* and *10 Nights in a Barroom* had garnered a majority audience for the theatre, that audience was not apt to subsist indefinitely on a diet of dramatized injustice and misery. Fortunately, if not inevitably, another accepted theatrical dish was concocted which could be called "wholesomeness" or mush-and-milk. Now that the pious ones had braved God's bolt in attending those moralizing tracts, *Tom* and *10 Nights,* could there possibly be anything wrong in partaking of "wholesomeness"? Certainly not—and it was found that sweetness and sunshine was a marvelously salable product, as it continued to be down to and including the pure presentations of John Golden (*Turn to the Right, Lightnin', Three Wise Fools*).

When we say the dish was concocted, that is precisely how it came about in the case of *The Old Homestead.* There was an ambitious low comedian-dancer named Denman Thompson whose specialty, ironically, was material shading toward blue. He might have lived out his life getting laughs from the lower belly except that while playing Pittsburgh, a city with five rivers for dampness, he was seized with a severe attack of rheumatism.

This proved fatal to the career of Denman Thompson, the dancer. As a biographer said, "It looked as if he must abandon his profession or submit to a lower place in the ranks."

It is easy enough to understand why he sought material that was more words than action, but what inspired him to go from blue to white-on-white is not so easy to see. He devised a sketch called *Joshua Whitcomb* about dear, sweet, rustic, innocent, sincere and simple Uncle Josh of Swanzey, New Hampshire. He tried it out in 1875. The response was at least encouraging enough for him (and a collaborator he found) to add a second and third act during 1876 and 1878. Rechristened *The Old Homestead,* they opened it in New York to indifference, and a tour of New England was as cold. Then the tide turned in, of all places, Denver, Colorado. There have been many instances of such a shift in public attitude, and they are no easier to explain than the fact that the tide can turn five thousand feet above sea level.

From then on, helped by tremendous applications of "modern" exploitation, with scenes from the play plastered on fences and walls, there were few empty seats for the rest of Thompson's life. Twenty-four years later, the New York *Dramatic Mirror* reported:

> MEMPHIS—Denman Thompson in *The Old Homestead* to large houses Jan. 28–29.
> NASHVILLE—Denman Thompson in *The Old Homestead* 30, largest house of season.
> CHATTANOOGA—Denman Thompson in *The Old Homestead* 31, delighted packed houses.
> KNOXVILLE—Feb. 1, Denman Thompson in *The Old Homestead,* SRO.

Thompson was Uncle Josh (he never played anything else) until his death in 1910, and he is said to have made over three million dollars, which should have relieved his rheumatism.

Since this was another source of sustenance for the growing theatre, it is worth checking on *The Old Homestead*'s appeal. To begin with, it was considered marvelously realistic. "Theatregoers," said a commentator, "had been sated with the artificial in plays and players." Meaning, perhaps, Eliza's skill on ice or saloonkeeper Slade's remarkable pitch to Mary's forehead. Here now were such touches of realism as "A load of hay drawn by oxen lumbers across the stage and enters the barn." Or the haymakers gathering around an old well sweep and, after drinking the pure water, singing:

The moss-covered bucket that hangs in the well . . .

While Denman Thompson, they felt, was so authentic he wasn't even an actor. They quoted comments such as: "An old Philadelphia lady summed it up correctly after she had seen Mr. Thompson as Uncle Josh, 'That man is not acting—he portrays a living character.' " And: "When Denman Thompson performed *The Old Homestead* in Keene, New Hampshire, the people wanted their money back. They insisted 'It warn't actin'; it was just a lot of fellers goin' around doin' things.' " While one enthusiastic critic wrote, "When Joshua says he will 'go down into the cellar and set my mousetrap,' we have a touch of the actual that no dramatist on earth could have furnished out of his imagination."

There were sociological reasons, too, for its great appeal. Country people were becoming aware of the city and its advantages, and the young folks wondered if they should stay home and miss the excitement. While those in the city (largely from the country here or from the country in Europe) were finding the price of the material advantages—horsecars, bathtubs, gaslight—getting higher and higher in strain and disillusionment. It was all the result of competition which required a rat alertness, and that brought the question: Was the sparkling champagne any better than the pure water from the bucket? Was knowing the latest slang any better than being colloquial like simple Uncle Josh?

Though Eugene Field called *Homestead* "altogether the best American play yet produced," its story was about as predictable as sunrise. Act I and Josh is setting his mousetrap, the oxen are lumbering into the barn, and the hands are singing four-part

Denman Thompson in *The Old Homestead.* The fourth time he played Paducah, Kentucky, they thought he was better than ever.

hosannas at the well, when the terrible, incredible news comes that son Reuben, pride and joy, has pilfered at the Cheshire Bank. Reuben, hurt, falsely accused but too homespun to cope, too ashamed to stay, runs away from it all. Josh, plain patriarch, too good, too wholesome, to have possibly sired a bank robber, gets his spirit up to go look for his child so as to stand by him. The prospect of this sweet-souled innocent going farther into the wicked world than ten miles from Swanzey is cause for incredulity and suspense as the curtain gently falls.

Act II. Here is Josh in the palatial mansion of his boyhood chum, Henry Hopkins, who has made a million dollars in New York City but finds nothing so satisfying as reminiscing about their blissful childhood together. What became of . . .? Who married whom . . .? Remember the time . . .? You are made to feel and sigh that their former life was sweeter than the palatial present can ever be. And how endearingly old-fashioned and virtuous Josh appears in this contrast. "You might as well leave a sasser of taller alongside the fireplace; I may want to grease my boots before you get up in the morning." Incidentally, all actors playing the boyhood friend and other good city folks always helped the audience response by slowly shaking their heads in kindly, bemused admiration of such saintly simplicity. Dear old Uncle Josh. Curtain.

Act III. Before Grace Church, Broadway, New York. It is possible that most of the audience had never seen stained glass, and the effect of the light through the windows of the church as painted on the drop provoked a sanctified awe. It is snowing this night, which aids the pathos. And there is music coming from behind the stained glass. The program of the New York opening informed: "*The Palms* rendered by Chauncey Olcott and *The Old Homestead* choir." A Policeman enters, "hand on Reuben's collar."

POLICE: Come on; you can't stop here.
REUBEN: Hold on, officer—let me explain.
POLICE: You can tell the judge all about that in the morning.

A young man named Jack has entered.

JACK: Say, what are you going to do with him?
POLICE: [*Roughly*] Is that any of your business?
JACK: Oh, no! Oh, no; it is not any of my business but he's a friend of mine. He isn't a bad sort of a fellow, officer.
[*Taking note from breast pocketbook and pressing it in Policeman's hand*] He's all right.
POLICE: [*When Jack passes money, takes sly glance at it and changes tone*] Oh, well, if he is a friend of yours, that makes all the difference in the world.
[*Exit, swinging club*]
REUBEN: That was very kind of you, sir. . . .
JACK: Now tell me, what did the King of Clubs want to take you in for?
REUBEN: [*Pointing*] I fell asleep in that doorway.
JACK: A little tired out, I suppose? A little discouraged, eh?
REUBEN: [*Nervously*] No, sir; I was sleeping off a drunk.
JACK: I thought so. [*Feeling Reuben's arm*] Well, look here, old fellow, you're all over a-shake! You need a good strong milk punch to brace you up. Have you got the price?
REUBEN: Not a cent.
JACK: Oh! Well, here's a dollar note for you. . . .
REUBEN: [*Gratefully shaking hands with Jack*] Thank you, sir, thank you! . . .

They exit and Uncle Josh instantly enters, posts a letter in a box to the folks back home and has some conversation with himself.

JOSH: Well, I guess I'll have to do as Henry says, give it up for tonight and take a fresh start in the morning; can't find Reuben nowhere.

A Salvation Army band passes and Josh is amazed to see such "soldiers." The postman comes to collect the mail in the box and Josh summons the Policeman. "Catch him! Catch him! He took my letter out of that box!" Once it is explained "this man is appointed by the Government to collect the mail," Josh can only say, "Gosh all fish hooks!" Then Jack returns.

[Jack stops, surprised at seeing Josh. Looks Josh all over. Josh puts right hand on watch and left hand in pocket]

JACK: *[Astonished]* Why, no!

JOSH: What's the matter?

JACK: It is.

JOSH: How do you know it is?

JACK: My preserver!

JOSH: Sho'!

JACK: Why, you saved my life!

JOSH: Well, that's the first time I ever knew I looked like a life preserver.

JACK: I met you in Swanzey.

JOSH: *[Very slowly and knowingly]* Well, I guess not! I have had that two or three times before.

[Turns up stage and balances first on one toe and then on other in a country smart way as much as to say, "I know a thing or two!"]

JACK: *[Laughing]* Yes, I did. About three weeks ago. Don't you remember?

JOSH: Now, look here; I have been tackled by about a dozen of you fellers since I have been here, and I'm gittin' kind o' tired on't. Now if you don't want ter get your feathers ruffled up, you go look for squashes somewhere else! I just hitched on to a feller and I feel pretty darned "kinky." Ain't quite so green as you think I be. I take the papers. Play none o' yer hunker slidin' on me, by gosh!

JACK: Don't you remember about three weeks ago giving a poor miserable wretch money enough to go to his home? I am the man.

JOSH: You be darned. You ain't?

JACK: I can convince you.

JOSH: *[Putting his hands in his pockets]* Well, that's what you'll have to do before I talk to you much longer.

JACK: I can tell you the last words you said to me.

JOSH: Well, let's hear them.

JACK: Go home and try to be somebody. It isn't too late.

JOSH: *[Taking hands from pockets and slapping them together]* By gum! That's what I said!

[Jack holds out his hand to shake. Josh puts hands in pockets again quickly]

Hold on! Hold on! Tell me what you said and then I'll give up.

JACK: I told you I would try and if I didn't win, I'd give Old John Barleycorn the toughest scuffle he ever had for the underhold.

JOSH: Well, that's just what you said. And there's my hand. I'm glad to see you.

JACK: And I am glad to see you, old gentleman and old friend. [*Taking ten-dollar bill from pocket and handing it to Josh*] Allow me to return your ten dollars.

JOSH: [*Taking money*] Now, by gosh! I know it's you. How de-do! [*Shaking hands*] I guess your mother was glad to see you, wasn't she?

JACK: Yes, overjoyed!

JOSH: I knowed she'd be!

JACK: Did you find your boy yet, Mr. Whitcomb?

[*Organ plays piano—some very pretty church service*]

JOSH: [*With feeling*] No, sir; I didn't, and I have been trampin' up and down these streets for more'n a week searching for him everywhere; and I have seen more wickedness and misery in that time than I ever thought could exist in a civilized community. I am dreadfully afraid he has been led off, and took to drink. Henry Hopkins says drink is the ruination of more than half the young men of New York.

JACK: Well, Henry Hopkins isn't far from being right.

[*Organ stops. Commotion outside*]

JOSH: There's a row! Don't go too near or you'll get stabbed. A lot of rowdies outside—

JACK: Here comes my dollar investment and about as drunk as they make them.

[*Voices outside shouting "Good night, old feller," etc. Enter Reuben staggering. Josh recognizes him. He falls into Josh's arms and then falls on his knees. Josh bends over him*]

JOSH: My boy Reub! Reub! Reub!

[*When Reuben falls, Policeman runs on, and Jack stops him*]

Why, it's my boy Reub!

[*Organ in church plays "Wedding March," piano, till curtain, and then forte till final curtain*]

CURTAIN

[*Second curtain: Policeman with head bowed. Reuben stands with his head on Josh's shoulder. Jack removes his hat and stands with bowed head*]

The clerics, who once could have almost as much influence at the box office as present-day critics, all became tub-thumpers for *The Old Homestead.* This was one:

> I beg to add my recommendation of that most excellent moral play. I have seen it twice, and have advised my people, more particularly the young man's guild and the older boys of the Sunday school, to go and see it. I consider your play equal to a dozen sermons, bringing home as it does so forcibly the lesson of the Fifth Commandment. God bless and prosper you in the good work you are doing through your play among the young men and boys of New York.
>
> Rev. Edwd. Wallace Neil
> Church of St. Andrew-the-Martyr

If it is wondered why the devout thought this opus better than the Shakespeare they had shunned, the explanation, no doubt, is in what the citizen of Cincinnati told Mrs. Trollope, who was visiting there from England. "Shakespeare," Mrs. Trollope was informed, "is obscene, and thank God we are sufficiently advanced to have found it out!"

Denman Thompson had his *Old Homestead* as Forrest had his *Metamora,* and there were other shays that carried stars for a lifetime. The one that the public today has heard most about is *The Count of Monte Cristo* and its star, James O'Neill. O'Neill had two disdainful sons, one of whom had a bad enough conscience to compel him to write what has been called "probably the greatest of American plays" (Clive Barnes, in the *New York Times*). The play, of course, is *Long Day's Journey into Night* by Eugene O'Neill, and it projects the gist of the father's story.

It may not be sad enough to make us remove our hats and bow our heads, but there is pathos in the fact that but for the accident of a genius son, James O'Neill would have been another actor who sculptured in air—delighting audiences through almost all his life, then thrillingly remembered by those who saw him but can no more make the next generations understand the wonder of him than we can reproduce the effect of Olivier's scream in *Oedipus.* Which is what O'Neill feared at the end of his career, for he had not established his reputation in Shakespeare or in any other traditional way but had simply electrified audiences more than five thousand times and made a fortune as Edmond Dantès in a melodrama, *The Count of Monte Cristo.*

Part of O'Neill's feat was to get himself accepted in a play which was not written by Shakespeare, did not inveigh against any sin of the day, did not advocate any cause such as abolition, or make people weep wholesome buckets. Actually, what the play celebrated was a rather questionable human aspiration: good old revenge. This was plain entertainment, and the only excuses for going—aside from wanting a hell of a grand evening—were the assumption that the book was a sort of classic, written by a "good" author; the play contained nothing in bad taste such as "By Gad!" or the exposure of a feminine ankle; and Mr. O'Neill was a terrific actor. The time had come when that was enough.

The story of *Monte Cristo* can be sketched if you accept the convenient way things once happened in plays. Edmond Dantès is a young sailor. He is arrested on his wedding day, falsely accused of some political involvement, and confined to a dungeon below the Château d'If. After eighteen years, an imprisoned Abbé, trying to escape, mistakenly digs his way into Edmond's cell. The Abbé falls ill and tells Edmond of a great fortune hidden on the island of Monte Cristo, which he can find if he escapes. The Abbé dies, Edmond puts the corpse in his bed, gets in a sack intended for the corpse, is thrown by the guards into the sea and thus escapes. Clambering up a rock to bring down the curtain of Act II, Scene 3, he shouts:

"Saved! Mine, the treasures of Monte Cristo! *The world is mine!*"

He now proceeds to ruin the three men who did him wrong. As they rightfully fall, he ticks them off: "One!" "Two!" . . . and "Three!" makes the final curtain.

With almost no education (although the *American Dictionary of Biography* speaks of his "intellectual attainments"), at age eighteen O'Neill made his first stage appearance in Cincinnati. He was an extra who was supposed to help overpower Forrest in a climactic scene, but the great man's reputation and personality so overawed young O'Neill that he failed completely in the assignment. Then came traveling-show experiences, which included losing his trunks and wardrobe more than once to satisfy landlords.

Before long he was making good in an impressive way with the best company in New York, and he moved on to become the lead with the famous McVicker's company in Chicago. That he had what it takes is attested by Harrison Grey Fiske, editor of the leading theatrical publication of that time, as he describes O'Neill after he had found his great part:

> His face is beautiful—beautiful in its cameo-like profile, and beautiful in its mobile expressiveness. His eyes are large, dark, and lustrous, dreamy in repose, flashing in action. His mouth is sensitive, yet firm, the shade of sadness blending with its smile giving a strange interest to the whole countenance. His movements are grace itself; his attitudes are superbly picturesque. His voice is rich, mellow, and musical; and it is susceptible of a wide range of expression. His speech is just tinged with a bit of the brogue that adds to, rather than detracts from, his many singular graces.

While he was at McVicker's he once played Othello to Booth's Iago and Booth was heard to say in the wings, "He plays it better than I do!" The audiences thought he was good, too, according to a letter to a Chicago newspaper years later (and kept by O'Neill in his scrapbook), as quoted by the Gelbs in their superb biography of son Eugene. The letter speaks of the time when James was playing Macduff to Booth's Macbeth:

> The house was packed to the doors and when Macduff announced the foul murder, the curtain went down on a roar of applause. . . . Men and women stood up, waving their handkerchiefs and crying "O'Neill! O'Neill!" This applause and shouting were deafening. O'Neill came before the footlights, blushing like a boy. The audience had no desire to say to Mr. Booth by their applause that they did not appreciate his great acting. But they did want Mr. O'Neill to know that his fine acting had highly registered.

Appraisals such as this were to wound O'Neill when he thought, long after, of his lost chance, as his son has told us in *Long Day's Journey*.

Here also at McVicker's he was cast as Edmond Dantès in *The Count of Monte Cristo*. Realizing his strength in this part, he bought the rights, and that was his great, successful mistake. Harrison Grey Fiske wrote of O'Neill's effect:

> In the role of Dantès he demonstrates his mastery of the technique of the stage art, and exhibits the versatility of his talent. Whether as the rollicking nimble sailor of the prologue, or the emaciated convict making his bold stroke for liberty, or the gentle-voiced, sad-eyed priest, or the opulent Count of Monte Cristo, he is equally effective. . . . No scene is unreal or improbable in which O'Neill appears; he shuts the door on reason . . . and we sit entranced beneath the wondrous spell of the actor who can . . . clothe dreams with flesh and blood . . . and charm us with its heroes and their marvellous exploits.

They came to see him and they conquered him. Though he brought home fifty thousand taxless dollars a season, it was not enough satisfaction as he recalled the range of his success pre-Dantès and as the public spurned him when he offered them

JAMES O'NEILL in *Monte Cristo* (*left*). They waited to see him again in Atchison, Kansas, after he rested at his summer home in New London, Connecticut, with his sons Eugene and Jamie.

Hamlet or melodrama or anything else, but returned with religious regularity to hear him say the lines that were now part of the everyday language: "The world is mine! . . . One! . . . Two! . . . Three!"

His sons thought it was ridiculous, thought he was ridiculous, a ham and a tightwad because he could not forget the poverty of his childhood and the embarrassments of being broke when he was trying to be an actor. Their mother, his wife, was small solace, she was usually high on dope. And that about summed up his well-paid defeat except for the fact that one of his goading sons became a Nobel Prize playwright and apologized, after his father's death, in a magnificent play. All of which was of no concern to James O'Neill's audiences as he forced his way through the grind of one-nights and brought them his trammeled talent.

1905–6

BANGOR [Me.]—James O'Neill in *Monte Cristo,* to full houses and satisfaction; company and performance good.

FITCHBURG [Mass.]—James O'Neill in *Monte Cristo* Mar. 19; big house; star excellent as usual, but company mediocre.

NEW BEDFORD—James O'Neill in *Monte Cristo* Oct. 23; fair business.

FALL RIVER—James O'Neill in *Monte Cristo,* matinee and evening; excellent company, attendance good.

HOLYOKE—James O'Neill in *Monte Cristo*; good company; fair house.

SHAMOKIN [Pa.]—James O'Neill in *Monte Cristo* Nov. 7; delighted big house.

JACKSON [Miss.]—James O'Neill in *Monte Cristo* Mar. 13; well received by large audience.

VICKSBURG—James O'Neill in *Monte Cristo* Mar. 14; play, cast and attendance good.

SAN ANTONIO [Tex.]—James O'Neill in *Monte Cristo* Mar. 23–24; excellent, to good business.

GALVESTON—James O'Neill in *Monte Cristo* Mar. 20; pleased big house.

To the end of the season . . . Next season: *Monte Cristo.*

This was possible because he and other stars of that era had a capacity that no actor of merit appears to have now: the ability to repeat indefinitely yet sustain the quality of performance. Producers now have difficulty in signing stars to more than a season because the stars maintain they cannot perform one part longer without disintegrating, artistically and mentally. In contrast, this was the appraisal of O'Neill's performance by the leading trade publication as late as 1905:

> There is scarce a new word of commendation to be said. . . . His many appearances in the role—they number in the neighborhood of four thousand—have not dimmed Mr. O'Neill's enthusiasm. . . . He acts earnestly, forcefully and with the gracious bearing that won for him the admiration of the public in the days of his youth. In no single instance did he fail to give the fullest value to a spoken word, nor was there in his performance a gesture, an attitude or an expression of countenance that one wished here done otherwise.

Until the end—1914 . . .

The theatre was pushing forward and becoming more American each season. New plays better than *10 Nights, The Old Homestead* and *Monte Cristo* were beginning to be written, but the better they were, the greater the risk, the more select the audience and the shorter the run. The United States theatre has been, is, will be for a bit longer, a commercial proposition. To operate, to keep its houses open so as to hold the land and pay the investors, it must have hits, popular wide-audience successes. *10 Nights, The Old Homestead* with Thompson, *Monte Cristo* with O'Neill in any opera house could pay for the bad weeks of the "just-god-awful" or "good-but-too-advanced" or the "beautifully-produced-classics for limited tastes." The profit-based theatrical grocery could not, and still cannot, deal only in truffles and caviar; it has to carry staples.

Another attraction as reliable as salt was *Lotta!* She guaranteed packed houses for years, from New York to the whistle stops, in plays that were not worth the paper they were on even as she did them. It didn't matter, she was *Lotta*, a personality, of a category of theatre that once charmed the patrons and beatified managers. Never mind the title of the play, just put up the sign: "*LOTTA!*"

She came out of the West at the time when stars rose in San Francisco, New Orleans, Cincinnati, all over, for the theatre was national. So it did not necessarily mean she came from the sticks, although much of her earliest training was as crude as the mining camps where she began. Yet the audience there could be sharp, for in the crowd were persons who had been in great cities in many countries, had seen great actors, read the great books and had the imagination and wit to get themselves to the California-Nevada-Colorado extravaganza, the Gold Rush. Mark Twain was out that way and was not lonesome for intelligent company.

Lotta had been taken to California when she was six and her name was still Charlotte Crabtree. Her story is included in one of the most enjoyable theatre books ever, *Troupers of the Gold Coast* by Constance Rourke. She had a mother of the sort that makes the husband-father disappear and the daughter visible with sublimated aura. Mrs. Crabtree had no acquaintance with theatre, but when she heard that children were sometimes excellent money-earners as entertainers, she easily achieved the maternal conviction that her child was as good as any and probably better.

There was a woman in California, not Mrs. Crabtree's kind, to be sure, but someone who might help Lotta, especially as this person had taken a fancy to the child. She was Lola Montez, now semiretired after having worked in some very royal beds in Europe. She taught Lotta to dance and, in view of the little girl's prodigious talent, it must have been a most satisfying instruction. Lotta could sing, too. So perhaps could a million other moppets but none with the infectious good nature, sense of joy, of Lotta.

Mother and her about-to-be precocious star went up to the camps, and immediately Lotta was a riotous success. The miners littered the barroom and grocery-store stages she danced on with nuggets, when that was still an original gesture. They loved her, she loved them, and mother had a hot heart for the returns.

They completed the tour and came back to San Francisco. Mrs. Crabtree knew they had something, but as she contemplated that sophisticated city, she had difficulty seeing where it could

Lotta. New York City and Anderson, Indiana, loved her.

be used. At this time, San Francisco was a theatrical mecca where Laura Keene (who would be the star of the play in Washington the night of the Lincoln murder) was staging in a single season elaborate productions of *Hamlet, Macbeth, Richard III, Othello, Midsummer Night's Dream, Much Ado,* even *Coriolanus.* Could this city have need of a child just singing and dancing? Then Mrs. Crabtree saw the light—the people wanted plays, stories, so why not put Lotta in a play?

There were old comedies and farces galore, and the twist was to have this comical, lovable child play the grown-up leads. Or, strictly speaking, play the leads and do her stuff. We have an account of this in a description of Lotta doing a scene in which she was to tiptoe in and put a bottle on a table. Mother had an idea, and at the next performance, just as Lotta put down the bottle, she gave one of her infectious laughs, startling and delighting the audience. That was good—now could she top it? She did a handspring on her next exit and brought down the house. In other scenes, cues were found for songs and dances. It was the building of a legend.

It was a long struggle to perfect it, with many more mining-camp tours before the child had discovered her range—a long enough time for her to reach sixteen, and then they went to New York. When she appeared there, the New York *Clipper* gave its judgment:

> She can dance a regular breakdown in true burnt cork style and gives an Irish jig as well as we have ever seen it done. She has a pleasing countenance, looks charming on stage . . . and knows exactly how to put an audience in good humor. She would prove a valuable star to any music house in the country. Her style is certainly not intended for a first-class audience, concert halls being her proper stamping ground.

There followed a year playing the Eastern cities, breaking in more plays until she had the requirement of that time: a repertoire. On returning to New York, Mrs. Crabtree was given the best theatre in town, Wallack's, because it was midsummer, when show business was notoriously poor in New York, and it was one of the hottest summers folks could remember. Lotta packed them in for six weeks.

She was soon able to write back to San Francisco, to a friend of the family:

> Yes, we started out quite fresh, and so far things have been prosperous. I am a continual success wherever I go. In some places I create quite a theatrical furore, as they call it. . . . Your heart would jump with joy to see the respect I am treated with here amongst the theatre people. I'm a star and that is sufficient, and making quite a name. But I treat all and everyone with the greatest respect and that is not what everyone does, and in consequence I get my reward.

Her public and national love affair, the only kind Lotta would ever have, was beginning. She had the first-class audience because she had them all—all could not get enough of the adorable, clever girl who seemed to return all the love they gave, often to the extent of eight encores. There was more than cuteness to all this; there was a calculated-innocent spice, as Constance Rourke observes:

> The hoyden in a dozen aspects became Lotta's substantial part. She rolled off sofas and showed far more than an ankle: pulling up her stockings as she ran on to the stage in *Nan the Good for Nothing*: the movement, in an age when even allusions to stockings were considered depraved, became indescribably comic. She lifted herself to tables and swung her feet—another dashing innovation. Her short skirts were daring.

When she played San Francisco again, she gave the California theatre its first three-hundred-night season with play after play:

Little Nell and the Marchioness
Pet of the Petticoats
Family Jars
The Irish Diamond
Captain Charlotte
Firefly
The Little Detective

and more—often doubling parts, offering an almost inexhaustible variety of characters.

She was on her way to a thousand theatres and opera houses, always the same, always the image of Lotta, like an amaranth for she never seemed to age. Even at fifty, friends and reporters marveled at her appearance of someone twenty-five or thirty.

She quit at forty-four and retired to a home near Boston. There could be no question but that she was the richest woman of the stage. There was not only her theatre income, beginning with those mining-camp nuggets; Mother Crabtree through the years had been scouting the towns they played, exercising her gift for spotting precisely where land would increase in value, investing and reaping.

Mother died, then Lotta at age sixty. There began a gold rush to stake claims to her four-million-dollar estate—claimants declaring their legitimate or bastard connection. Finally, the courts decided and the money went where Lotta had willed it, to public charity, to some of those people she never met except out front as they applauded. To the end, she returned the affection.

Finally, after the theatre's tortuous start, there was Lotta and *10 Nights*, *Uncle Tom*, *The Old Homestead*, *Monte Cristo* and an almost bewildering variety of attractions. It was a good business, one that could afford the classics, too: dedicated, brilliant, beautiful people would arrive to take you to almost anywhere that appealed to Shakespeare's imagination. Now there was a place in the town where you could weep, hiss and cheer, and be filled for a night with ennobling, exhilarating excitement. It helped you celebrate your American luck or it helped you bear up as you waited for the hard-work award that Horatio Alger promised you should have.

•

Charles Frohman, 1905, meditating on his empire in his office in his Empire Theatre, New York, could enjoy the past and anticipate a future in an American theatre that must inevitably grow in size and greatness—so he had every reason to believe.

A boy from Sandusky, Ohio, one of his first jobs when he got to the great city was working for the producer of Hazel Kirke, a hit that soon had a dozen companies on the road. That was where he learned how to book shows. Then he got the nerve and money to produce Shenandoah, and that was his own hit.

From there to here: an organizer of The Syndicate. There were complaints from the old-fashioned who preferred a theatre put together by players, but now everything was to be determined by the businessmen, for what player, what star, what writer, could handle a network of more than a thousand theatres from coast to coast? And supply sufficient product to keep them lighted? So they had made their contribution, the Syndicate people, had organized the business, and now they, the schemers, negotiators, enforcers, were accepting their munificent compensation. Let the actors have the applause. And with the formula perfected, they saw no limit in this growing country.

This year, there were 111 new productions in New York going out, the cream of them Frohman's—plus those from last season and seasons before, still on the road. And it was his pleasure to pay the stars handsomely—those who didn't resist. All in all, that great future theatre would be grateful, would know what it owed to him, Charles Frohman from Sandusky, now going to London every year to check on things at the Duke of York, his theatre there.

He was with those who went down on the Lusitania, 1915. Aged fifty-five.

Life on the Road or The Well-Known Strangers

In 1905, the Interstate Commerce Commission reported there were 2,272 connecting railroads in the United States—with names like the Cedar Rapids Route; the Cincinnati, Hamilton & Dayton; the Black Hills Line; and the Natural Bridge Rail Road. Unlike a later time, they were as willing to carry passengers as freight. In fact, their advertisements indicate they were doing their best to improve the passengers' comfort, were in competition for the travelers' favor.

It was in this year that the Pennsylvania Railroad inaugurated "the fastest long-distance train in the world," eighteen hours each way between Chicago and New York. That was on June 11. On the eighteenth, the New York Central met the challenge with the 20th Century Limited, same time. Twenty-five thousand people gathered at the Chicago station to see the Limited leave on its first run.

Train travel, pre-airconditioning, could be dirty. With the smoke and soot coming in through the open windows, one could watch one's clothes change color. The Lackawanna Railroad advertised that it had solved the problem by using anthracite. It had a series of ads showing "Miss Phoebe Snow," always spotless in her white linens. One caption:

Miss Phoebe Snow,
About to go
Upon a trip to Buffalo:
My gown stays white
From morn to night
Upon the road
Of Anthracite.

But the real sensation was the news from the Chicago & Northwestern Railway that their new Overland Limited was now electric-lighted from Chicago to California. There was a reading lamp in every berth, they said.

That was 1905. Things were getting better. As people expected.

THE best account of American theatrical touring as it was some fifty years previous to 1905 is in the diary of Mrs. Sam (Emilie) Cowell, published as *The Cowells in America* 1860–61.

When you read of this genteel couple, you feel they should never have strayed from a cot and garden down in Surrey, but Sam, who had changed from acting to "dramatic singing," decided to partake of the wealth of America. He would tour the hinterlands in concert, and, naturally, his good and loving wife accompanied him. They brought with them their thirteen-year-old daughter, Sidney, to complicate the adventure, but left Florence, seven, and Joe, four, at home.

Dramatic singing appears to have consisted of story-songs sung in character, to judge from some of Sam Cowell's material.

As I vas a-valking down by the sea-shore,
Vere the vinds and the vaves and the vaters did roar . . .

Or:

A Hero's life I'll sing,
His story shall my pen mark;
He was not the king,
But Hamlet, Prince of Denmark.

Or:

> *In Vestminister, not long ago,*
> *There liv'd a Ratcatcher's daughter. . . .*

All with comic or convoluted plots.

Although there is evidence that Sam Cowell had been appreciated in England, in America he often received indifference, so that he was constantly pawning his watch and borrowing and paying back and pawning again to survive and reach the next stand. Which is distressing to read, because anyone taking the tour as it was logged by Emilie deserved better.

They began in Taunton, Massachusetts, after a journey of "two hours from Boston," and sweet Emilie was not above the well-known English complaint:

> How strange that people so enlightened as the Americans should continue the pernicious system of overheating their houses, with the sulphurous fumes arising from the furnaces and hot air-pipes. The cold is felt with increased severity when one ventures into the open air, and I cannot help thinking that to this cause is attributable the extraordinary number of deaths from consumption, and other diseases of the "lungs and larynx" which fill the columns of the newspapers and make the churchyard populous.

But the subject is rarely mentioned again. Soon she seems too distracted to be bothered—except in the railway cars. From Taunton to Providence was "another two hour journey" and "As we entered the car, the atmosphere so heated and vitiated by the number of persons assembled, almost turned us sick, especially as the outside was so keen and frosty." From Providence to Worcester was a "journey of 43 miles—the usual two hours." At New London, "wait up until half past 12, vainly hoping that a steamer will leave for New York but the storm was too violent."

Similar trials of transportation, whether on land or water, are prevalent through the year-long entries:

> Pittsburgh to Cincinnati, 17 hours, fare $10 . . .
>
> Arrive late, owing to *two* breakdowns on train. . . .

We are on the mighty Mississippi, and God grant that we may get safely to New Orleans! Three times, on her way from Cincinnati (which she left last Tuesday week) she has been stuck on a sand bar —once for 36 hours—and once she was fast sinking, and about half the cargo had to be thrown overboard, before help arrived. . . .

Here we are, "hard and fast"—on a sand bar! The Captain says that we are hard aground and may not get off for days. . . .

Montgomery to Atlanta. In the train all night—an eleven hour journey. The seats of the car were narrow and uncomfortable, and in no way could we compose ourselves for repose.

Not all of their plight was due to the conditions in America, for one of their complications they brought with them. Emilie's comments are reluctant and forbearing, but we learn that Sam-dear liked to tipple. He tried to reform. Once, on March 7, he promised to touch no more spirits until July 4. Emilie's entry for March 8 said: "Sam endeavoring to keep his resolution, was so ill that at night he could scarcely get through his first song. Was obliged to get some brandy. Sudden abstemiousness made him very ill, before he must become so (please God) by degrees." March 14: "Sam did not get back until 6 in the morning." But he was a trouper, he didn't miss a performance.

Emilie was also troubled by some of what Mrs. Trollope had cited as "the domestic manners of the Americans," particularly one habit that proved loathsome even to the Americans—in time:

I think the thing which has struck me most unfavorably [is] the disgusting habit of spitting. Not wishing to be fantastical, I cannot help saying that I was nearly made ill, in the railway carriage yesterday; by the "hawkings" and expectoration going on in all directions.

And again, while making the twelve-and-a-half-hour "jump" from Louisville to Nashville.

Up at 5 a.m. and left, by train at 6:30. . . . We had a terrible journey, and, of course, I was ill, nearly all the way! What is the matter with me? Am I growing old! But silver-haired old people are travelling with us who do not seem to be affected by the ceaseless jolting, the stifling fumes from the stove, the nauseating hawking and spitting, and "greasy sweat" that pervade the cars. . . . Did not get to Nashville until nearly seven o'clock.

The *dining saloon* on a Mississippi steamer was another strain:

Dinner was at 12. Sam was asleep so we [she and Sidney] sat down in company with some most repulsive looking people, and a swarm of children. They almost prevented our eating anything! The children put their filthy little hands into their plates, the grown up people used their knives to cut their food, convey it to their mouths, to take salt from the salt-cellar, to cut the butter, to help themselves to vegetables with—in fact the knife was supreme, the fork a superfluity.

These inconveniences did not distract her from observing Americans and their peculiar customs and recording their odd ideas:

Oh, what a dirty place! . . . Everything is covered with thick dust, there being no *paving* in Memphis, or so little as not to be worth mention. . . .

Almost opposite our windows is a house on which is painted (in big, black letters, on a white ground) "Negro mart." and below "Nevill and James Slave dealers." . . . When ladies walk alone they are followed by a negress "slave" as it is not considered respectable to be quite unprotected. "Niggers" slouch about in every direction. They have all a sort of shambling lame kind of walk; indeed I am told that there really is a malformation in the negro's foot which induces this peculiarity. There is no hollow under the foot, and the heel protrudes very far at the back. For the most part they seem contented, gay and *insouciant*, and I have observed a few faces so full of diabolical meaning that I cannot but pray that they may never have the power of doing the harm they seem to meditate.

The American experience was wearisome and suspenseful because money was so often low, but they paid their debts and she was able to end the story with "Happy days have preponderated over the sad ones, and our lot has been one to be grateful for." All in all, she was an excellent attendant trouper.

In the slow trains of the next forty-five years, with schedules not much better than those the Cowells endured, there were as many as four or five thousand actors crawling over the United

States and Indian Territory to provide pleasure and enlightenment for American opera house-goers. Life was not easy then, but there were many who had more comfort, less strain and tension than the actors.

Trains and curtain times set the pace and the trains could be quite unobliging with their predilection, so it often seemed, for leaving at daybreak, not the most convenient time for people who retired no earlier than midnight. Sometimes the passengers sat on slat seats, as hard as the wood they were made of, and at best there was the pricking, dust-absorbing velour stretched over what felt like iron filings.

In the latter part of this period, the stars sometimes had private cars, but these were not salons of comfort either. The springs would compare unfavorably with those of a truck today; the track was bumpy and induced swaying, and because the cars could be stifling hot it was necessary to let in the cinders and dust. In any event, the conditions for the great star had little meaning to the majority in the average or cheap companies traveling at the smallest expense that farsighted managers could devise. "You never know when you'll hit trouble. You hit a town where the bank has gone up and you're lucky if you can take in enough to get out."

It was an era of the "junctions." With a network of short independent railroads, touring involved many changes. What the actors disliked most were the broken-night jumps, where you had to change trains in the middle of the night. If you were spendthrift enough to get a sleeper (assuming one was available), it might be sidetracked at the junction and picked up by the succeeding train, permitting you to sleep through (if the switching and jolting didn't shock you awake), but actors were reluctant to do this because it might mean, if you arrived too early in the next town and checked in at the hotel, having to pay for *two* accommodations for the one night.

[NOTE: *Actors Equity Association contract, 1972:*

Rail Transportation. Day coach transportation for the Company is limited to ten (10) hours and night transportation shall include individual first-class sleeping accommodations. If the train schedule requires transportation in excess of ten (10) hours or after 10:00 P.M., a roomette or other first-class sleeping accommodation shall be furnished each actor.

Air Transportation. The Actor shall not be compelled to travel by air without his written consent. . . . If air travel is consented to by the Actor, it must be on CAB certified and scheduled first-class Air Lines, including chartered flights on such air lines and not on non-scheduled or private airlines. The cost of baggage transportation, not to exceed two hundred (200) pounds, will be borne by the Manager. . . .

The Manager agrees to reimburse the Actor for the premium cost of air travel insurance up to the amount of $60,000.00, purchased by the Actor. In the event of a delay in travel, the Manager, if the Actor is traveling other than first-class, agrees to pay such costs as are normally paid for by the airline for first-class passengers.]

Few train connections were immediate or direct inasmuch as trains found it difficult to be on time and there had to be margin. This meant troupes often found themselves spending the middle-of-the-night hours in dim, cold or overheated stations, in silence except for the cricket of the telegraph. Even in the daytime, these junction stations, surrounded by tracks bordered by factories or tenements, were uninteresting places to wait for the whistle of relief. And because the connecting trains were as often late as not, there was tension—it could be the only train that day, or you might miss connections, or arrive too late for the night's performance, in which case there was a night's salary lost, because actors were not apt to be paid for work not performed. Managers felt a sort of Puritan virtue in not rewarding the idle.

[NOTE: *Equity contract, 1972:*

Should any performance be lost through unavoidable delays in travel, said lost performance shall be compensated.]

Because it was so vital to make the trains (the usual weariness of the actor involved the risk of oversleeping), the players were inclined to use the hotel nearest the station, and it could often save hack fare as well. Such hostelries were ordinarily not the best, but the poorly paid troupers were not seeking luxury. They were also inclined to accept what was convenient though dreary out of the feeling "It's only temporary," one night—in a few hours they would be gone and anyhow there wasn't time to hunt for better.

[Note: *Equity contract, 1972:*

Two (2) weeks prior to the play date the advance agent or company manager will submit to the company a list of available hotel accommoda-

Lincoln, Nebraska, had its Opera House as good as any where the shows that played everywhere else came for at least one night. The great Edwin Booth played *Julius Caesar* here April 12, 1888.

tions at different price ranges. Within one (1) week thereafter the Actor shall indicate his acceptance. . . . If the Actor has complied with this requirement and does not receive accommodations upon arrival, he shall not be required to rehearse or perform until such accommodations are forthcoming.]

This meant, in aggregate, that they were spending their lives in faded, frequently filthy ("Don't look under the bed") rooms, with temperatures at extremes, where the electric light was small improvement on the candle; places noisy with drunks, singing chambermaids in the halls, doors crashing; beds with sags, lumps or thinly covered springs; broken window shades, broken windows, no closets, no bath—and, despite prayers, sometimes bugs that made acquaintance in the middle of the night. There were places where the players had to accept these accommodations in bitterness because the "reputable" places did not accept "show people."

On arrival, the actor would be anxious to get to the theatre to see what problems it might present. He would look at the list posted by the stage manager on the callboard to learn which dressing room was his. Unless the opera house was on a second or third floor (over stores), he would probably be billeted in the basement, or cellar. This might put him next to the boiler so that his makeup would be running with sweat before he got his costume on—or she got into her dainty dress. You could say it was better than being next to the alley door and suffering the subzero drafts. The lighting was often installed by someone who never thought actors might want to see themselves in a mirror as they made up. The room could be closet size and three or more might have to use it, in which case trunks were left in the hall and clothes were hung on any available nails. Stagehands could be tramping about above, sending down a sprinkling of dust and flaking whitewash. The accumulated dirt and the rubbish from previous companies did not contribute to their sense of worth.

Some theatres had assorted signs to provide cynical amusement:

WE KNOW THE THEATRE IS ROTTEN!
HOW'S YOUR SHOW?

DON'T BLAME THE ORCHESTRA.
THEY ARE TOO BUSY
AT THE FOUNDRY TO REHEARSE.

THE DRESSING ROOMS ARE SWEPT OUT EVERY SUMMER.

[NOTE: *Equity contract, 1972:*

The Manager agrees to provide the Actor with safe and sanitary places of employment.

Stage and Backstage Area. All stages shall be cleaned and properly heated. The Manager shall use his best efforts to insure comfortable healthful temperatures at all times.

Dressing Rooms. All dressing rooms shall be properly heated and shall have adequate lights, mirrors, shelves and dressing equipment. . . . Floors shall be washed or vacuumed at least once each week, and dressing rooms cleaned at least once each working day. . . . Peeling paint and loose plaster shall be repaired. . . . Each dressing room shall contain at least one washstand, with hot and cold running water.]

Whatever the circumstance and whatever happened, the actor knew it had been worse. For instance, there was the theatre Sol Smith had played at Natchez.

The new theatre at Natchez was situated at the extreme end of the main street, and in a grave-yard. . . . The dressing-rooms for the gentlemen were under the stage, the earth having been excavated to make room for them. Human bones were strewn about in every direction. The first night, the lamplighter being a little "pushed" for time to get all ready, seized upon a skull, and, sticking two tallow candles in the eye-sockets, I found my dressing-room thus lighted.

There is reason for Equity stipulating running water because water was something theatre owners on occasion did not provide. Often the actors had to wear their makeup home to the hotel and remove it there. In fact, the whole business of getting and staying clean was one of the tricks of the trade. Actors, partly because of the common prejudice dating from England, where they had once been classified by law with "strollers, vagabonds, vagrants, harlots and trollops," and also for the reputation of the show, were supposed to present a good appearance. A smart spick-and-span company might suggest a prosperous, ergo a good, show. Then, too, wardrobe was the actor's chief asset after talent and must be kept in condition. This was when "ad lib" actors advertising for jobs in the trade press would say: "Snappy dresser on and off. Complete wardrobe with dress suit and dinner clothes."

On Sundays, the only day when they might be stopping long enough for things to dry, they could do their wash. In the Western part of the country there was help from those self-effacing public servants, the Chinese with their laundries. "The Chinks do it quick." Dry cleaning was in the future, and so actors carried fuller's earth, sprinkled it on serge, suede and what not, brushed it off and there you were, standing on the station platform as neat as a pin.

Their ways of maintaining cleanliness and health were impressive. As stated, their hours were about as regular as glad tidings, and the actor of any duration in those years needed a digestive system made of noncorrosive metal. Most of the food of America was bad and the bulk of this subsistence was fried. The waiters never asked how you wanted your meat prepared, everything was a well-done gray. Further, the troupers had the problem of getting sustenance, bad or worse, at the times they wanted—after finishing work at 11 o'clock or at 5:30 in the morning when a cup of coffee might brace them for the trip. You ate what you could get when you could get it, but there is no record that any actor had ulcers, an affliction that seems to have come with the discovery of "proper diet."

The best explanation for their ruggedness is that they could not *afford* to get sick. The show had to go on because otherwise there would be no salary, and, anyhow, who wanted to be left behind in a strange, suspicious town? So the men would sweat through the performances in armor, then change in icy dressing rooms; the women would work on drafty stages in thin dresses—all defying pneumonia. To be disabled by colds or cramps would suggest you lacked professional qualifications.

Occasionally, to be sure, someone would get sick, and this could be frightening—who knew if the native doctor had more to recommend him than a diploma from one of the mills then existing. So as long as possible they stayed on their feet. For all Sam Cowell's hangovers, he never missed a show and resorted to a doctor only once. Emilie noted:

> Sam so frightfull ill with diarrhoea that I wonder he got through the Concert at all. . . . The doctor was here, twice today, and by the evening the pills seem to have done a little good. I asked the doctor,

if Sam was in danger. He said, if this continues he was in danger of Flux. I do not know what that is, but fear it is something dreadful.

The tour was through limbo. Contact with citizens was usually too brief to be meaningful. Though actors by their very nature extended themselves, they had reason to be reserved in their trust; like a Jew or a Negro, they could never know when the townsmen's prejudice might show, particularly if the actor shared the Jew or Negro's risk of being odd, not true to the prejudged concept. Part of the offstage audience expected the actors to be libidinous; some expected them to be "artists"; many, if not most, expected them to double in life for whatever character they assumed on stage: it would be assumed that the dame who played the seductive French maid ought to be interested in any man's offer while the villain would have to extend himself, be amusing, to relax suspicion.

Isadora Bennett gives an example of how far auditors would identify the actor with his character in the play. She was eleven, standing at the back of the house in a small theatre of western Canada while members of her family were on stage in *The Squaw Man.* Two cowboys beside her began to be disgusted with the sissiness of the English fop in the play and presently began shooting to express their disdain. Isadora stamped her foot and said, "Now you *stop* that! That's my *brother!*" They stared at her, Isadora recalls, as if she were the second bush to catch fire and then turned and watched the rest of the performance confused, in silent stupefaction.

The players were briefly the best-known people in town and yet they were lonely. Under the focus of lights and the spectators' concentrated gaze, they became vividly familiar in the short time between overture and final curtain. Yet no one knew them and they would be gone before they knew any of those who had been so close and friendly in the auditorium dark. The show done, the husbands and wives in the company would go to their rooms, write letters home to their darlings staying with grandparents or aunts, or, if they had no darlings, would write to professional friends from other tours, then retire to noisy beds to get the strength to reach a different roost tomorrow. About the extent of socializing would have been the waitress asking, "Is it a really good show?" or the clerk's "Hey, I saw you, you were slick!"

Except that their beds were colder, it was the same for the single people in the company. The women could not afford quick liaisons—in a period of female hair-pulling and hat-pin stabbing, God alone knew what might happen. Besides, who wanted to encourage the rustics in their goatish ideas? So they wrote letters and some found solace in pamphlet religion.

The men did little better unless, like James O'Neill, they found distraction in after-the-show saloons. They hesitated to tie up with the women in the company for if it got serious, it could hobble your career if your partner's talent was less marketable than yours, and you might have to split, one touring in California, one in the East. Frequently, women of the town would make themselves available, some desperately willing to do with the stranger what they would never consider with a resident, while others were tramps who could be trouble, either as jailbait or because their generosity included a dose.

Married or single, young or old, the actors did not belong in the town; they were outside its business, social life, friendships, its community concerns or religious affairs. There was only one place where they were wanted, needed, and when they stepped through the stage door and saw "The Platform before the Castle" or "The Square of the Village of Falling Waters" or "An Open Place on the Banks of the Seine, Paris," or "A Chamber in the Carlyle Mansion," they were home. For three hours, they would glow in the warmth of lights and applause, they would have a dramatic existence larger, more colorful, more envied than that of any who put down their dollar or half-dollar or quarter to watch. This, plus the thin possibility of hitting it, getting famous and prosperous, was why it was worth catching the next train.

The life was demanding, grueling, but they signed up for another season. They survived because the ordeal, of necessity, included camaraderie and professional respect. It has been said that the theatre is and has been a place free from the prejudices of the ordinary population. This may be because if someone can show talent, can help the show, can support and lift his fellows—if he knows his business onstage, can help maintain morale off, can *troupe*—who cares about religion, color or even intelligence? What partner ever rejected a good straight man because he misspelled or was born to the wrong faith?

However, the prejudice against the incompetent, the unprofessional, can be formidable. Better he should be in a jute mill even though he is supporting a broken-backed mother and three idiot sisters and has to pass a kidney stone every week—*get him out of my scene!*

In illustration, there is the story of the aspiring, talentless would-be ingenue who got the manager's interest in a bedroom audition. He introduced her to the director and he, too, wanted to retain her for her fresh, warm company and gave her a part. But at rehearsal she was breaking the rhythm for everyone, she was frightening in her lisping potential for disaster in performance. When they had finished a just-once-more try and there was an awkward pause, the second woman spoke for the cast. "Just remember this, dear," her well-projected voice advised, "you can't fuck the whole *audience!*"

The players would return to the challenge next season because invariably they would have seen and experienced something impressive: the grandeur of the human spirit under stress, the beauty of courageous endurance. Given this test of survival through enemy territory—analogous to the covered-wagon treks—they would discover each time how much larger than life people could be. In old age, they would recall someone's wit that kept them warm when stalled in a blizzard, someone's magnificent scorn in squelching a native's insult. (Once as a train pulled into a North Dakota hamlet to pick us up, I heard a station baggageman say, "Well, now we'll get the fairies out of town," and the character man's smooth and cultured response: "And to all you sodomists staying here in Gomorrah, we wish you continued success.")

The survivors would remember the sensible sympathy in grief, and, most of all, the almost incredible good nature. I spoke of this once to a very old actor who had been there. He didn't deny it, and he diminished the wonder of it only slightly when he explained: "If you complained, if you couldn't keep up, you got a reputation, and what manager was going to send you out to complicate things on the tour? That's why they were a very select group of people. My boy, we were *troupers!*"

•

Whatever the statistics as to the number of actresses compared to actors on tour in 1905, we know they were equal. When the all-male theatre of Shakespeare's time was discontinued and females were given the privilege of playing female parts, the world's first profession with absolute sexual equality was established. (In contrast, female writers, as exemplified by the Brontës, Evans, Dupin, et al., found it advisable to present themselves as men.) No one ever attempted to say the actor was more essential than the actress, and all the discrimination outside the theatre with respect to employment was nonsense to those on stage—even though it had been only the year before, 1904, that women had been first permitted to be ushers in a theatre, at the Majestic, New York.

While suffragettes were in the streets screaming and fighting for opportunity in the man's world, equality on the job was such an old thing to the ladies working in the theatre that the issue had no meaning. Actresses as a matter of course paid their part of the checks, lugged their own luggage without expecting or simpering for male help, negotiated their own contracts, got their own hotel rooms and gave orders like a man.

This sometimes confused the common folk. Could such women be ladies or did it mean they had abandoned that position of virtue by stepping down to the level of licentious man? As suggested by their use of cigarettes.

In 1905, twenty-two years before the Lucky Strike people put the faces of Broadway stars—Gertrude Lawrence, Nazimova,

Billie Burke, Florence Reed—on billboards with endorsements urging the women to light up, the actresses, many of them, were puffing away. However, except for those who, like Bernhardt, could afford the notoriety, they were inclined to be discreet about it. They tried to do it out of sight of the civilians, in their hotel rooms, dressing rooms or in the company's special railroad coach. They knew the public was not ready to see wives and sweethearts blowing smoke, even in New York. For there, in the year before, the newspapers reported that a New York City policeman had halted an automobile in which a woman was smoking a cigarette, saying, "You can't do that on Fifth Avenue!" She was arrested.

When Katie Emmett, playing with The Waifs of New York company in Jackson, Michigan, read about this, she asked, "What do they want women to do, chew?"

☛ 7

Gentility in Makeup

It has been mentioned that the Reverend Timothy Dwight, president of Yale, promised that anyone attending a theatre could lose his immortal soul. In 1898, when Dwight's reverend grandson was president of Yale, the university was pleased to award an honorary degree to an actor, Joseph Jefferson. Three years later, Harvard did as well by the great comedian.

The gentlemanly Jefferson graciously accepted, without public comment on the theological and academic shift of position.

It might be said that the rise of man and his civilization is due in good part to the scorn of snobs. There is considerable evidence indicating that men and women have been stung to improve and prove themselves because self-elected superiors gave them the down-the-nose stare.

There is no story more odd than the way the select for several ages applauded the actors and simultaneously viewed them with haughty disapproval if not contempt. Even after the American pious surmounted their fear of joy and were paying well to relish the genius of actors, they could gasp in disapproval if a son or daughter expressed a wish to take up that trade, or, worse, to marry one of the creatures in it.

The rejected players responded as best they could. Sometimes they had luck, as when the young lawyer came to the rescue of the Jeffersons in Springfield, Illinois. Frequently, however, discretion meant doing your act with an eye on the law, "toeing the line." Finally, they chose to "raise the profession" (from where their oppressors had put it) by their aristocratic behavior, to surpass their detractors in the genteel style. The upper caste might be rich in money and/or morals, but they were usually wanting in manner.

Like most social developments, this was not consciously planned. It happened, though, and the supreme example of the gentleman with style among American actors was Mr. John Drew. If Mr. Drew was invited to an exclusive club, his presence could make the place seem like a lair for louts. Men of the Four Hundred might spend more on clothes, but they could never carry them like Mr. Drew, and the clergy should wish that God had such grace in *His* robes.

For John Drew and many others, there was no difficulty in assuming this mantle of gentility because they were not, like most of the opposition, self-made, first-generation gents. They came from a long line of theatrical aristocrats, and however subculture that might seem to outsiders, they were royalty in the kingdom of the stage. They were educated and cultivated, even those who had hardly seen a school—all had been taught by Shakespeare. Drew came from a line of actors tracing its ancestry back to the Bard's time and his mother was *the* Mrs. John Drew. As a small child, she had played with such greats as Macready, and then, a professional at age seven, she was brought by her mother to the United States, where, as Louisa Lane, she continued her success, playing Lady Macbeth when she was sixteen.

Her greatest fame and importance to America came after she married John Drew and became manager of the Arch Street Theatre in Philadelphia. America has never had a production theatre of higher standards. The *Oxford Companion to the Theatre* notes that "she ruled her theatre and family with unwavering rectitude and energy." Her talented daughter Georgiana married Maurice Barrymore and this gave brother John Drew his niece Ethel and nephews Lionel and John.

Drew and his associate stars were models of polish and decorum, true nobility by inheritance and bearing. They did much to forward the general acceptance of actors, and, of course, as soon as the public decided the players were no worse than anyone else, the actors became no better and today are as disreputable in appearance and rude of speech as the general democratic run.

There were actors of such genius and spirit as to *command* respect whether they dressed for it or not. Joseph Jefferson, at the end of his life, was friend and fishing companion of the President of the United States, and there could be no doubt but what most Americans considered this Grover Cleveland's good luck. No American actor has been as beloved as Jefferson. For seventy-one years he had the public's admiration for his genius and good nature. Much of his charm must have come from his father, though there was not much time to absorb his parent's happy disposition.

After the Springfield-Lincoln experience, the family went on trouping into the South. Some of this, as Jefferson recalls it, sounds like the most idyllic training a young actor ever had:

> Business was bad [in Tennessee], and on one occasion the gentlemen of the company, myself included, walked from Gallatin to Lebanon—not, however, for the exercise.
>
> Upon our return to Nashville it was time to think of going South . . . but the Cumberland River had fallen so low that no steamboat could navigate it. In this dilemma there was but one course left: the company must come together, buy a barge, fit up a cabin, and sleeping apartments. This was done . . . and we all departed down the river in the queerest looking craft that ever carried a legitimate stock company of the old school. To a boy of my age this was heaven. To stand my watch at night gave me that manly feeling that a youngster, just before he grows his beard, enjoys beyond everything.
>
> We stopped at Clarkesville and gave one entertainment playing *The Lady of Lyons*. I acted Galvis. This was another manly stride for me; I was getting on. . . .
>
> The river was full of ducks, which I could sometimes shoot from the deck of the flatboat. . . . There was a small set of scenery on board

that had been brought in case of an emergency. . . . Now the time came when it could be displayed and utilized in a manner "never before attempted in the annals of the stage." When we reached the Ohio the river had widened out, and some stretches were from five to six miles in length; so, if we had a fair wind blowing downstream, by hoisting one of the scenes for a sail we would increase our speed from two to three miles an hour. . . . The wonder-stricken farmers and their wives and children would run out of their log-cabins and, standing on the river bank, gaze with amazement at our curious craft. It was delightful to watch the steamboats as they went by. The passengers would crowd the deck and look with wonder at us. For a bit of sport the captain and I would vary the picture, and as a boat steamed past we would first show them the wood scene, and then suddenly swing the sail around, exhibiting the gorgeous palace. Adding to this sport, our leading man and the low comedian would sometimes get a couple of old-fashioned broadswords and fight a melodramatic combat on the deck. There is no doubt that at times our barge was taken for a floating lunatic asylum.

Jefferson's father died in Mobile, where the yellow fever was raging. The mother and son, thirteen, had no choice but to go on, eventually reaching Texas, where they heard the guns at Palo Alto and acted in the Spanish Theatre at Matamoros two nights after the city fell. Often they played in hotel dining rooms and even in barns, with nothing to separate them from the audience but the row of tallow-candle footlights.

He rose slowly in his profession without attracting special attention until he played Asa Trenchard in *Our American Cousin*. Then in the 1850's when several people were trying to dramatize *Rip Van Winkle*, Jefferson played in one of these versions and saw possibilities for himself as Rip if a workable play could be made. He produced one that he put together in 1859, but it didn't catch. In 1865, he was in London and spoke of his interest to the skillful and prolific actor-writer, Dion Boucicault. Boucicault later gave his version of what happened:

He [Jefferson] was anxious to appear in London and all his pieces had been played there. The managers would not give him an appearance unless he could offer them a new play. He had played a piece called *Rip Van Winkle*, but when he submitted this for their perusal they rejected it. Still, he was so desirous of playing Rip that I took down Washington Irving's story and read it over. It was hopelessly undramatic.

"Joe," I said, "this old sot is not a pleasant figure. He lacks romance. I daresay you make a fine sketch of the old beast, but there is no interest in him. He may be picturesque, but he is not dramatic. I would prefer to start him in a play as a young scamp, thoughtless, gay, just a curly-headed, good-humored fellow such as all the village girls would love and the children and dogs would run after." Jefferson threw up his hands in despair. It was totally opposed to his artistic preconception. But I insisted and he reluctantly conceded. Well, I wrote the play as he plays it now. It was not much of a literary production, and it was with some apology that it was handed to him. He read it, and when he met me I said: "It is a poor thing, Joe." "Well," he replied, "it is good enough for me." It was produced. Three or four weeks afterward he called on me, and his first words were: "You were right about making Rip a young man. Now I could not conceive and play him any other way."

Boucicault was right and Jefferson was right. After its success in London, a ritual began in America: going to see Jefferson, year after year, as Rip. Taking yourself, then your children, then your grandchildren. It was still the time when audiences waited in murmuring excitement to see the mystery behind the curtain, to witness the magic. Presently, there was the hush and they were in the Village of Falling Waters. Gretchen is discovered washing clothes. The sounds of a chorus and laughter come from the inn.

GRETCHEN: Shouting and drinking day and night! Hark how they crow over their cups while their wives are working at home, and their children are starving.

Men enter and immediately there is a plot to worry everyone watching. The town's cruel landlord is here and to save him from ruin, they must trick Rip into signing a certain paper. Here he comes!

[*Rip enters, running and skipping, carrying one small child pickaback, and surrounded by a swarm of others hanging on the skirts of his coat. He is laughing like a child himself. He is dressed in an old deerskin coat, a pair of breeches which had once been red, now tattered, patched and frayed, a shapeless felt hat with a bit of the brim hanging loose. One of the boys carries his gun*]

The entrance, the costume, the business, could catch any star's attention and the action that follows would attract, too, for now they succeed in getting Rip addled with drink.

RIP: Well, here's your good health, and your families' good health, and may they all live long and prosper!

Then the innocent signing of the paper and then the disgraceful disclosure that he has given away an unknown fortune in land to the villains he trusted. And then the virtuous wrath of his wife, Gretchen:

GRETCHEN: Out, you drunkard! Out, you sot! You disgrace to your wife and to your child! This house is mine!

RIP: [*Dazed, and a little sobered*] Yours! Yours!

GRETCHEN: [*Raising her voice above the storm, which seems to rage more fiercely outside*] Yes, mine, mine! Had it been yours to sell, it would have gone along with the rest of your land. Out, then, I say—[*Pushing open the door*] for you no longer have any share in me or mine.

[*A peal of thunder*]

MEENIE: [*Catching Rip's coat*] No, Father, don't go!

RIP: [*Bending over her tenderly, and holding her close to him*] My child! Bless you, my child, bless you!

GRETCHEN: [*Relenting*] No, Rip—I—

RIP: [*Waving her off*] No, you have driven me from your house. You have opened the door for me to go. You may never open it for me to come back. [*Leans against the doorpost, overcome by his emotions. His eye rests on Meenie, who lies at his feet*] You say I have no share in this house. [*Points to Meenie in profound despair*] Well, see, then, I wipe the disgrace from your door. [*He staggers out into the storm*]

GRETCHEN: No, Rip! *Husband, come back!!* . . .

Now comes the magical heart of the play.

SCENE—*A steep and rocky cove in the Kaatskill Mountains, down which rushes a torrent, swollen by storm. Overhead, the hemlocks stretch their melancholy boughs. It is night, Rip enters, almost at a run, with his head down, and his coat-collar turned up, beating his way against the storm. . . .*

Having reached a comparatively level spot, he pauses for breath, and turns to see what has become of his dog]

RIP: [*Whistling to the dog*] Schneider! Schneider! what's the matter with Schneider? Something must have scared that dog.

This scene is a whimsical monologue as elves and dwarves appear and he talks to them. Though they never speak, they enlist his help in moving out a keg of elixir. The ghost of Henry Hudson appears and he and Rip sit down to have a draught of the elves' brew. There follows a savory opportunity for the actor as he pantomimes the effect on Rip. He is obviously headed for a trip.

RIP: Are you goin' to leave me, boys? Are you goin' to leave me all alone? Don't leave me; don't go away. [*With a last effort*] I will drink to your good health, and your family's—[*He falls back heavily, asleep*]

The full wonder of this American folklore classic is in the following scene. The curtain rises and you cannot see Rip—the leaves of years have covered him. There is suspense as he stirs beneath the pile and then appears, unrecognizable. "His hair and beard are long and white, bleached by the storms that have rolled over his head during the twenty years he has been asleep."

And in the rest of the play, all in the audience can fantasize for themselves as Rip comes home. What if *they* could go away to some merciful place and sleep for twenty years and return? Would they now be appreciated? What would it be like to talk to people they knew so well who now don't recognize them? Could scores be settled, forgiveness granted?

What a wonderful range for an actor! But the fact is that no other actor but Joe Jefferson has ever been able to do what he did. The sweetness he observed in his father flowed through the play. How could anyone censure the man, blame him for anything—even for leading them to Galena, Illinois—even for being an impractical dunce, toper, derelict husband and father in the village of Falling Waters?

As Booth was the greatest tragedian America has known, Jef-

JOSEPH JEFFERSON. He could bring *Rip* back to Denison, Texas, any time.

ferson was our greatest comedian. This was not because of hokum material to the public's taste or because of personality, and not only because he was a master technician. "He had inherited," one critic has written, "a massive technical knowledge of acting. This he was expert in applying. Every detail of his performance was governed by a design that he had worked out minutely. But he had mastered the art of concealing his art. His playing of Rip Van Winkle produced the illusion of spontaneity, of casual, even careless, fluence."

The performance had more than all these things; it had his character. It was this that audiences felt and remembered, as he remembered that comical and inspiring glance from his father looking back as he led them, he hoped, to an audience. Which is why one writer wrote, "The most remarkable thing about Jefferson, is not what or how he acted but the way he made everybody feel about him." While Mary Shaw, an actress, said, "He was the most lovable person I ever met in or out of the profession. With great gentleness he combined tremendous strength, which one felt all the time." And Laurence Hutton added, "He was one of the gentlest, sweetest, cleanest characters I ever knew. He never did a mean or selfish thing. He never said an unwise or an unkind word."

For thousands of nights, Joe Jefferson took audiences up into the mountains with him—"His Rip Van Winkle never lost its spell for his audience because he created it afresh every time he presented it"—and he does not appear to have regretted his success as James O'Neill did his. But then Jefferson did succeed in doing more. His Bob Acres in *The Rivals,* which he toured with Mrs. Drew in their old age, was a national event and deepened the love for him. It was reported that the day he died a photographer placed his picture draped with crape in the display window and men passing by bared their heads. Something was gone and it would be a long time before it was forgotten. My grandfather, who never touched a drop in his life, poor man, seized every opportunity to say, "Und here's to your gute health, und your family's gute health, und may you all live long and prosper." He was never as good as Jefferson, but he was loyal.

It is impossible ever to leave the story of Jefferson without recalling the origin of the legend of the Little Church. An old comedian, George Holland, had died; a man Jefferson always admired—"A bright and cheerful spirit, in this world for eighty years, for time could not age his youthful heart"—and Jefferson offered his services. It is best to let him tell the story as he does in his autobiography for it reveals how honestly and sensibly sentimental he could be.

I called at the house of the family, and found them in great grief. The sister of Mrs. Holland informed me that they desired the funeral to take place from the church, as many of Mr. Holland's friends would like to mark their love and respect for him by their attendance, and that the house in which the family lived was too small to receive the large gathering of people that would be likely to assemble. The lady desired me to call upon the pastor of her own church, and request him to officiate at the service.

I at once started in quest of the minister, taking one of the sons of Mr. Holland with me. On arriving at the house I explained to the reverend gentleman the nature of my visit, and the arrangements were made for the time and place at which the funeral was to be held.

Something, I can scarcely say what, gave me the impression that I had best mention that Mr. Holland was an actor. I did so in a few words, and concluded by presuming that probably this fact would make no difference. I saw, however, by the restrained manner of the minister and an unmistakable change in the expression of his face that it would make, at least to him, a great deal of difference. After some hesitation he said that he would be compelled, if Mr. Holland had been an actor, to decline holding the service at the church.

While this refusal to perform the funeral rites for my old friend would have shocked under ordinary circumstances, the fact that it was made in the presence of the dead man's son was more painful than I can describe.

I turned to look at the youth, and saw that his eyes were filled with tears. He stood as if dazed with a blow just realized; as if he felt the terrible injustice of a reproach upon the kind and loving father who had often kissed him in his sleep, and had taken him on his knee when the boy was old enough to know the meaning of the words, and told him to grow up to be an honest man. I was hurt for my young friend, and indignant with the man—too much so to reply; and I rose to leave the room with a mortification that I cannot remember to have felt before or since. I paused at the door and said:

"Well, sir, in this dilemma is there no other church to which you can direct me, from which my friend can be buried?"

He replied that "there was a little church around the corner" where I might get it done; to which I answered: "Then, if this be so, God bless 'the little church around the corner' "; and so I left the house.

The Landmarks Commission of New York has marked the Little Church Around the Corner for preservation, which is as it should be, not only because it is an architectural gem and a proper place for actors to get married so long as that custom survives, but also by way of memorializing what someone has called "a bit of decency in an otherwise Christian world."

It became increasingly preposterous to damn out of hand an institution which produced Jefferson. And Edwin Booth.

Edwin Booth was the theatrical equivalent, although later, of such Americans as Copley and Irving and Cooper. He helped prove to the world that original genius could also flourish in America. He changed permanently the nature of acting, revealed the greatness of its scope and was another man with character. In fact, it was his character that forced respect even as the nation was wont to curse his family for bringing as harsh a sorrow as the people could know.

It has been mentioned that Junius Brutus Booth, well born and well educated in England, came to America to avoid a wife and to grasp some of the opportunity in the New World. This meant, among other things, that the ten children he had by the woman he brought with him were not legitimate. Whatever this may have meant to the sons and daughter must have been mitigated by their deep love and respect for their mother. There is reason to believe that life on the Maryland farm bought by Junius was rather ideal except for one problem—money. It was not that Junius was experiencing failure in America. He had the power to shake audiences and to rev their hearts with excitement —he has been called the founder of the American tradition of tragic acting—and he was successful throughout his career. He suffered "the curse of drink," and that is why insufficient funds got back to Maryland when he was trouping.

In desperation, Mrs. Booth finally sought a solution and sent her son Edwin, the year he was sixteen, to accompany the family provider when he set out on that season's tour and see if he could keep his father a bit more practical. Junius did not approve. It seemed absurd that the foremost tragedian in the United States, a man who could enthrall the French of New Orleans playing Orestes in Racine's *Andromaque* in the language of the audience, who could play Shylock in Hebrew, should be shadowed by a callow kid who did not even know what it was to need sustaining spirits.

The idea was not to Edwin's taste either, but he was dutiful. He had no intention of acting as he accompanied his father, but these were times when if you got near enough to a stage, you might be asked to hold a spear at the least.

In Boston, the opening night of *Richard III*, an overworked prompter demanded relief and Edwin was told to play Tressel. The following account is included for the benefit of present-day fathers who may be overplaying their efforts to make their sons geniuses or to lure them into the father's trade. This is the extent of what happened when Junius heard his son was going to act.

He summoned Edwin to his dressing room and interrogated him: "Who was Tressel?"

"A messenger from the field of Tewksbury."

"What was his mission?"

"To bear the news of the defeat of the king's party."

"How did he make the journey?"

"On horseback."

"Then where are your spurs?"

Edwin looked down and realized he had not thought of spurs.

"Here, take mine," the father said.

Edwin took them and after the scene returned to the dressing room to find his father deep in thought. Presently, Junius noticed he was back.

"Have you done well?"

"I think so," said Edwin.

"Give me my spurs," said Junius.

Junius did not intimidate Edwin, at least not enough to drive him home, and Edwin continued to be his father's guardian and his mother's emissary in the succeeding seasons. When Edwin was eighteen, they went to California, crossing the isthmus to get there.

In San Francisco, Edwin continued to play small parts with his father or to stand in the wings and watch the old man's skill. Junius was beginning to fight age, but he could still rouse the audience, make them forget everyone else on stage, in *Othello*, *Richard III*, *Hamlet* and the rest of his repertoire. Up in the mining area, though, hard times had set in and the people there felt no need for imported tragedy. For this reason or perhaps even for the son's sake, Junius invited Edwin to go his own way.

It was painful but fortunate. Edwin began to establish his independence and career. The price was high, he was sometimes destitute, but the necessity to work at whatever he could get brought his essential experience. He toured the mining camps, alone on horseback, carrying his banjo and offering solo entertainment, or he traveled with miserably poor companies. On returning to San Francisco, getting the lead in a melodrama, *The American Fireman*, he caught attention, with one critic predicting he would attain "a high rank in the profession." He played Fred.

Mrs. Jerome and her son, Fred, are eating supper in their humble apartment.

MRS. JEROME: [*Sighing*] O Frederic, I have a strange foreboding as if something dreadful was about to happen.

FRED: Now, don't talk in such a melancholy way, when I feel so happy.

[*Distant fire bell heard*]

Hark! what's that? Fire! I'm off, mother.

MRS. JEROME: Oh, no—not without your supper!
FRED: Supper—and do you think I'd stop for that? No! for while I remain to eat, some poor family may lose their all, which, were I present, I might aid in saving; the meal would choke me did I attempt to feast while others suffer. No, no, never.
[*Exit hastily, center door*]
MRS. JEROME: Brave boy! Heaven give you strength to save the unfortunate!
[*Watches off center door, as scene closes. Music*]

This is an abbreviated version of that climax. Actually, some say it included sentiments such as "What is my death if I save the city?" and "A San Francisco fire-boy is the noblest work of God!" Which feels like leg-wrenching until you consider the iron-faced, low-keyed bombast of modern TV.

Some people are puzzled, wondering how this could possibly be worthwhile training for the greatest tragedian of his century. How could he even *do* it with a straight face? The answer is in the actor's "gift of belief." When you consider how easy it is to make the whole act of acting ridiculous—

. . . forc[ing] his soul so to his own conceit . . .
Tears in his eyes, distraction 'n 's aspect . . .
For Hecuba!
What's Hecuba to him, or he to Hecuba,
That he should weep for her?

—you appreciate how necessary it is for the player to believe so as to convince his audience. When an actor loses belief, he can infect the audience with sullen boredom, and it is this necessity to believe which is the hazard for the actor; it explains why so many good ones can appear, sometimes to their ludicrous disadvantage, in plays that don't play. The mistakes, however, can be instructive: the actor learns how far he can or cannot take an audience, by what means he may succeed against the odds in forcing or beguiling attention and respect. It can be precious knowledge later when he finds himself alone onstage with "Now I am alone."

Before long more important parts began to come Booth's way,

encouraging him to stay in California when it was time for his father to return east. Junius crossed the isthmus again—where his purse was stolen—and appeared in New Orleans during one of the city's regular yellow fever epidemics. The six-performance engagement was successful, netting Booth a thousand dollars, and he proceeded homeward on a steamer to Cincinnati, but the first day aboard he was seized with fever and on the fifth day of misery he died. Mrs. Booth came to Cincinnati to get the body. It is said that the thousand dollars he was bringing her was stolen from the corpse. Edwin, when he heard of his father's death, blamed himself bitterly for not going with him; it was the first of several great sorrows he was to keep.

On learning of the end of Junius Brutus Booth, Rufus Choate declared: "What, Booth dead? Then there are no more actors!" There was no reason for Choate to suspect the son might be much greater. Edwin had not yet shown himself to New York but was, in fact, going in the other direction, to Australia, with and opposite Laura Keene. When he returned, he was twenty-one, a man "who looked unusual and unique without trying to," and, unfortunately, now man enough to drink. He got engagements, though, in San Francisco, with the critics scolding, "If he will but apply himself *industriously*, *unceasingly* and *perseveringly* in his profession, he will ere long rank the foremost of living actors!" But this was not his mood, and when he appeared in Sacramento as Richard III, his father's great part, a reviewer commented, "It was palpable that the part had not been studied with the deep concern which an actor of so much promise as Mr. Booth owed not only to an audience but also to himself."

He drank, was indifferent, got fired from one engagement, but he knew he had power when he wanted to use it. "Want to see some good acting?" he asked J. J. McCloskey as he came to his best scene in the melodrama, *The Marble Heart*. "I haven't seen it yet," answered McCloskey. "You'll see it now," said Booth and went on stage and so moved the audience and impressed McCloskey that years later he told reporters, "I suppose very few know that Booth was a great melodramatic, romantic actor . . .

and those who knew him in the early days are not so sure that it was not a mistake for him to follow the great tragedian roles rather than those of the romantic, picturesque school."

Booth went east, determined to be recognized, but the New York managers were indifferent and would not offer a theatre. He took to the road, guest-starring, taking what his manager could get. In Richmond, he played a theatre being stage-managed by Joe Jefferson. "There was a gentleness and sweetness of manner in him," Jefferson noted, "that made him far more winning than his father." Jefferson cast his sixteen-year-old leading lady, Mary Devlin, as Juliet opposite Booth's Romeo. Booth wrote to his mother, "I have seen and acted with a young woman who has so impressed me that I could almost forget my vow never to marry an actress."

Baltimore, Chicago, Detroit and more until, finally, Boston, which was important because the Brahmins there had convinced almost everyone that they were the final arbiters of everything from art to beans. The theatre he appeared at was second-rate, but there were important people who came to see the great one's son. Edwin had barely begun to speak when Dr. Samuel Howe and his wife, Julia Ward Howe, were sent into shivers and, looking at each other, they whispered, "This is it!"

"Quite a triumph," commented the Boston *Transcript*. "Young Booth's success was decided. . . . It brought back the most vivid recollections of the fire, the vigor, the strong intellectuality which characterized the acting of his lamented father."

That was enough, New York was eager for him now. He opened at the best theatre, the Metropolitan, in *Richard III* (the manager's choice), and though he was still rough, brought the audience to its feet. He was a star! With the enthusiastic approval of his co-players because, then and until his last performance, he was the soul of consideration and courtesy to all who worked with him—the gentleman.

One thing about his new success annoyed him intensely, the constant comparison, especially in the press, with his father. He determined to root out the similarities and to have a style of his

EDWIN BOOTH. They told themselves in Springfield, Ohio, they would never forget the night he was there.

own. This enhanced his appeal; the old style of declamatory acting, his father's and Forrest's, was becoming passé, especially after Booth presented the famous parts in a reasoning, human manner. Where previous stars had stood still and orated the soliloquies, Booth spoke them thoughtfully and moved about in keeping with the impulse in the words. It was the difference between a character and a man; audiences were fascinated and thrilled by this new realism. And held by the softer, more intimate voice and his eyes. The eyes! No one could forget being transfixed by those eyes.

It soon cost more for the tickets when Booth came to town, but few were deterred, judging by the business. After all, how many actors had played *Hamlet* for one hundred nights as Booth did in New York? None, ever. There was no one like him, and in every town they waited for his return, even while he was away abroad conquering Britain and "Shakespeare's second home," Germany. Many were like Lincoln, who said he preferred to read Shakespeare except when it was Booth performing.

The repertoire of parts brought to his countrymen in every state included Hamlet, Macbeth, Lear, Othello, Iago, Shylock, Richard II, Richard III, Brutus, Richelieu, Bertuccio (*The Fool's Revenge*), Ruy Blas, Don César de Bazan, and sometimes Sir Edward Mortimer, Sir Giles Overreach, and Claude Melnotte in *The Lady of Lyons*. Later he would shorten the list to those parts where he felt he gave the most: Hamlet, Brutus, Richelieu, Bertuccio and Lear.

He was an idol, it was generally agreed that the nation had never had such genius on its stage; he was married to Mary Devlin, he adored her and their child; yet spells of melancholy dogged him, abetted by "his father's curse," drinking. He was performing in New York and too addled with drink to open the telegrams telling him Mary was dying at their home in Boston. When he reached her bedside too late, that was the end of his drinking and the beginning of another sorrow that would weigh on him forever.

Not long after, he was playing in Boston when word came that Johnny, John Wilkes, his younger, headstrong brother, so loved by their mother, had done something which seemed impossible to believe, had killed the President of the United States, the President who had brought the nation through the war. It was incredible, but Edwin was finally forced to accept the fact. It was not only the end of his career as he saw it—his mother, his poor mother who had borne so much for her love of his father, all the family, his daughter, would now live forever in disgrace.

"I don't believe it," said John McCullough on hearing the news.

"Well, I do," snarled Edwin Forrest. "All those goddamned Booths are mad!"

Sniffed a clergyman on learning that it had occurred in a playhouse: "Would that Mr. Lincoln had fallen elsewhere than at the very gates of hell."

Booth instantly retired from the stage. But a year later, when a committee of honorable citizens called to assure him the public would not be vindictive, he returned in *Hamlet*. The New York audience rose at the sight of him and cheered until, his face wet with tears, he bowed in acknowledgment. The play continued and so did his career, giving America the best he had to offer.

He built an elaborate theatre, the Booth in New York, costing over a million dollars, and proceeded to mount the most distinguished productions theatregoers had ever seen. He was not a businessman, the advice given him was bad, the dream could not amortize the theatre, and he had to declare bankruptcy. For the opera houses and their patrons from coast to coast, it was their good fortune, for Booth took to the road to recoup and, for the rest of his life, New York was but another date.

The Walter Hampden Library of The Players Club has his route book for the season 1887–88, which is representative of all his tours. Few people can appreciate the exhaustion of acting, particularly Shakespeare. There is the strain of the intense control of self and audience, the exertion of movement (including dueling), speaking at a projected level, changing costumes, the tension of making all look effortless—and today few actors can appreciate what it meant to do all this *on tour*, especially as it was then.

With the aid of John McLeod, Librarian of the Association of American Railroads, I have worked out the traveling times involved in the '87–88 tour. It is true that Booth often had a private car, but it was still an unrelenting pace, September 12 to May 19—one that most moderns might not want to cope with even by air.

You can glance down the list and compare the distance-times that are familiar to you now with what they were then:

BUFFALO Sept. 12–14 / 3 performances
LV. 6:45 A.M. / 258 miles / 7 hrs, 30 mins
to DETROIT Sept. 15–17 / 4 perfs
LV. 6:50 A.M. / 739 miles / 31 hrs, 50 mins
to MINNEAPOLIS Sept. 19–24 / 7 perfs
LV. 8 A.M. / 154 miles / 8 hrs, 15 mins
to DULUTH Sept. 26 / 1 perf
LV. 11 A.M. / 160 miles / 7 hrs, 15 mins
to EAU CLAIRE Sept. 27 / 1 perf
LV. 9 A.M. / 194 miles / 8 hrs, 28 mins
to OSHKOSH Sept. 28 / 1 perf
LV. 7:58 A.M. / 85 miles / 3 hrs, 22 mins
to MILWAUKEE Sept. 29–Oct. 1 / 7 perfs
LV. 1 P.M. / 85 miles / 3 hrs
to CHICAGO Oct. 3–22 / 21 perfs
LV. 11:20 P.M. / 488 miles / 21 hrs, 40 mins
to KANSAS CITY Oct. 24–29 / 6 perfs
LV. 6:40 A.M. / 277 miles / 11 hrs, 35 mins
to SAINT LOUIS Oct. 31–Nov. 5 / 7 perfs
LV. 8 A.M. / 341 miles / 10 hrs, 30 mins
to CINCINNATI Nov. 7–12 / 7 perfs
LV. 7:15 A.M. / 244 miles / 7 hrs, 20 mins
to CLEVELAND Nov. 14–16 / 4 perfs
LV. 5:35 A.M. / 113 miles / 4 hrs
to TOLEDO Nov. 17 / 1 perf
LV. 4:30 A.M. / 207 miles / 7 hrs, 25 mins
to ERIE Nov. 18 / 1 perf
LV. 2:26 A.M. / 103 miles / 8 hrs, 9 mins
to YOUNGSTOWN Nov. 19 / 1 perf
LV. 10:50 A.M. / 68 miles / 2 hrs, 45 mins
to PITTSBURGH Nov. 21–26 / 8 perfs
LV. 7:15 A.M. / 354 miles / 9 hrs, 30 mins

to PHILADELPHIA Nov. 28–Dec. 10 / 14 perfs
LV. 6:35 P.M. / 324 miles / 13 hrs, 15 mins

[Through cars had to be transported by lighter across New York City harbor.]

to BOSTON Dec. 12–24 / 14 perfs
LV. 8:30 A.M. / 234 miles / 7 hrs
to NEW YORK Dec. 26–Jan. 7 / 14 perfs
LV. 2:15 A.M. / 187 miles / 7 hrs, 30 mins
to BALTIMORE Jan. 9–14 / 7 perfs
LV. 9:45 A.M. / 159 miles / 5 hrs, 3 mins
to RICHMOND Jan. 16 / 1 perf
457 miles / 14 hrs, 2 mins

[A special private train is indicated for this jump. There was no regular service that would have made them in time for the performance.]

to CHARLESTON Jan. 17 / 1 perf
LV. 7:30 A.M. / 115 miles / 3 hrs, 22 mins
to SAVANNAH Jan. 18 / 1 perf
LV. 7:10 A.M. / 192 miles / 6 hrs, 30 mins
to MACON Jan. 19 / 1 perf
LV. 3:35 A.M. / 103 miles / 2 hrs, 40 mins
to ATLANTA Jan. 20–21 / 3 perfs
LV. 11:15 P.M. / 291 miles / 12 hrs, 35 mins
to NASHVILLE Jan. 23–25 / 4 perfs
LV. 7:15 A.M. / 230 miles / 8 hrs, 45 mins
to MEMPHIS Jan. 26–28 / 4 perfs
LV. 10:45 P.M. / 310 miles / 11 hrs, 10 mins
to CHATTANOOGA Jan. 30–31 / 2 perfs
LV. 8:50 A.M. / 143 miles / 6 hrs, 30 mins
to BIRMINGHAM Feb. 1–2 / 2 perfs
LV. 3:50 A.M. / 96 miles / 3 hrs, 20 mins
to MONTGOMERY Feb. 3 / 1 perf
LV. 7:30 A.M. / 180 miles / 6 hrs, 20 mins
to MOBILE Feb. 4 / 1 perf
LV. 2:25 A.M. / 141 miles / 5 hrs, 15 mins
to NEW ORLEANS Feb. 6–11 / 8 perfs
LV. 10:45 A.M. / 411 miles / 22 hrs, 30 mins
to GALVESTON Feb. 13–14 / 2 perfs
LV. 6:25 A.M. / 50 miles / 2 hrs
to HOUSTON Feb. 15 / 2 perfs

LV. 9:05 A.M. / 265 miles / 10 hrs, 45 mins
to DALLAS Feb. 16–17 / 2 perfs
LV. 6:55 A.M. / 26 miles / 1 hr, 5 mins
to FORTH WORTH Feb. 18 / 2 perfs
LV. 8:50 A.M. / 88 miles / 4 hrs, 40 mins
to WACO Feb. 20 / 1 perf
LV. 12:45 A.M. /110 miles / 5 hrs, 45 mins
to AUSTIN Feb. 21 / 2 perfs
LV. 6:30 A.M. / 80 miles / 4 hrs
to SAN ANTONIO Feb. 22–23 / 2 perfs
632 miles / 24 hrs, 59 mins

[*To make this performance, a nonscheduled train must have been used.*]

to EL PASO Feb. 24 / 1 perf
LV. 11:50 A.M. / 804 miles / 33 hrs, 40 mins
to LOS ANGELES Feb. 27–Mar. 3 / 8 perfs
LV. 1 P.M. / 482 miles / 23 hrs, 15 mins
to SAN FRANCISCO Mar. 5–24 / 21 perfs
LV. 9 A.M. / 103 miles / 4 hrs, 10 mins
to STOCKTON Mar. 26 / 1 perf
LV. 8:57 A.M. / 48 miles / 1 hr, 53 mins
to SACRAMENTO Mar. 27 / 2 perfs
LV. 12:20 P.M. / 781 miles / 32 hrs, 20 mins
to SALT LAKE CITY Mar. 30–31 / 3 perfs
LV. 8:03 A.M. / 660 miles / 30 hrs, 42 mins
to DENVER Apr. 2–7 / 7 perfs
LV. 8:30 A.M. / 568 miles / 23 hrs, 45 mins
to OMAHA Apr. 9–11 / 4 perfs
LV. 7:45 A.M. / 58 miles / 3 hrs, 50 mins
to LINCOLN Apr. 12 / 1 perf
LV. 11:35 A.M. / 184 miles / ARR. Beatrice, Neb. 1 P.M.
LV. Beatrice 3 P.M. / ARR. Manhattan, Kan. 11:40 P.M.
LV. Manhattan 2 A.M. / ARR. Topeka 3:55 A.M. / 16 hrs, 20 mins
to TOPEKA Apr. 13 / 1 perf
LV. 1 A.M. / 162 miles / 7 hrs, 10 mins
to WICHITA Apr. 14 / 2 perfs
LV. 10:30 A.M. / 218 miles / 8 hrs, 15 mins
to LEAVENWORTH Apr. 16 / 1 perf

LV. 9:18 A.M. / 42 miles / 1 hr, 42 mins
to ST. JOSEPH Apr. 17 / 1 perf
LV. 10 A.M. / 198 miles / 9 hrs, 15 mins
to DES MOINES Apr. 18 / 1 perf
LV. 3:40 A.M. / 144 miles / 6 hrs
to CEDAR RAPIDS Apr. 19 / 1 perf
LV. 5:10 A.M. / 136 miles / 7 hrs, 10 mins
to DUBUQUE Apr. 20 / 1 perf
LV. 7:30 A.M. / 102 miles / 11 hrs, 20 mins
to DAVENPORT Apr. 21 / 1 perf
LV. 8:05 A.M. / 92 miles / 3 hrs, 17 mins
to PEORIA Apr. 23 / 1 perf.
LV. 7:40 A.M. / 73 miles / 7 hrs, 20 mins
to SPRINGFIELD, ILL. Apr. 24 / 1 perf
LV. 11:55 P.M. / 59 miles / 2 hrs, 5 mins
to BLOOMINGTON Apr. 25 / 1 perf
LV. 4:25 A.M. / 153 miles / 10 hrs, 50 mins
to TERRE HAUTE Apr. 26 / 1 perf
LV. 1:30 A.M. / 73 miles / 2 hrs, 45 mins
to INDIANAPOLIS Apr. 27–28 / 3 perfs
LV. 7:10 A.M. / 64 miles / 2 hrs, 28 mins
to LAFAYETTE Apr. 30 / 1 perf
LV. 10:45 A.M. / 109 miles / 3 hrs
to FORT WAYNE May 1 / 1 perf
LV. 2:40 A.M. / 94 miles / 3 hrs, 55 mins
to KALAMAZOO May 2 / 2 perfs
LV. 7:10 A.M. / 49 miles / 1 hr, 55 mins
to GRAND RAPIDS May 3 / 1 perf
LV. 6:40 A.M. / 131 miles / 5 hrs, 5 mins
to BAY CITY Mar 4 / 1 perf
LV. 6:50 A.M. / 15 miles / 50 mins
to EAST SAGINAW May 5 / 2 perfs
LV. 7:40 A.M. / 138 miles / 8 hrs, 55 mins
to ANN ARBOR May 7 / 1 perf
LV. 7:15 A.M. / 186 miles / 8 hrs, 3 mins
to SPRINGFIELD, OHIO May 8 / 1 perf
LV. 2:30 A.M. / 24 miles / 55 mins
to DAYTON May 9 / 1 perf
LV. 3:25 A.M. / 166 miles / 7 hrs, 40 mins
to LOUISVILLE May 9 / 1 perf
/ 700 miles / 34 hrs, 10 mins
to WILLIAMSBURG, VA. May 14–19 / 7 perfs

[There were seven performances in Williamsburg because theatregoers came from Washington. Booth never played the capital after the assassination.]

The repertoire was *Julius Caesar, Hamlet, Othello, K & P* (as the company manager listed *The Taming of the Shrew*, suggesting a tab version may have been used), *Macbeth, King Lear, The Merchant of Venice.*

There were 258 performances at 72 stands, 48 of them one-nights.

The gross was $634,971.85, the net $459,903.51. To get this attraction, some theatres asked only 5 percent of the gross. Booth shared the returns with his co-star and the manager of this tour, Lawrence Barrett. Booth's share: $249,927.54. The weekly salaries of the company, other than the stars, totaled $1,480. Supernumeraries, hired locally, not included.

In Kansas City, they played a theatre not yet completed, without a roof; the set was boxed to keep out the wind and the audience sat bundled up and shivering. They were given an ovation. In places like Oshkosh, Macon, Waco, Lincoln, crowds waited for Booth's arrival at the railway stations.

At this time, Booth was fifty-five. His health was failing. It was his fortieth year on the stage, and he continued on until he was fifty-eight and then gave up, worn out by the labor and grief. His second wife had lost her mind and had tormented him unmercifully in the process. He had wealth—he had recovered to the extent of more than half a million—and, when this was known, it brought him the respect of those who do not feel competent to judge until they have heard the returns.

Was he truly the great artist? Can we tell from this distance? We have the witness of many playgoers of sensitive and experienced judgment, including the critics, and, though there have been many fine actors, none has made a similar impression in such a range of great roles. There is also the recorded opinion of the professionals he worked with, who were the most capable of taking his measure. They considered him incomparable. J. J. McCullough, a proud actor-manager, persuaded Booth to come to San Francisco after twenty years' absence and played in his support. His explanation: "I will always gladly be second to Edwin."

Actors appreciated his intelligence and his extraordinary equipment. When he came to London, Ellen Terry felt hostile because of her fear he might steal thunder from her employer and idol, Henry Irving. But when she met Booth in Irving's dressing room, and Booth turned to her as they were being introduced, she gasped. Later she recalled, "I have never in any face, in any country, seen such wonderful eyes."

David Belasco said Booth's voice kept him awake all night after he first heard it. Charles Copeland wrote: "Its sweetness and strength spoke to the inner even more than to the outer ear. It stirred not only the blood but the spirit."

The best biography of an American actor is Eleanor Ruggles' *Prince of Players*. She tells of hearing that voice long after Booth was gone:

> Edwin Booth made two recordings in 1890, but for some time I was half afraid to hear them—afraid that Booth's voice and style might not measure up to the enthusiastic descriptions I had at second hand.
>
> It seemed my plain duty to listen, however, and so I did, at the Harvard Theatre Collection in Cambridge, Massachusetts, not three miles away from where Booth lies buried in Mount Auburn Cemetery. I listened while Booth's voice sounded, faint but distinct, out of the crackling surface noise in Othello's address to the senators:
>
> *Most potent, grave, and revered signiors . . .*
>
> I had expected rant, but these were quiet tones. The diction was exquisite, the delivery formal and grand but stirring and unstilted. A few reminders of an older method had to be got used to: the elecutionary use of "me" for "my", of "oll" for "all", and—a definite flaw to the modern ear—an occasional singsong cadence, as "my *boy*ish days." The voice itself, though, was the most beautiful speaking voice I had ever heard, with great poetry and feeling, yet with no straining for effect, and I suddenly understood the ecstatic, nostalgic praises of the men and women, my own grandparents, for example, who had heard Booth in life.

The second record was of Hamlet's "To be, or not to be." The surface noise was much more obstructive this time, with fearful sputterings and banshee wails. I tried playing the disc over and over, following the words of the speech on a printed copy until by degrees they became clear. It was a moving revelation. Booth had been more than fifty years a dweller in that country of which he was speaking so softly and intimately:

> *The undiscover'd country, from whose bourne*
> *No traveller returns.*

Yet through the screeches and burrs of that ancient record penetrated a voice that was saturated with magnetism of the living man and an emotion that seemed to breathe itself out of a whole lifetime's "acquaintance with grief."

I have heard Hamlet's famous lines given by twentieth-century actors less conventionally, and, perhaps, from an intellectual point of view, more interestingly than Booth delivered them. But not from anyone else have I heard a rendering that so touched and thrilled with that overwhelming, mysterious quality of "something more"; that extraordinary poignant and yet robust appeal, which, I suppose, is genius, and which sweeps away reservations in the listener, making the mere originality and intellect so much cultivated by our contemporaries seem superficial and insipid.

To judge by these fragments of his art, Edwin Booth really was an actor whose greatness would tower over the talents of today. We should all have more faith in the claims of our grandparents.

It is perhaps only the myth of my own making that says there was posted on the backstage callboard of the theatre at Epidaurus this advice: "*If you would have the audience forget that you are an actor, never forget that you are an actor.*" Booth, with his intelligence and the requisite duality of the good actor, used his endowment of physique and voice with consummate skill. Although "he approached his task reverently and thought of himself not as an entertainer but as an interpreter of great dramatic literature," he was always in perfect control of his work through command of himself as illustrated by the story of the rat:

He had just finished one of the most tremendous outbursts of passion in *Othello* and had aroused the audience to the highest pitch of excitement, when he moved upstage in, apparently, pitiable anguish, and said in a low tone to his nephew, Wilfred Clarke, standing in the wings: "Will, did you see that big rat run across the stage?"

The same was true of Jefferson:

> He knew that he always acted best when the head was as cool as the heart was warm. . . . Once when, as Caleb Plummer, he permitted himself to be overcome by his personal emotion, and to allow this to confuse itself with the emotion of the character, he lost control of the effect altogether, and had to ring down the curtain.

In the last years of Booth's life, he made a generous gift to his profession. He purchased a stately house in Gramercy Square and had it converted by Stanford White into a club, The Players —"Where gentlemen of the theatre can meet the gentlemen from other walks of life."

Whatever is made of that word now in a world of more indifferent manners, it must be observed that Booth and Jefferson were gentlemen. It has been cynically said that it is easy to be honest if you have the money and to be gracious if you have the leisure. From all that one can learn of America's greatest comedian and tragedian, it seems conclusive that these two, rich or poor, in any circumstance, had sufficient soul to be gentle.

A splendid company, following them on tour, benefited from their example:

Mrs. Fiske
Richard Mansfield . . .

No, the list is too long—and who dares to be responsible for the order of the billing?

•

In 1893, upon the death of Edwin Booth, Joseph Jefferson became the second president of The Players Club. In 1905, when Jefferson died, he was succeeded in that office by Mr. John Drew.

☛ 8

Moist Eyes and Wet Pants

Auburn [N.Y.]—*Burtis Opera House.* The Sunshine of Paradise Valley *to good houses. Jan 27.*

Wellington [*Kan.*]—*Woods Opera House.* The Hidden Hand. *Good business. Jan 29.*

Springfield [*Mass.*]—*Gilmore Court Square Theatre.* A Railroad Ticket. *Less gunpowder and crash box would improve the piece. Jan 29.*

Toledo [O.]—*Valentine Theatre.* The Great Diamond Robbery *to the capacity. Jan 30.*

Plainfield [*N.J.*]—*Stillman Theatre.* The Tornado, *good business. Feb 2/3.*

HARRIET Beecher Stowe was oh! so right. She had said: "If the barrier which now keeps young people of Christian families from theatrical entertainments is once broken down by the introduction of respectable and moral plays . . . it will be . . . five bad plays to one good."

The bad plays came thick and fast and oh! it was fun for the legions who enjoyed bad plays. Gone were the years when the actors' chief stock in trade was the royalty-free works of the Bard. Now the difference was that instead of plays for George Washington and the burgess class only, the hostler, hod carrier, laborers of every sort, clerks and minor officials were getting into the theatre to gulp their dish of tea. If you consider the pretentious air-pudding-with-wind-sauce that the upper classes have often been prone to swallow, you are not sure which group has had the better or the more foolish taste.

This development distressed the self-appointed guardians of morals, it made them fearful to see the common ones happy. As they saw it, a cultivated person might afford the risk of such vulgarity but the ordinary ones should be encouraged (by restriction if need be) to confine themselves to the Bible and Literature that was uplifting in the proper sense. Should not something be done, asked the agitated, to thwart those writers, managers, actors who pandered to the "baser instincts" with dramatized threats to virginity and stimulus to violence expressed in the uncadenced language of the gutter?

Because writers, managers and actors were now pandering to the common taste for all it was worth. There was a big avid public out there, and now, thanks to democracy on a continent ripe for the pickings, that public had the money and could not get enough of the simplified life as expressed in these popular plays, the black and white of it, the heroic, valiant, chivalrous, pure and wholesome good versus the wicked, flagrant, despicable, vile and odious hot-crotched bad!

It was exciting to see how good people got caught in trouble yet always escaped. Out on the farm or "here in this dead burg," about the biggest event was falling out of bed, while those characters at the opera house could go through and emerge from more thrilling calamities than the Jews had thought up for the Old Testament—almost. And on alternate nights, you could enjoy the woes of the upper class. It was interesting to see how the society folks also had strife; how the wife, elegant of dress and speech, suffered as much as her plain sisters in the audience. It was interesting to see how good and kind husbands could be married to wives no better than sluts, and a pity it was that the husbands were too noble to say so.

They went and loved it all, and if you wonder how they could afford it, how even a small town could support an opera house with a different company and show six nights a week, fall to spring, you must remember that the opera house got about all of the entertainment dollar. Consider how it is divided today: theatre (legitimate), movies, ballet, opera, nightclubs, television, radio, magazines, comic books, paperbacks, records, tape, concerts (classical and pop), store-bought games, baseball, football, basketball, skiing, boating, bowling, golf, tennis, photography and other hobbies, travel and more.

In meeting this demand for plays, it was not possible then any more than on television now to provide unique and expert stories every evening. So, as now, formulas were used, resulting in the machine-made plays, and there were a lot of skillful operators to run the factory. One product, as mentioned, was the domestic drama, which could have a background of marble and potted palms or cracked plaster and the kitchen sink. The important thing was that it should have a moral and be sad.

Today's soap opera doesn't seem to work up much more than a whine and a sigh, but there was a time when the characters in plays *suffered* grandly and could jerk enough tears to threaten the kidneys with desiccation. Again, why people paid to buy such sadness is strange. In a time of infant cholera, Tb, scarlet fever, smallpox, typhoid, they had an excellent supply of funerals which should have met the demand for morbidity. Also, it was an era of financial panics that should have satisfactorily dispirited everyone. Still they were not gratified, they had a tapeworm for "a good cry."

When they didn't get it at the play, there were recitations, and every club, church group and lodge had someone who could supply an evening's doleful entertainment. If they were adequately lugubrious, they would be acclaimed as "just perfect, I don't know when I've cried like that." Before me is a crumbling pamphlet entitled *The Most Wonderful Collection of Famous Recitations Ever Written.* Some random lines will give the flavor and indicate the subjects that satisfied. The reader is asked to hold his hand near his heart.

. . . Into a ward of the whitewashed walls,
Where the dead and dying lay . . .

I stood at eve when the sun went down,
By a grave where a woman lies. . . .

Beside a Western water-tank, one cold December day,
Inside an empty box-car, a dying hobo lay. . . .

. . . I have ruined my health in the struggle for wealth!
Said the banker in piteous tones. . . .

. . . More than a month after, we heard from the poor young thing,
He'd gone away and left her without a wedding ring. . . .

With trembling hand I took the letter from him,
I broke the seal and this is what it said:
Come home, my boy, your dear old father wants you,
Come home, my boy, your dear old mother's dead. . . .

There are more of these cadenced sobs, including two of the most famous: "The Face on the Barroom Floor" and "Over the Hills to the Poorhouse."

The public that found pleasure in this went down to the opera house with a minimum of two handkerchiefs to enjoy their two outstanding favorites in the lachrymose genre. The first was *Camille*. The list of great actresses who played this is impressive. It includes Bernhardt and Duse—and, in a different medium, Garbo. It was a very effective piece, and though it had only one good part, it didn't matter—people would have gone to see almost any actress if only the prompter was throwing the cues.

Camille represented quite a step for an audience so lately rigidly Puritan. Hawthorne had helped them advance when he insisted that Hester deserved some sympathy even if she did do it without a license. Now there was Camille's story, which was presented so extensively that only a few got through life without sobbing over the woes of this consumptive French call girl—even when played by actresses looking as sturdy as the oak. For thirty years and more, indestructible actresses were trouping and dying all over the country. The play was a ticket-printer, it and that other guaranteed purge, *East Lynne*. And why did a harassed people need *East Lynne?* Especially when you consider that it opened in New York in 1863, in the middle of the Civil War. Yet it was one of the greatest hits.

A second-rate actress, Lucille Western, had commissioned a writer, Clifton W. Tayleure, to dramatize the popular novel. Today when a critic's disfavor could close even *The Walk on Water*, one is inclined to be perversely pleased when reading that Miss Western and her *East Lynne* surmounted the snarls of disapproval they originally received. "Trash," wrote one critic, "sickly nonsense," and added, "Miss Western plays with earnestness and abandon; but she exhibits profound and general ignorance of the art of acting, and also a cheerful indifference to the laws of English grammar." Miss Western was another who could weep all the way to the bank, especially since the extent of Mr. Tayleure's take was the flat $100 she had paid him for his job while *her* percentage averaged $350 per night. People wasted no sympathy on writers. It was said they so enjoyed their afflatus they were quite indifferent to mere cash.

It requires concentration to follow the story of *East Lynne*. It opens with Archibald Carlyle bringing Lady Isabel (Miss Western's role) to his home, East Lynne. His sister Cornelia (called Miss Corney) disapproves, but she makes the gesture:

> MISS CORNELIA: I hope you will be contented at East Lynne.
> ISABEL: Contented! Why, of course I shall. The dear old place! I was very happy here when a child; and it was here that poor Papa died, too.

The next scene is a garden in *West* Lynne. Richard Hare enters "disguised with heavy black whiskers," and this is what he confides to the audience:

> RICHARD: Here I am at length, after my absence of nearly two years, once more in sight of the dear old home. But, alas! I dare not enter even for a moment. I am a fugitive from justice. . . . Ah! the garden gate is open, and I see my sister Barbara standing in the door. Hist, Barbara, come out! Don't you know me?—it is I, Richard!

Barbara enters and we learn she had hoped Archibald Carlyle might marry *her*.

Next, Lord Mount Severn shows up at *East* Lynne and wants to know how dared Archibald marry his ward, Isabel, while he was away and without his permission. Archibald says he found Isabel was being ill-treated by Lady Mount Severn. He wrote His Lordship for permission to rescue and marry Isabel and, not hearing, presumed there was no objection. Lord Mount Severn begins to relent, only showing concern for Isabel's future security.

LORD M.S.: But you cannot keep her as a peer's daughter, I presume.

ARCH.: Our establishment will be small and quiet. I explained all this to Isabel at the first, so your Lordship now perceives, I hope, that there was nothing clandestine in my conduct toward Lady Isabel.

His Lordship offers his hand.

An oily character named Francis Levison now arrives and tells Isabel he always meant to marry her, he was just short of funds, and he still yearns for her.

ISABEL: I will not listen to this language, sir! How dare you presume to address me thus?

Barbara comes to East Lynne to ask Archibald to meet her brother tonight to help him. Isabel, who has been listening, enters after they leave.

ISABEL: Oh, misery, misery. Oh, how palpable to all eyes must be that woman's love for my husband! . . .

And more—it's a long speech. Levison enters and says he has seen Archibald and Barbara together and it looks like hanky-panky. Isabel panics.

ISABEL: Only prove this and I will quit this house forever.

LEVISON: With me, Isabel?

ISABEL: Ay, with you. I care not who shall be the instrument of my vengeance.

[*Exeunt*]

In plays like this, time flits. By the time Isabel flaunts off with Levison, we learn she has had two children by Arch. So she is leaving something behind which she may recall when she subsides.

We then see Archibald in deep remorse because she has gone.

We then see Isabel in deep remorse—"very pale and very ill." Levison appears. She says he had promised to come back and marry her *before*—and now we learn she has had a *third* child, Levison's. Levison makes excuses, he was delayed on business, then levels:

LEVISON: Well, Isabel, you must be aware that it is an awful sacrifice for a man in my position to marry a divorced woman.

ISABEL: [*Rising*] Stay, sir! You need not trouble yourself to find new excuses now. Had you taken this journey on purpose to make me your wife, nay, were the clergymen standing by to perform the ceremony, *I tell you, Francis Levison, I would not have you!* [*Sinks in seat exhausted*]

Curtain down, curtain up, and we see Archibald and Barbara married and happy together. A visitor arrives, Madame Vine, who is to be the children's new governess.

ARCH.: [*Looks closely at Madame Vine as he goes out*] I've seen those features before, I'm certain of it; but where can it have been? [*Exits slowly as if in deep study*]

There is some more plot before we get to the great sad scene. (Incidentally, without meaning to confuse may we mention that Levison is found guilty of the murder that made Richard run away.) Now we come to the chamber where Willie, Isabel's child, is dying as he talks to "Madame Vine." There will soon be a rustle in the audience as folks reach for their linen.

WILLIAM: Madame Vine, how long will it be before I die?

MAD. V.: What makes you think you will die, William?

WILLIAM: I am certain of it, Madame Vine; but it is nothing to die when our Savior loves us.

And we hear that his only concern is whether he will meet his mother there, in heaven. Archibald enters.

ARCH.: Madame Vine, do you not perceive a change in his countenance?

MAD. V.: Yes, he has looked like that since a strange fit of trembling that came over him this afternoon.

ARCH.: Oh! it is hard to lose him thus.

Arch leaves the room, Willie is expiring, Madame Vine is frenzied, "throws off cap and spectacles." As Beatrice Lillie used to say, Now this will *kill* you! Because Madame Vine is *Isabel!*

She now does what she's supposed to do, she pays. In a scene long enough that millions got what they paid for: red eyes. Ending:

ARCH.: You are growing faint, Isabel. Let me call assistance. [*Takes her head in his arms*]

ISABEL: No, do not stir—it is not faintness—it is—death! Oh, but it is hard to part so! Farewell, my once dear husband until—eternity!

[*Soft music*]

ARCH.: Until—eternity . . .

[*She falls back in his arms and dies. He lays her gently down and stands in attitude of deep grief, as if invoking the blessing of Heaven for her soul*]

CURTAIN

Tomorrow night's attraction might be Booth with a grander, louder form of self-pity as Lear. Or more probably it would be a melodrama to thrill the breath out of you, for this was the most popular product of all. Craftsmen of amazing ingenuity were constantly devising new plots and new climaxes to fit the purpose of every melodrama, which was to demonstrate the triumph of virtue over vice, meaning love over lust. This could occur anywhere and did, for it added novelty if you could vary the scenery. So it happened in Soho, the Bowery, Down East, anywhere that could be made to provide a perilous situation.

The skill of these playmakers was in keeping with the times.

America was learning what was to be the basis of its economic conquest of the earth: how to stamp out, assemble or spin in mass production about everything anybody would buy. Bathtubs, shoes, hats, underwear, furniture, stoves and, soon, cameras and autos. There were men who could do the same with plays, and the most notable manufacturer was Owen Davis. He had studied Greek at Harvard, but he discovered that the exciting way to make money was knocking out mellers, sometimes two and three a week.

Davis never looked the type, he looked more like a banker who operated down the block from the Emporia *Gazette.* After he had composed so many melodramas even he couldn't be sure of the number, he decided to reform and wrote *The Detour,* which was respected, and then *Icebound,* which got the Pulitzer Prize. "But," says a biographer, "his pride on that occasion was certainly no greater than the experience when Gus Hill put on his *Through the Breakers.* This, according to the billing, was 'a drama of real life produced with a carload of elaborate scenery, two sensational scenic effects, the height of mechanical realism, in addition to being a play of real strength and originality, with a cast of New York favorites.' "

The emphasis was on effects more than story. A show could have a shipwreck, the next a high pier or precipice atop which there would be the struggle to see who would be thrown to a fully described death, or a train wreck, or rails to tie virtue to in the path of the oncoming express, or a dungeon with rising tide, or waterfalls for turbulent drowning, or anything else a writer's fiendish mind could imagine, including the greatest of all inspirations, the spinning saw eager to divide the heroine or hero in slabs.

All this called for acting with stamina. The grimaces alone could lame a normal being and, in addition, heroines had to resist in struggle, heroes and villains had to fight, climb, leap and often lift and carry fainting damsels who might be unfeelingly overweight. The theatres in *Cahn's Guide* always listed their traps (trapdoors)—

CALAIS [Me.]—Music Hall.
Depth under stage, 3 feet
5 traps, center

GRAND JUNCTION [Col.]—Park Opera House
Depth under stage, 10 feet
3 traps

MAQUOKETA [Ia.]—Grand Opera House
Depth under stage, 4 feet
1 trap, located center

MILFORD [Mass.]—Music Hall
Depth under stage, 5 feet
6 traps

—for melodramas more often than not involved exits underground or entrances from dungeons. What better effect than a hand pushing up the lid of a hellhole and an evil face appearing, snake eyes glancing about, and a black mustached, lecherous, depraved skunk rising to perform something foul? In the course of which, actors often acquired bruises, sprains and slivers.

When electricity came to the theatres, it was as if it had been perfected for the melodramatists—now the effects could be heightened, lightning was added to thunder. *Through the Breakers* advertised, as they all did, its elaborate scenery, and this could include a panorama of the wicked city or gloomy slums or the blissful valley—"looking so real you feel you could walk right into it."

Lithography was another development exploited by the producers. Often the scenes depicted in the posters (cf. Eliza crossing the ice) were, like some of the next-week movie trailers today, better than the show. There was no hesitation in promising more than the actual on the assumption that the consumers would be satisfied with what was delivered or, if not, the show would be gone before resentment could be effective. As an example of this oversell, the mastiffs pursuing Eliza in the posters were much more vicious-looking than the hounds that yelped in reality (and then only because Eliza was carrying a concealed hunk of meat to tantalize them into action). Or, whereas the heroine was actually saved in the play, on the fences and walls she was shown hurtling to destruction.

The producers of these shockers—or of Shakespeare—did not have to hire artists and arrange with printers to execute such scenes. If a producer decided he had the right people and sufficient scenery, and if he heard the mills were doing well in New England or anywhere else, and it was his hunch that he could make profit if he booked Such-'n'-Such, all he had to do was order the paper for Such-'n'-Such from a company that had it in stock and then all he needed to do was paste the place and date of performance across the bottom of each poster.

This was the ad of

The Metropolitan Printing Co.
Greatest & Largest Show & Mercantile
Printing House in the World
213-227 West 26 Sreet
New York City
We have stock paper for sale
for the following attractions:
A Heroine in Rags
The Limited Mail
A Midsummer Night's Dream
A Guilty Mother
Only a Working Girl
Under the Gaslight
Brownies in Fairyland
The Black Crook
Dangers of Paris
Dangers of a Great City
Down on the Farm
Hamlet
In the Heart of the Storm
Richard III
Nellie, the Beautiful Cloak Model
Uncle Tom's Cabin
Woman Against Woman
When Knighthood Was in Flower
and 444 more titles.

There were five principal characters in the usual melodrama: hero, heroine, light-comedy boy, soubrette and the heavy. Beyond this, the cast might have many more. The plot could have murder, arson, burglary, skulduggery and treachery in any form—everything except actual rape. They were content to let pursuit imply the possibility.

One famous chase that resulted in an immortal line had the villain after her in the street, after her in the shop, after her on the pier, after her on the trestle. Finally, she was safe behind the locked door of her room until a ladder appeared at the window and the dastard's head came up to stare at her cowering against the opposite wall. Then the dastard inquired with a gentle rasp: "Why do you fear me, Nellie?"

Another sample of melodrama is from *The Naval Cadet.* This starred James J. Corbett, the immensely popular prizefighter. He finally located the heroine in a cellar dive. "So you've come for the gal," sneered the villain, then glided forward with an ugly knife in his teeth. Gentleman Jim would calmly take off his white gloves, lay them carefully beside his silk hat and step forward. Wild was the audience as evil was vanquished. This was inevitable for the same reason that poverty was honorable and innocence unassailable.

Under the Gaslight was an early thrilling success that paved the way for the flood of blood and thunder, and who can wonder? At the climax, the hero is tied to the railroad tracks.

VILLAIN: I'm going to put you to bed here on the railroad track.
HEROINE: [*Locked in the station and observing from the window*] Oh, heavens!
VILLAIN: In ten minutes, you will hear the thunder of the locomotive. Then remember me! *remember me!*

Gloating, the villain leaves. The train is coming, we hear the thunder, the whistle, see the trembling light from the headlight shining brighter and nearer.

HERO: Oh, how my neck tingles on the track!

The heroine frantically tries to pull open the station door. No chance. The train is close with a juggernaut roar, the theatre is shaking—how can it sound much louder? She finds an ax! She chops her way out, releases him, the train roars past! He takes her by the hand.

HERO: You were a brave girl to resist.

He leads her forward and clinches the curtain, saying: "*And these are the women they refuse to give the vote!*"

Picture! Curtain!

Under the Gaslight. Carrollton, Georgia, had never been so excited.

When all "modern" locales and situations began to pall, there was rescue—the Western was discovered. Same plot, same characters, now augmented by treacherous aborigines and enough gunfire to supply a war. The hero in Western regalia or frontier army spick-and-span looked larger than ever, the heroine more fragile, the villains less human. Never fear: "And another redskin bites the dust!"

It was the stuff dreams and nightmares were made of. Young girls and old maids could feel hot as they wondered what would have happened if the hero hadn't saved her, if the villain *had* got her in his power. Boys could quake and wonder if they could be/will be as valorous as the hero. And in the minds of all echoed those brave and menacing and dolorous lines that forced the heart!

> "Curse you, Jack Dalton! . . ."
>
> "Drop that gun or you're a dead man! . . ."
>
> "Behold thy promised bride!
> Consent to make her mine or
> down yon boiling cataract,
> I'll hurl her to destruction! . . ."
>
> "Willie! Don't you know me,
> Willie! I am your mother! . . ."
>
> "Firearms and bullets have I none.
> But this right hand is sudden death
> and this left hand is six weeks
> in the hospital! . . ."
>
> "You shall die the death of a dog! . . ."
>
> "I, Hawkshaw, the detective! . . ."
>
> "Place a hand on that poor girl
> and I'll kill you with as little mercy
> as I would a reptile! . . ."
>
> "When you say that,
> smile! . . ."
>
> "Stop that man—
> for God's sake stop him
> before it is too late! . . ."
>
> "I ain't fit to breathe the same air
> with you, ma'am. . . ."
>
> "Rags are royal raiment
> when worn for virtue's sake! . . ."
>
> "Defend your life! It is my knife
> against your sword! . . ."

"Don't dare address this lady
in that manner again! . . ."

"I'll—do anything,
only let me live! . . ."

"Foiled at last—
and by a woman!"

"Stand back—hands up!
You know what this is
—a bomb! . . ."

"Thou cur! . . ."

Theatregoers and moviegoers are more sophisticated today. They sit in the placid audiences pondering the significance of pauses, waiting for the meaning which will not be divulged, postpone reactions until post-mortem determination of what they should have seen, heard and thought, and torpidly watch the conflict of gray versus gray, the sonofabitch villain against the bastard hero for control of the shitty business with the hero winning so he can learn that he has lost.

What is there to hiss, what to cheer? So it now requires strength of imagination to feel the almost unbearable excitement when the scoundrels enjoyed their work, when heroines struggled to save it to reward a noble heart, when heroes not only looked like heroes, they had names to prove it—like Archibald Carlyle!

With effort, you may be able to feel the eager anticipation, the sense of thrills in store, the tearful relief guaranteed, the prospect of escape when you could look in at the opera house and see the announcement:

NEXT WEEK

Mon. *Her First False Step*
Tue. *The Fast Mail*
Wed. *A Fight for Love*
Thr. *The Tornado*
Fri. *Because She Loved Him So*
Sat. Mme. Modjeska in *Macbeth*

Perhaps there was one night a week for those who liked Shakespeare and stuff like that. Come Monday there would be more of what *most* people liked, including *Confessions of a Wife* and *The Robbery at the Lighthouse!*

•

Sometimes, instead of a different company each night, a single company would come for the week with a new play for each night. In 1905, the leading impresario in this type of business was Corse Payton, an actor who knew the box-office value of the superlative. Having no legitimate claim to exceptional talent, he nevertheless made himself unique by billing himself as

CORSE PAYTON
The World's Worst Actor

It got the attention he wanted, made him different, and people were amused, especially as the brag wasn't justified—everyone had seen someone even worse. But it was comical and refreshing to hear him give his curtain speeches and advance his claim.

> Woonsocket [R.I.]—*Corse Payton has got some new jokes in his rag-time speech this season, one of which is that he is the only actor in the business who looks like 30¢ and isn't ashamed of it.*

Any actor who worked for Corse Payton got experience. *In one season, he was offering* Woman Against Woman, Only a Farmer's Daughter, The Runaway Wife, A Desperate Game, East Lynne, Her Lord and Master, Taken from Life, The Eagle's Nest, Young Mrs. Winthrop, A Noble Woman, On the Rappahannock, The Girl I Left Behind Me, The Private Secretary, The Player, Jim the Penman, Aristocracy, Quo Vadis, A Child of the State, My Kentucky Home, The Prodigal Daughter.

> *Fall River* [Mass.]—The Prodigal Daughter. *At the matinee the attendance was a record, there being over 2,700 people in the house, which seats 1,960.*

At the height of his inverted fame, the buttons on Corse Payton's coats were always coins of solid gold.

Expressive Music

1905—*Some of the Year's New Songs*

"Captain Jinks of the Horse Marines"
as sung by George Lingard

"45 Minutes from Broadway"
as sung by George M. Cohan

"Glow Worm"
as sung by May Naudain

"I Want What I Want When I Want It"
as sung by William Pruette in Mlle. Modiste

"In the Shade of the Old Apple Tree"
as sung by Frank Morrell

"Mary's a Grand Old Name"
as sung by Fay Templeton

"Nobody"
as sung by Bert Williams

"She Is Ma Daisy"
as sung by Harry Lauder

"Will You Love Me in December as You Do in May?"
as sung by Janet Allen

In a land saturated with music, where the citizens have trained themselves not to hear as they concentrate on their work or studies, it can be difficult to conceive how precious song could have been when melody was rare. Today, the car in the desert speeds along picking music from the air. Factory workers move to Muzak, a stimulant designed not to reach consciousness. Housewives can have a symphony orchestra accompany them as they dust. Perfume, automobiles, better interest rates are sold with the help of music. Composers write for passengers in elevators and rouse tone-deaf millions to go to work.

Once, the tunes were homemade or church-supplied in hymns. The instruments were few: whistle, harmonica, banjo, guitar, fiddle, jew's-harp. Only the cultured rich heard other strings and brass. The songs, the best of them, were anodynes for the misery of slave work or to alleviate loneliness, frustration, the grief of man's hard lot.

Then came the professional music-makers, bringing melody to the opera house as effective as a spring of May wine. People who had been limited to Old Hundredth and intoning such humility as "Low we bow the adoring knee . . . scarce we dare to lift our eyes" were now striding down Main Street, hanging out the clothes, diminishing gravity as they hummed and promised themselves a hot time tonight. Although the change was not quite so fast as that may suggest. I talked once to a man who had heard that classic when it was first offered in a theatre. Instead of the eventual oom-pah beat, he said it was sung largo, with a slow and almost stately swing:

There'll . be . a . HOT time . in . the . OLD town . to . night.

But it was rhythm and that is what people were eager to feel at the opera house then and until Cole Porter. *A Trip to Chinatown* had a rhythmic song you heard tonight and remembered till the day you died. Strolling on Maple Avenue on a summer evening you could hear Irma Pierce trying to get through her Mozart exercise so she could get good enough to accompany her friends singing the show's hit:

The Bowery, the Bowery!
They say such things, and they do strange things on
The Bowery! The Bowery!
I'll never go there any more!

Everything can be better with music, including funerals, a fact that has been unmercifully exploited by the pitchmen. To wit: "Like everything else today, carpet height has gone to extremes. That's why the Hoover . . . makes the world's favorite vacuum cleaner just a little bit better"—to background music on the harpsichord! But despite all this abuse, there continues to be pleasure in music and words, or music and dance, or music, words and dance together as in American musical comedy.

As the plight of the Negro inspired the novel and then the play, *Uncle Tom's Cabin,* which was the breakthrough for popular American drama, so the spirit and character of the Negro can be credited with the beginning of the American musical theatre. The origin involves a comedian, Dan Rice, affectionately called "Daddy" Rice. One day he observed a shuffling, some say deformed, Negro, and he conceived of a comic dance which became famous as Jim Crow. The song for the dance began:

Come listen all you gals and boys,
I'm just from Tuckyhoe;
I'm goin' to sing a leetle song,
My name's Jim Crow.
Wheel about, and turn about,
And do jis so—
Eb'ry time I wheel about,
I jump Jim Crow.

What Rice had done was sink a shaft into a bonanza of dances, music and humor as created by the American Negro—an ore the whites converted to theatrical gold. Rice in his blackface act was immediately the rage, and it is reported his success in Europe was even greater than at home. Joseph Jefferson tells us that in London Rice acted in two theatres nightly. Jefferson remembered him well because, though he was only four at the time, he had worked up a good imitation, and when Rice saw it, he made up and dressed the child in exact duplication of himself, carried him on stage in a bag, stopped in the middle of his act and announced:

O Ladies and Gentlemen, I'd have for you to know
That I've got a little darky here that jumps Jim Crow.

He dumped out the miniature of himself and they danced and sang together. Jefferson says they had the house cheering, and he says the coins tossed to the stage for him totaled twenty-four dollars to prove it.

The theatre has never had compunction about stealing success. Soon there were comedians jumping Jim Crow all over the place, and ten years after the Rice and Jefferson act, there was presented a whole evening of cork-faced entertainment—"the novel, grotesque, original and surprising melodious Ethiopian Band, entitled *The Virginia Minstrels,*" said the announcement in New York papers. And a new all-American form of entertainment had been devised that was to have a full life.

From that night on the phrase "Gentlemen, be seated" provoked a delightful anticipatory lift. What happened was that the curtain went up and here stood the performers of the evening in a semicircle—all men, a solid row of black-faced, big white-lipped comics, singers and dancers wearing striped trousers, swallow-tailed coats, oversize collars and white gloves. A dignified Interlocutor was center, and at one end of the line was Mr. Tambo (with banjo) and at the other, Mr. Bones (with bones). Now the Interlocutor would begin and, playing straight, would ask Tambo and Bones alternately questions, the answers to which convulsed the audience:

INTERLOCUTOR: Mr. Tambo, when was the first theatrical business spoken of in the Bible?

TAMBO: Oh, I know that.

INTERLOCUTOR: Then tell us, Mr. Tambo, when was the first theatrical business spoken of in the Bible?

TAMBO: I know that, that was when Eve appeared for Adam's benefit.

INTERLOCUTOR: Mr. Bones, how does the hairdresser end his days?

BONES: He goes the way of the wigged.

TAMBO: He curls up and dyes.

All the examples remaining of minstrel humor are equal duds to us today, but the minstrels did originate one gag that has suffered as many repetitions as any two-liner ever heard:

INTERLOCUTOR: Mr. Bones, who was that lady I saw you with last night?

BONES: That was no lady, that was my wife.

This was in the "first half." The second act, as we would call it, they called "the olio." This was really a small vaudeville show consisting perhaps of a humorous sketch, a quartet of singers, a monologue by the chief comedian and a miniature review. And now the hilarious Act III, called the "afterpiece." However much fun the show had been until now, you always knew the best was yet to be. The afterpiece would be a burlesque of everything that had gone before.

Burlesque, meaning caricature, was a standard commodity before striptease changed the point of view, and there were brilliant practitioners. With the broad gestures of blackface, all life was satirized, and we must take their word that it was witty. Since we are not familiar with what was being burlesqued we are lost. Enough to say the persistence of minstrels indicates it was all rollicking stuff, and for seventy years folks went home to repeat the humor to those who had missed it, invariably backing out of failure with "Well, it was funny the way *they* did it!"

There were the Christy Minstrels, the San Francisco Minstrels, the Dockstader Minstrels, the Haverly Minstrels (their ad said, "The only [perhaps the first] American minstrel company that ever visited Great Britain. World tour in contemplation"), the Primrose Minstrels, the Bryant Minstrels—names as proud as Ringling Brothers and Barnum & Bailey would become in the circus world.

STOP THIEF!

Warning to Managers AND THE PRESS

"Who steals my purse steals trash; 'tis something, nothing;
'Twas mine; 'tis his, and has been slaves to thousands;
But he that filches from me my good name,
Robs me of that which not enriches him,
And makes me poor indeed."

COLUMBIA THEATRE, Chicago, Dec. 15, 1888.

TO MANAGERS AND THE PRESS:

We are credibly informed upon what we consider reliable information that one Fred A. Thomas, of Paterson, N. J., is booking a BOGUS ''Original J. H. Haverly Mastodon Minstrel Company'' in New England. There is but one GENUINE HAVERLY MINSTREL COMPANY in existence, and that is under the personal management of W. S. CLEVELAND. Any manager permitting the FRAUDS to appear in his house will be pursued to the full extent of the law and be forever debarred from playing a Haverly attraction in his house. The real Haverly Company will shortly appear in New England, and the Haverly-Cleveland route may be seen in all the amusement journals. No manager can have a shadow of excuse in aiding and abetting a pirate after this fair warning.

Fraternally,

J. H. HAVERLY,
W. S. CLEVELAND.

For the information of managers the names of the gentlemen who represent us in advance are supplied: Chas. E. Cleveland, Business Manager; Charles H. Day, General Representative, Will H. Slade, Special Agent; Joseph Freebury, Programmer and Lithographer. All others representing themselves as such are confidence men and subject to arrest.

"THEY SHALL NEVER AGAIN BE DIVIDED." W. S. CLEVELAND
THE GREAT & ONLY
W. S. CLEVELAND'S
ALL UNITED MINSTRELS
POSITIVELY THE LARGEST & BEST IN THE WORLD
COMING BY SPECIAL TRAIN
MILLETT'S OPERA HOUSE
Matinee and Night, WEDNESDAY
FEB. 15
NO CHANGE OF DATES
NO POSTPONEMENT

One after the other, season after season, the minstrels came to the opera house and found it sold out for their performances. The impact of this exhilaration in Centerville, Hillsboro, Riverton, Newport and Old Town has never been appreciated. The audience folks didn't just watch and listen; they imitated, and those who couldn't tried. The barber with the high tenor now lived to hear people say he ought to be in a show. The clerk at Mayer's Men's Store, indisputably the best dancer in town, could dream of the life he should have had on the stage cakewalking in blackface. Housewives in the privacy of their work could flat and sharp and feel assured that with the advantage of training they could be in recital, with some decent appreciation. To keep their dreams up to date, they hurried to the next minstrel to hear the latest.

Now the shows are gone. For a time, amateurs would attempt a recall, but that went out of style, too. When, fifteen years ago, my daughter's first-grade teacher announced the class would have a minstrel show with everyone blacked up funny and the little girls' hair done up in pickaninny rags, and when my wife and another mother went to the teacher to suggest that caricature of a hard-pressed minority would not be good instruction for the children, the teacher burst into tears. She could not understand such interference and how anyone could fail to be amused by a minstrel show—and besides, she said, there wasn't a Negro child in the class.

It was not race consciousness that finished the minstrels—they were gone before the Negroes began to break out of the white conception. What did the minstrels in was plain American competition. When the first enthusiasm began to pale, the famous companies began raising the ante of size and novelty. That familiar opening semicircle could now have as many as 40 men. One troupe had a population of 110 members, including two bands of 14 musicians each, a sextet of saxophone players, two drum corps of 8 each, two drum majors, and a quartet of mounted buglers. Others offered The Siamese Twins! The Hindoo Ballet Dancers! The Trick Elephants! The Chinese Giants! The Headless Man! Since they did not dare raise the traditional prices, the promoters of this "only branch of the theatrical art . . . which had its origin in this country" managed to budget themselves out of existence.

The banjo is almost silent, bones-players are not in demand, the faces with the ear-to-ear grins are as out of fashion as Lincoln's shawl, yet a residue of the minstrels remains that has precious value to Americans, and this is due to Dan D. Emmett and Stephen C. Foster. Emmett was with Bryant's Minstrels when they needed a fast "walk-around" (cakewalk) to close the show. He was given four days to fill the bill. What he provided he called "Dixie's Land," a song that had Abraham Lincoln leaning out of his box in Chicago yelling, "Play it again! Play it again!" No one knew "Dixie" would be appropriated by the South to raise its war spirit nor that it would be so effective.

Stephen Foster was never on the payroll of a minstrel show, but in view of the songs he supplied, they should have made him wealthy. Instead, Christy paid him fifteen dollars for the privilege of putting his, Christy's, name as composer on "The Old Folks at Home." Close your eyes and you can see Christy taking bows at the Grand Rapids/Omaha/Riverdale/Oneida/All Over opera houses after the quartet had melted the audiences singing "his" song. Eventually Foster had enough success to write to Christy: "I have concluded . . . to pursue the Ethiopian business without fear and shame and . . . to establish my name as the best Ethiopian song writer." Writing this letter was about the most Foster ever did for himself; he was another talent who would have made more by paying 90 percent to an agent.

Born in a town called Lawrenceville near Pittsburgh on the Fourth of July, 1826, he had no formal training in music whatever. He taught himself to play the flute. When he was seven, a servant took him to a Negro church—this and the popular songs and dances of the blackface performers were the chief musical influences in his life. He got as far as college, Jefferson, but he found it impossible to forgo playing the flute, writing music and daydreaming, and after a few days he canceled out.

His first minstrel song to be a hit was "Oh! Susannah," and any American who can hum can name others: "Camptown Races"; "Massa's in de Cold, Cold Ground"; "My Old Kentucky Home"; "Old Black Joe"; "Jeanie with the light Brown Hair"; and more. The Jeanie inspiration was his wife, Jane Denny McDowell. They were opposites, to say the least. While he dreamed, she was practical. A devout Methodist, she disapproved of his drinking and firmly advised his giving up the song business for something worthwhile.

The time came when he could not find a market for his songs. The family accompanied him to New York in search of the public that had passed him by. His wife gave up and took their daughter back to Pennsylvania, while he lived on in a room on the Bowery. One morning a chambermaid found him; he had fainted and was bloody from the fall. They took him to Bellevue Hospital, where he died. All that was in his pockets was three pennies and a scrap of paper with the scribble "dear hearts and gentle friends," causing everyone to wonder whether that might have been another precious song if he had lived.

When you consider two of the handicaps of the minstrels, it is astonishing they could have been popular so long. They had neither story nor women. Two years after Foster died, in 1866, there was a show that had plenty of both, plot and females, and it was to be a success of such proportions that American musical comedy was then and there established.

The story of how *The Black Crook* came about is full of enough preposterous happenstance to make it appropriate to theatre lore. Two gentlemen, Henry C. Jarrett, a theatre manager, and Harry Palmer, his backer from Wall Street, had imported a French ballet troupe. They were going to present it at the Academy of Music in a Parisian success, *La Biche aux Bois*. The dancers arrived and the Academy burned down before they opened.

What do you do with a ballet troupe and no place to put it? They heard that William Wheatley, manager of the most fashionable theatre in town, Niblo's Garden, had signed a con-

It was a revelation to Waukesha, Wisconsin.

tract to do a melodrama called *The Black Crook.* How they got the idea of suggesting to Wheatley that he put their dancers in his play which, as written, had no place for them, has never been explained. But Wheatley, who was having reservations about the script, thought it a good idea. The only objection came from the author—"It would spoil his play." However, the author was hungry, so they were able to make him swallow the desecration by accepting $1,500 and a royalty contract. The author then lived handsomely ever after until he got in the way of a train and was killed.

Wheatley decided to do well by the hybrid and even went to England to buy the scenery, props, costumes and machinery for the production. He paid $3,000, while the figure that flabbergasted the public even more was the $500 paid to have the one hundred tons of stuff shipped to New York. The newspapers estimated the whole show could not have cost less than $35,000 to mount, possibly as much as $50,000, colossal figures at the time.

The Black Crook has been described as a combination of romantic French ballet and German romantic melodrama. It was the *production* that got them—that and the dancers, about which more in the next chapter. The *Tribune* said: "The scenery is magnificent; the ballet is beautiful; the drama is—rubbish. . . . The last scene in the play, however, will dazzle and impress to even a greater degree, by its lavish richness and barbaric splendor. All that gold, and silver, and gems, and light, and woman's beauty can contribute to fascinate the eye and charm the sense is gathered up in this gorgeous spectacle." Here was a lesson for the future: the story may be rubbish, but extravagantly produced rubbish can be money.

The sophisticated first-night audience—all the reports said it actually was smart—arrived for the 7:45 curtain and was enthralled until the end at 1:15. They got up to make room for audiences that came for 475 performances in the next sixteen months, paying $1,100,000. Duplicate companies were shipped on the road to stun folks in every theatre existing that could house the lavish production. It circuited the country for years.

This was a spur to practically every manager or would-be impresario in the land, except those forever committed to *Uncle Tom's Cabin*. No one could produce another *Black Crook*—they didn't have all those French dancers—but the public appetite was so whetted that for a time you could put music to almost anything and stand a chance to profit. Then an even greater impetus to musical theatre arrived in 1878, and this was to advance the genre to a point that even the present hasn't caught up with.

On November 25, a production of *Pinafore* by William S. Gilbert and Arthur Sullivan opened in Boston. It was wildfire. A month later, another company opened in San Francisco. Immediately after, a company appeared in Philadelphia. Back in Boston, by August of the next year, nearly three hundred performances had been given by a variety of companies, including one made up of children. There was no reciprocal copyright agreement with England, so the script and score could be grabbed by anyone here.

The free-royalty aspect, however, was not the determinant. Anyone who listens again to the wit in the text and the music will find it still impressive and will understand the impact on a world that had never heard anything remotely like it. And all done with decorum; the staid Philadelphia *Public Ledger* approved and invited the attendance of the "pure minded." For those too pure to accept, there were "church-choir companies" to bring the sugarplum to them. In the next years, there were juvenile companies, black companies—at one time in New York, there were five professional companies playing simultaneously, and as for the amateur stagings, there were undoubtedly too many.

Now each year one of these gay satiric gems appeared: *The Pirates of Penzance*, *Patience*, *Iolanthe*, *The Sorcerer*, *Princess Ida*—until *The Mikado* came to excite the public as if it were the first one. The country went *Mikado*-mad and one effect was to set the women to buying anything Japanesy to decorate their homes . . . an English fad that had inspired Gilbert to write the show in the first place.

When you look at the titles of the songs from the great hits that gave delight before 1905, most of them lie on the page in dead silence. Except for those from the G & S cornucopia. Even the present rock-bound generation is not apt to get through the list without hearing some of the melody from Sullivan, some of those perfect ebullient lyrics from Gilbert:

"My Name Is John Wellington Wells"
"A Policeman's Lot Is not a Happy One"
"Three Little Maids from School Are We"
"We Are Gentlemen of Japan"
"The Flowers That Bloom in the Spring"
"A Wand'ring Minstrel I"
"I'm Called Little Buttercup"
"My Object All Sublime"

A people long depressed by the assurance of eternal damnation was lifting its spirits with music. The hired man in Saginaw was whistling "Yankee Doodle Boy" from *Little Johnny Jones.* Piano racks in Topeka held copies of "Brown October Ale" from *Robin Hood.* The matrons and madams in Springfield were being Lillian Russells in their mirrors singing "Come Down, Ma Evenin' Star" from *Twirly Whirly.* Men shaving in the morning in Walla Walla were humming "Always Leave Them Laughing When You Say Goodbye" as sung in a show called *Mother Goose.* Sweethearts were singing "Toyland" from *Babes in Toyland.*

The music for that last show was by Victor Herbert, the outstanding composer of operettas. Unlike Stephen Foster's, his was the good life. He was an Irishman turned English who grew up German and became American. Born in Dublin, he was taken to his grandfather's in England when his father died during his infancy. At seven, he began piano lessons, and when grandfather became aware of his talent, he issued an edict that the child be taken to Germany for training. Training he got: "My lessons were no fifteen-minute affairs, and then away at something else. I was under the constant eye of my master, and I could not help making rapid progress."

His first two major works were a suite and a concerto, introduced by the Stuttgart Orchestra. He was then old enough to marry, and this brought a turn in his life when his wife was offered a contract by the Metropolitan Opera Company in New York. In America he played cello with many leading orchestras and became the conductor of the Pittsburgh Symphony. He resumed composing and the operetta world was enriched with *The Fortune Teller* ("Gypsy Love Song"); *The Wizard of the Nile* ("Star Light, Star Bright"); *Mlle. Modiste* ("Kiss Me Again"); *Naughty Marietta* ("I'm Falling in Love with Someone"; "Ah! Sweet Mystery of Life"; "Italian Street Song"); *Sweethearts* and more.

People handing their stubs to the ushers in the road opera houses hardly knew of the problems of the professionals who provided their joy. When the overtures lifted the customers' hearts in Cedar Rapids, Beacon Falls, Iron River, Valley Stream, Sweetwater and Dry Creek, they felt anyone who could create such pleasure might be tickled to death to work for nothing. The composers, though, preferred life, and the man who made it worth their while to set America to music was Victor Herbert. Dining one day at Shanley's Restaurant, Herbert heard the orchestra playing one of his songs. It struck him that there was something not right in this royalty-free use of the work of living composers and he sued Shanley's. It took four years for the case to reach the Supreme Court and the decision was in favor of Herbert.

He then called a meeting of composers, lyricists and publishers and proposed they organize to promote and protect. This was the birth of ASCAP—the American Society of Composers, Authors, and Publishers—a powerful defender of and collector for its members. Any Stephen Foster today will be properly reimbursed.

But even with the opera house putting melody in the heart of the town, it took some time to relieve the country of its lugubrious inclinations. There was still a market for "A Violet from Mother's Grave" (1881), "A Flower from My Angel Mother's Grave" (1883), "A Handful of Earth from My Dear Mother's Grave" (1883), "The Pardon Came Too Late" (by Paul Dresser, 1891), and particularly that classic of rue, "After the Ball" (1892), as examples. But the show tunes stayed persistently cheerful, and they also perked up the public mood with the dances they inspired. In a country that generally had gone only as far as hoedowns and square dancing, it was now exciting to see the full potential. There was instruction from the sensational, short-skirted Lottie Collins, although one rustic was dissatisfied. He was heard to complain, "She kicked so fast you couldn't see a thing."

There were operettas, musical comedies and extravaganzas of burlesque, the most famous burlesque being *Evangeline*. This was a takeoff on Longfellow's popular poem, and it came about because Edward E. Rice, a Bostonian by birth, and a friend of his, J. Cheever Goodwin, a reporter on the Boston *Traveller*, went to see Lydia Thompson and her "high-kicking blondes." As people do, Rice and Goodwin said they could write something better than what they were seeing, and the difference was that they did. *Evangeline*, in one company or another, also ran thirty years—some said it was even more popular than *The Black Crook*. All of which annoyed a critic writing in the New York *Dramatic Mirror* in 1880:

> The vitality of the extravaganza is something wonderful, considering the length of time [six years] it has been before the public. Some of the old pointless puns and gags have been eradicated, only to be replaced by new puns and gags just as witless and just as inane as their predecessors. . . . When it is all over, the question arises, what is there in *Evangeline* that should ever have gained for it the amount of public favor it has enjoyed?

It is a question impossible to answer some ninety years later except for one blessed feature of that show. It is one thing to discover a helpful drug, to invent a man-saving tool, to compose a perfect poetic statement or to stir moondust, but the person or persons who can think up a gag that will have audiences crying with laughter for a hundred years should be canonized unsubject to recall.

We don't even know who created this bit of joy in *Evangeline*. Longfellow had given Evangeline a snow-white cow, and when they were considering the equivalent for the show, someone got the idea of a heifer with a man in the front legs and another in the rear. Furthermore, it would do a dance. We are told the audience split a gut then, and I will testify that I have never laughed harder in my life than I did the first time I saw a beast of this same breed sit down on a chair and cross its legs. That was unwritten theatrical literature of the highest order.

Another musical phenomenon of late nineteenth- and early twentieth-century theatre was the popularity of the Irish tenor. Anyone who could do the shamrock tad with a silver throat was in. Plays were written for him, elaborate productions mounted, and, shure as Irish eyes were smilin', even that segment of the audience full of the anti-Catholic prejudice then rampant would put down its cash to be charmed by Irish cuteness and to vibrate to a pitch so high they might wonder if the man had had the benefit of castration.

The most successful of the Erin-go-braghing tenors was Chauncey Olcott. When Charles Frohman was showing his prowess as a manager of stars, Olcott called on him and said he would like to have Frohman manage him. Frohman turned him down, saying he preferred to make his stars and since Olcott was earning $100,000 a year already, he considered him well made.

As for Olcott's vehicles, they were turned out by mechanics and had only as much reality and common sense as any pre-*Showboat* musical—which is to say, none worth believing. One of the most popular of Olcott's shows was about Edmund Burke (1729–97). The encyclopedia gives the impression that Burke was a sober and forceful politician who, though born in Dublin or because he was born in Dublin, devoted his life trying to help England govern itself with some sanity. To that end, he criticized her treatment of the American colonies, drafted the India bill, urged various radical reforms and then aged gracefully in the liberal manner by becoming yearly more conservative.

This is not to see that great one as the writers for Chauncey Olcott saw him. The following condensed paragraph of a review of Olcott's musical, *Edmund Burke,* tells you all you need to know about its literary quality and why it got by:

> In the old days of duelling and fine sword play, of satin knickers and silk polonaise, when men spent their days in rose gardens, their nights in ballad-making, when women sighed over impassioned verse and were carried off on bold chargers by ardent suitors . . . in those carefree stage-life days, there came to England . . . a young prophet. Perhaps the real Edmund Burke spent more of his time in essay-writing and speech-making, less in versifying . . . than did the stage Burke of Chauncey Olcott. . . . [But] should anyone prefer the author of "The Essay on the Sublime" to this charming figure . . . let him spend the evenings in libraries and not venture into the Majestic.

It takes columns for the reviewer to report the plot. It includes Burke's friend, Oliver Goldsmith, who can't get his play produced. It's called *She Stoops to Conquer.* And aside from Burke getting his girl, this is how it all ends: "He proceeds to defend the Prince [of Wales] against a gang of ruffians who would abduct him. In return the Prince promises the production of Goldsmith's comedy and for Burke a seat in the House of Commons."

The critic was happy to say *Edmund Burke* was "the best medium Mr. Olcott has found, and the generous applause of the audience throughout promises it a long run."

There are, of course, no films or recordings of most of the musical artists who delighted the public in 1905 and before. What would we make of them if we could hear "dear" Sam Cowell singing "Reuben Wright and Phoebe Brown"; Maggie Cline shouting "Throw Him Down, McCloskey"; the forgotten famous Florences and their song, "The Colonel from Constantinople"; Lottie Gilson singing "La-Didily-Idily, Unti-Unti-Ay!" or the fabulous Lillian Russell singing "The Silver Line"?

So far as research can tell, there has been no figure in the history of the American musical theatre, certainly no woman star, to compare with Lillian Russell. When she came to town, folks knew they would never see more beauty, style and charm in one warm package. Perhaps the best statement of this great lady's talent and effect is by Gilbert Chase in *America's Music*:

> To this day Lillian Russell remains one of the most deeply beloved and widely admired prima donnas of the American popular musical stage. Such latter-day celebrities as Marilyn Miller, Gertrude Lawrence, Ethel Merman and Mary Martin have never received quite the same unbridled adulation; nor has any of them become the single, supreme, unchallenged symbol of all that was most desirable and most glamorous in her period.
>
> "From early girlhood to the hour of her death," wrote Francis Wilson in 1922, "she moved in a court of beauty of which she was the undisputed queen." This beauty, which won her three husbands, the lifelong friendship of Diamond Jim Brady, and millions of advocates all over America, was combined with a temperament so generous that Lew Fields, after her death, called her "the dearest thing that ever was in show business."

Such panegyrics are so general they begin to make her seem mythical, but Chase makes her human as he states the case for her place in American musical history:

> Though she had little or no talent as an actress, she did not flaunt her beauty as a device to deflect attention from her dramatic shortcomings. She seemed almost unconscious of her physical endowments, apparently taking them for granted as gifts God intended her to preserve and cherish, but regarding them without vanity. Beyond argument, she was the best-dressed woman on the stage. She took her responsibility for the handsome and unblemished display of her expensive dresses so seriously that she bought substitute gowns of cheap fabric but identical in color to wear at rehearsals, in order to preserve her wardrobe in complete freshness for the opening-night performance.
>
> The daughter of an editor and a militant woman-suffragist, Lillian Russell was born in Cleveland in 1861. In spite of all feminist leanings, her mother recognized Lillian's exceptional beauty, and reared her with a full appreciation for her loveliness and a sense of her duty to protect it. With Lillian's naturally sweet face went an

LILLIAN RUSSELL. Folks in Huntington, West Virginia, marveled that a human woman could be so perfect.

equally sweet voice, which her mother placed under the care of Leopold Damrosch, one of the leading musicians of New York, when the time came to begin serious vocal training.

Her sumptuous beauty alone might never have carried Lillian Russell to the summit of success if she had been a less capable singer. . . . In *Princess Nicotine*, in 1893, she ventured to sing eight high C's at each performance, seven times a week. After one performance Nellie Melba went backstage to chide her, saying, "No prima donna sings fifty-six high C's in a week."

With her beauty and charm and high C's, who could care if she could not act? Or would we be less susceptible today? We may not have the hunger the audiences had then, that let them enjoy with such enthusiasm. We may be overfed.

On the other hand, something as real, as nonsynthetic, as Lillian might excite a dormant taste. Yet—it is difficult to imagine men now unharnessing the horses and pulling the carriage of any high-C Aphrodite. Now they would have to push her automobile and that doesn't seem the same. Lillian lived at the right time.

•

Advertisement
New York Dramatic Mirror, *April 1, 1905*

GRAND OPERA HOUSE PHILADELPHIA
LEW DOCKSTADER'S MINSTRELS
Week of March 10th in the heart
of Lent and 3 days of rain
$9013.50
Not so bad, eh?

10

Dirt: Imitation and Real

Notice was served on him by Anthony Comstock, head of the Society for the Suppression of Vice, that prosecution would follow if the performance was given. Daly and Miss Shaw decided to disregard the warning. Tickets for the opening night—October 30, 1905—were sold by speculators for $25.

Lloyd Morris, Curtain Time

In a surprisingly brief time, the opera house-goers from San Francisco to New York, in cities, towns and even in villages where the customers came in from the mud, became sophisticated and selective, causing jeopardy at the box office. Managers found their fickleness annoying because the managers had been so diligent in tendering product to fit the taste. In those early days when people felt more proper at plays that sermonized (preferably against sexual irregularities, offenses against property and murder, in about that order) the managers and their writers had willingly offered them plays that moralized, beginning with the very title:

The Way of the Transgressor
Sin of Temptation
Thou Shalt Not Kill

But the time came when such preachments palled, and that is always a dangerous and exciting time in the theatre. For, to hold attention, the theatre usually resorts to surprise, shock, if need be. When there is a threat of apathy, indifference, theatre people ask what can excite, make people nervous, for that's what they want—as repeatedly proven since the first Greek used slaughter to incite the spectators to come at dawn to get the best of the stone seats.

But you have to be sensitive, to gauge—there is risk. Send a shock wave that is beyond the public's capacity to absorb and you are a libertine, a disgusting pervert bent on corrupting society ("the young"); you may run one night, be threatened with arrest and have your kids catch spit. If you hit it right, there will be an uproar sending people running for tickets, and you can be acclaimed as a courageous innovator and champion of truth.

Until about now, the eighth decade of the twentieth century, the human female body was the best and handiest source of theatre excitement and moral disturbance. Originally women were covered from instep to chin to wrist, and it is a tremendous commercial misfortune that they have been bared so precipitately and entirely. If the process could have been slowed, there would still be money in the tease—one can only guess at the millions to be made if the female shoulder was yet to be seen in public. The estimate can be based on the gross of all those profitable shows that featured some form of revelation—like the *Follies* and particularly the *Artists and Models* series ("Sam, will you listen, don't artists always have undressed models? All we got to do is tell the girls not to move, not to even raise a tit, just stand there and pose, so who can complain?")—down to *Hair*, which featured a murky fifteen-second peek at the female everything, and included for good measure some bare boys hanging limp.

The first person in America to establish in a large way this law of diminishing cover equals expanded returns was Adah Isaacs Menken. Hers was a short life, thirty-three years, but enough transpired to put her in theatre history. Her primary claim to such fame was in a play called *Mazeppa, or The Wild Horse,* which she rode with a difference.

The play had been around with mild success. One scene called for the heroine to ride the beast up a mountainside—that is, a ramp ascending in sections masked by canvas rocks across the back of the stage, or, when possible, around the auditorium itself. In all previous performances, a dummy had been strapped to the back of the nag, but if you went to a Menken performance, you saw the *real* Menken! There is an account of her first rehearsal of this stunt, when she was thrown off. She was hurt but had the fortitude to mount again and risk it for how many performances only God kept count.

This could have earned her respectful applause in an era when men knew horseflesh and riding, but Menken provoked hysterical enthusiasm by riding Mazeppa naked! In a profound confirmation of the delusive eyesight of the wishful, although Adah wore white tights all over herself, the audiences were convinced *they saw her naked!* The vast majority of her male patrons had never seen anything so undressed before. They had not been to museums, had not seen art reproductions, had not studied anatomy, had not seen female flesh beyond hands, feet and face in pictures either still or moving; it was a time when if a man wanted to perceive what his wife or sister or anything female was made of under her wraps, he would have had to stun her to get a look. So, by gad, if they said The Menken was bare, she was naked! And according to all accounts, Menken was worth the look. She has been described as "exquisite," with a "beautiful figure and elegant legs," which is about as nice a word for legs as was ever spoken in panted breath.

She was born in New Orleans and her name was Adelaide McCord. It is said that she had a good enough classical education to be able to translate Homer when she was twelve. That she had a fine intelligence is to be believed because of the cultured friends she acquired. It is further said she was the daughter of a Presbyterian minister, which adds interest to her second marriage, to a musician named Alexander Isaacs Menken. For him she adopted

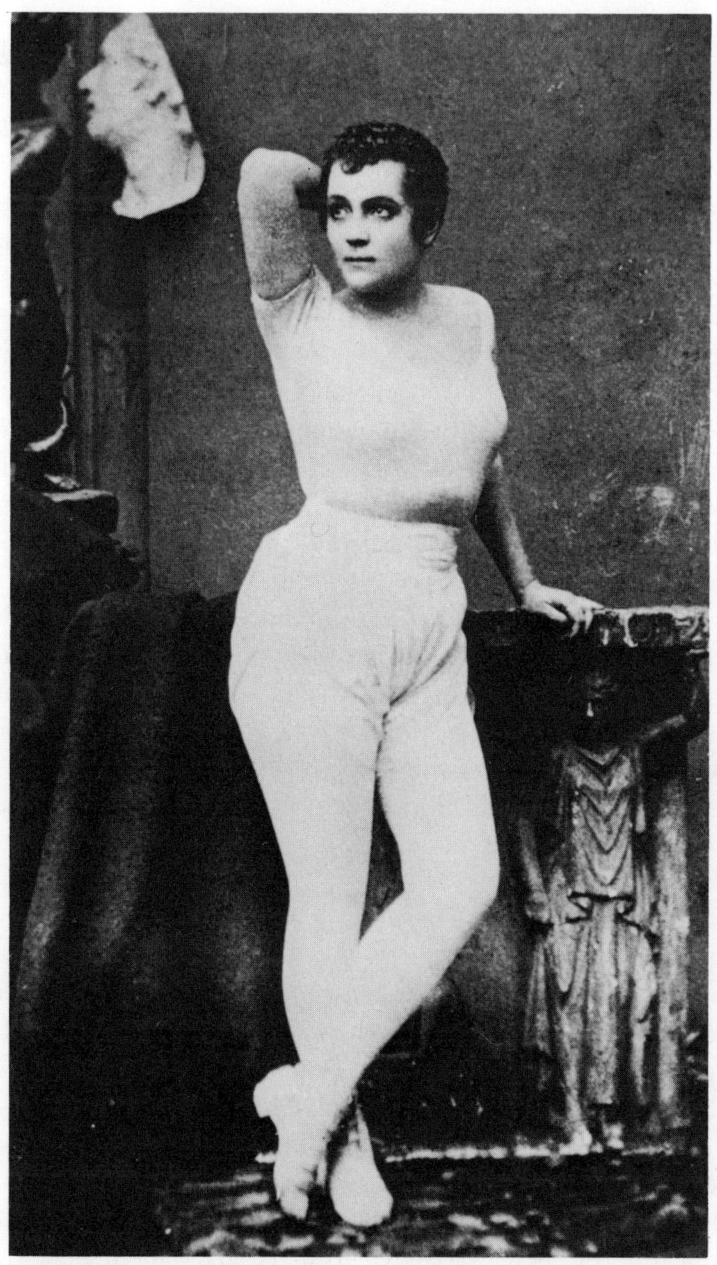

ADAH MENKEN. Man for man, they cheered as loud for her in Cripple Creek, Colorado, as in Paris, France.

the Jewish faith, which she kept until her death in exchange for his name. Her third marriage increased her fame, for that was to John C. Heenan, the prizefighter; then after Heenan, she had two lesser husbands. One historian-investigator claims her father was Auguste Theodore, a "free man in color," and her mother a Creole, explaining, he says, why Adah never went back to New Orleans after she became famous, because of the Louisiana law barring miscegenation.

Abandoned, so she said, by husband one, it was necessary for her to make a living, so she went on the stage as a dancer, first appearing at the French Opera House in her native city. She was a hit, she changed to acting, and appeared in many melodramas and also in support of Edwin Booth, James Murdoch and James Hackett. Her pictures show a creature of cuddlesome charm, with short Byronesque curly hair instead of the usual braids and swirls, and if the great men of the theatre found her Presbyterian-Jewish-Creole-Negroid features and intelligence enticing, they were not alone. The Menken, as she was called (or "Cleopatra in Crinoline," or "La Belle Menken," or "The Royal Bengal Tiger," or best, "The Naked Lady," after she had sent audiences everywhere into pandemonium, especially in Virginia City where they organized a Menken Shaft and Tunnel Company and sent her away laden with bullion and certificates of stock)—The Menken became the good or the good-and-intimate friend of Mark Twain, Charles Dickens, Dumas the elder, Swinburne, Rossetti, Sir Richard Burton, with photographs to prove it. And when she ended her one-hundred-night run in *Mazeppa* in Paris and took nine curtain calls at the final performance, she had in her audience Napoleon III, the King of Greece, the Duke of Edinburgh and the Prince Imperial.

After that came the beginning of fade-out, and, in Paris, alone, she died at thirty-three. Dumas only remarked, "Poor girl, why wasn't she her own friend?" and Swinburne, though ill for days on hearing the news, recovered to make jokes about her. Men! Heartless beasts!—just as the plays and novels of the time always said.

If Adah could provoke such interest in kings and men sophisticated enough to write in French, one can almost hear the public excitement when she came to Grand Forks, Saginaw, Macon and stops between. She may have been a better bare bareback rider than actress—what matters in theatrical history is that she taught the theatre managers a lesson which they learned with a vengeance. Those psalm-singing, "health-minded," solid folks out there in the audience wanted to see plain and think dirty, and America being the place where the buyer gets, they received as much as the market would bear, especially after the opening of *The Black Crook.* And once *The Black Crook* had come to town, a lot of innocence had left.

It's true *The Black Crook* had spectacular scenery, which was a plus even if most spectators hardly noticed. They were looking at those French dancers. One hundred of them in *tights!* Before this the men could have assumed a woman's leg must be something like their own. They didn't know how smooth it looked or how gracefully the lovely limb led up to man's desire. They could get the perspective when, at the finale, four of the creatures came right down to the footlights in tights "without a vestige of anything remotely resembling a skirt!" So, undress being relative, they might as well have been in their skins! Small wonder that the *World* cried ecstatically: "New York has never enjoyed the presence of so beautiful, varied, efficient, facile, graceful and thoroughly captivating a corps de ballet as the one herein introduced."

Although Americans considered themselves subject to religion, they paid their ministers next to nothing and, when possible, nothing. Consequently, the preachers they got often had a weakness of intellect and experience that no palms-together piety could make up for. In other words, they were not very smart. Consequently, they became wonderful publicists for sensational theatre and continued to be up to the day when everyone stopped listening.

What joy would fill a producer's heart when a parson would announce he had attended some notorious piece in order to report and protect his flock. In the case of *The Black Crook,* here is what one spiritual voyeur told his people. He told them about

> the immodest dress of the girls; the short skirts, undergarments of thin material allowing the form of the figure to be discernible; the flesh-colored tights, imitating nature so well that the illusion is complete; with the exceedingly short drawers, most tight-fitting, extending very little below the hips; arms and neck apparently bare, and bodice so cut as to show off every inch and outline of the body above the waist. The attitudes were exceedingly indelicate—*ladies* dancing so as to make their undergarments spring up, exposing the figure beneath from the waist to the toe, except for such coverings as we have described.

The show's press agent could not have done better. There had to be some in the congregation glancing at their watches to see how long before the Monday performance to see those undergarments spring up, something men had been waiting for on windy corners since puberty.

A Miss Olive Logan also helped the cause of exposure. She was an actress with an honest gripe; as she said, some actress who didn't know her business could get four times as much as the ones who did know, simply by baring herself. She published her reactions to *The Black Crook* as *she* saw it:

> When *The Black Crook* first presented its nude woman to the gaze of the crowded auditory, she was met with a gasp of astonishment at the effrontery, which dared so much. Men actually grew pale at the boldness of the thing; a deathlike silence fell over the house, broken only by the clapping of a band of claquers around the outer aisles; but it passed; and, in view of the fact that these women were French ballet dancers after all, they were tolerated.

She went on to use such golden terms as "disgraceful spectacle . . . jigging . . . wriggling . . . habiting themselves in a way which is attractive to an indelicate taste, [while] their inefficiency in other regards is overlooked."

As a result, with all this agitated help, fourteen of the sixteen theatres in New York were soon giving shows similar to *The Black Crook,* and soon this breathtaking erotica was the opera at the local house. Men—and women—in Little Rock, Austin,

Wausau, Mobile, might be trying not to be hicks, but the day those dancers arrived at the station, they were aware and anxious for a look, and, after that night, they could boast of their loss of ignorance and pose as sophisticates for the rest of their lives.

In time, there inevitably came an actress who did even better than Adah Menken had done. With the help of her playwright she showed how you could shock and excite without taking off even your beads. Olga Nethersole was an actress of beauty and talent who had a handicap: the public wasn't interested. Until *Sappho*. At the climax of this stylish shocker, the leading man picked up Miss Nethersole and carried her up the stairs, center, to his offstage bedroom. The rest was left to the audience's imagination, which was alert. The police of that time were wonderfully obliging even without managerial prompting; they came, saw him tote her up the stairs and arrested Miss Nethersole. The case went to trial and the newspapers carried all the testimony to the jury of its readers. Miss Nethersole was acquitted and business was tremendous when *Sappho* reopened. Olga had the public interest thereafter at every stand she played.

Toward the end of this era, two of the best playwrights since Shakespeare were in the business, however unintentionally, of enraging those people who took offense on behalf of the public. George Bernard Shaw might never have enjoyed so much fame if he had not written *Mrs. Warren's Profession*. Here he had this madam of a whorehouse, Mrs. Warren, looking perfectly well and intelligent, talking about how she had done what men want destitute girls to do, but instead of doing it for support in a poor but virtuous marriage with an early death from exhaustion, she had done it for money, independence and comfort. What particularly galled the objectors was that this woman's daughter was taught to *respect* her! And there was no scene with remorseful music, not the slightest show of regret. *Mrs. Warren's Profession* played one night, was closed by the police, cleared, reopened, all giving Shaw such a diabolical reputation that when *Man and Superman* was published, the New York Public Library put it on the reserved shelf "for special readers."

The other playwright who disturbed people more than Shaw's cerebrations ever did was the "unhealthful and injurious" Henrik Ibsen. They had a word for his stuff—"Ibscene." When *A Doll's House* was first presented, an audience sat perfectly still after the final curtain. They were waiting for the last act when Nora would return repentant to her husband. The stage manager had to appear and tell them that was all, they could go home. It was a dumfounding jolt that set wives practicing door slams, and made husbands irritable and nervous.

It can't be said that any of these plays were as immediately popular at the opera house as a female leg, but they were trouped and they gave tremendous satisfaction to the local literates who could scoff at the philistines "afraid or too dumb" to attend. Slowly, for an increasing audience, it began to be a theatre that was exciting beyond the thrills of melodrama. Great stars—Arnold Daly, Mrs. Fiske, Nazimova, Mansfield—were arriving with the radical playwrights, Shaw, Ibsen, Pinero and more, and it was daring to go to the opera house, the theatre. Who knew but what his world might be tipped, his life might be changed, because someone had written a play making the audiences *think!* Uncomfortably—about themselves!

Shakespeare sometimes made people ponder, but, even when audiences knew Shakespeare almost as well as the actors, he didn't have *this* effect!

•

New York—Season 1905–6

Mrs. Warren's Profession *by George Bernard Shaw*
Arms and the Man *by George Bernard Shaw*
John Bull's Other Island *by George Bernard Shaw*
Caesar and Cleopatra *by George Bernard Shaw*
Cashel Byron's Profession *by George Bernard Shaw, starring Jim Corbett*

☛ 11

Climax with a Wrong Ending

Edison was working in 1886 in his laboratory at Newark, busily completing perfections of the phonograph while waiting the completion of his new establishment at West Orange.

The phonograph had been worked out rather to his liking in the late months of the year. While he had been tinkering along on it, the notion came to Edison that he would like to give it eyes as well as ears. He dallied with the idea of a machine which recorded and transmitted not only the sound but the sight. He felt that it was a somewhat whimsical notion.

If Edison appraised this notion at all he thought it trivial. His work was the work of big things, machines and methods that deal with power, dynamos, batteries, ore crushers, cement mills and the like. His play was of the little things like the phonograph. This picture machine–phonograph was something to be done when another playtime came.

Terry Ramsaye, A Million and One Nights

How could change in America come any faster than it already had? Standing in 1905, looking 129 years back to when those men were sweating out the Declaration in the midst of those plaguing mosquitoes in Philadelphia, you thought of how, except for land surveyors like George Washington and a few others, none of those founding fathers had much conception of what was even 250 miles west—where Uniontown was now, where *The Ninety and Nine* was playing at the West End Theatre.

So how could the changes be any more astonishing? In as little as a couple of lifetimes, three at the most, people had not only occupied for all essential purposes the present 3,015,925 square miles of the United States; they had developed distribution systems for food and manufactures, had established schools for all, had even devised means of entertainment so that millions could sit down to a different show right where they lived every night—except, of course, in places where Sunday was not for pleasure.

What was needed except more of the same? You could work, travel, eat, sleep, learn, clothe yourself, keep warm—all but the impoverished, who, then as now, were often overlooked in appraisals of progress. The pioneering struggle was done; like that historian said: the frontier was gone, and all people had to do now was sit tight and let the progress continue. How *could* things change more or faster than they had?

To the extent things *might* change, everyone felt they had a good concept of what and how much, including the *Literary Digest*, a magazine that reflected the collective editorial judgment of the nation. The *Digest* said: "The ordinary 'horseless carriage' is at present a luxury for the wealthy; and although its price will probably fall in the future, it will never, of course, come into as common use as the bicycle."

There were other new inventions, including the Gramophone. Perhaps in time, these wind-up music-players would be among the common adornments of American life. In time. There was also the new thing called moving pictures, but even the inventor, Thomas Edison, had not summoned the multitudes to come see this, as he had when he announced the electric light. Nor had the people shown curiosity. It was considered a plaything of doubtful practicality.

The actors in 1905 were pretty well satisfied with things just as they were. True there was more grumbling about Klaw and Erlanger's monopolistic grip on the business. If you irritated that crude monster, Abe Erlanger, if you didn't do business his way, accept the terms, you could attend your own professional funeral. That's how it was and nothing could be done. Teddy Roosevelt could threaten to break up the trusts, but was he apt to get serious about *show business?* That would seem as foolish as calling out the troops to help a pretty girl cross the street!

On the other hand, the Syndicate system *was* efficient. With them, you could count on a full season's work. In fact, for about the first time since the business began, actors could see a lifetime ahead in the theatre. The opera houses would get better (it was becoming fashionable to call them theatres), there would be more of them, smarter people would devise better shows, and the audience would include everybody. (There was now even a ten-twent'-thirt' [10–20–30 cents] circuit of theatres for the cheaper crowd.) You could see the future and it was at least forty weeks a year behind the new electric footlights, subject to agreement on terms and billing.

There had never been so many thousands of actors working. It is possible, although not probable, that someone interested, watching, might be able to tell which ones would succeed most and might become stars: this one because of a musical voice that projected clearly; that one because of the intelligence to speak for Shakespeare; she because of her large eyes that could be seen, understood, from any seat in the house; he because of his skill with an audience—not only could he make them seem to move up closer, he could make them stop coughing and be quiet! It would not, of course, ever occur to the observer that some of these actors would soon be playing simultaneously in theatres all over the earth and would be more famous than the rulers of the various nations where they appeared.

In 1905, some of the unsuspecting actors could paste notices like these in their books:

William S. Hart

In *Home Folks:* "W. S. Hart was strong and convincing in the small opportunityless part of the villain and did the most possible with his part."

He had had better notices than this, six years before:

"W. S. Hart who is playing Ingomar, Orlando, Pygmalion, Sir John Oxon, and other leads with Julia Arthur, made a decided success in those roles . . . some of the critics stamping his work as 'perfect.' Henry Austin Clapp referred to Mr. Hart's performances as 'spirited, manly and discriminatingly intelligent.' "

He received that notice in Boston. Soon he would never troupe again and the most strenuous acting he would do would be to draw his gun and set his iron jaw in Westerns that would make even the males in China wish they could enter and cow a saloon full of toughs the way Bill Hart did always.

W. C. Fields

"The brightest spot in the cast is Mr. William C. Fields, a clever juggler and eccentric comedian."

—*Life,* New York

"Fields made good. He should be given more to do, more lines to speak and more business. He has added a new twist to the juggling act he did in vaudeville and it went like wildfire last night."

—*Evening Times,* Rochester, N.Y.

Later to star in a series of cheap films that would make him the world's most amusing-looking idol since Buddha.

Mary Pickford

In *The Gypsy Girl:* "Gladys Smith, as Freckles, displayed much skill in handling her pathetic role."

Little Gladys—to become Our Mary, adored by every person of every sex and age without exception.

Before Hollywood . . . WILLIAM S. HART . . .

. . . Mary Pickford . . .

. . . and DOUGLAS FAIRBANKS . . . in places like Alton, Illinois; Muskegon, Michigan; Mankato, Minnesota.

DOUGLAS FAIRBANKS

In *Fantana:* "Hubert Wilke, Frank Rushmore, Douglas Fairbanks and Philip Leight added unusually fine voices, acted with distinction, and added more than the usual share of manly good looks."

Fairbanks could not have known that the days of such lump praise were destined to be few, that he would be more famous than any actor could become by spending the next century in the theatre.

BUSTER KEATON

Appearing with his family in vaudeville. Joe, his father, believed in advertising in the theatrical papers:

> Joe, Myra and Buster Keaton.
> Peace on Earth and Good Will to Friends. A Happy NEW YEAR to all showmen—if you haven't seen Little Buster, the original, drop in at Tony Pastor's this week.

Out on Long Island, New York, Maurice Barrymore, a charming, brilliant, erratic actor, who had been out of his mind for over two years, died in 1905. It took some time for his children to get together at the funeral. Ethel was appearing in *Sunday* in Philadelphia. Lionel was in *The Other Girl* in Texas. John was with the Willie Collier company in Buffalo. After the service, they returned to their jobs in the theatre, where, so far as they could see, they would remain the rest of their lives.

Charles Chaplin, when he broke from the theatre and tried the new moving pictures, was discouraged. He is reported to have said to another comic, Chester Conklin: "I'm going to get out of this business. It's too much for me. I'll never catch on. It's too fast. I can't tell what I'm doing, or what anybody wants me to do. At any rate, I figure the cinema is little more than a fad. It's canned drama. What audiences really want to see is flesh and blood on the stage. I'm not sure any real actors should get caught posing for the flickers."

And when there began to be a studio on Fourteenth Street and another one a ferry ride away over in Fort Lee, New Jersey, "good" actors were loath to "pose." Those who did tried to keep it quiet. It was as if William Dean Howells were to write ads for Lydia Pinkham—whatever it paid, could one afford to risk one's reputation? There are more important things than the money, you know. People said.

Strange as it seems, there was a considerable lag in exploiting the new medium because no one knew exactly what to do with the films, how to present them. The theatre procedure was copied, presentations were made at specified times like plays, but this had been a bust. The direct comparison made the silents seem foolish, especially after you had seen them once. Who was going to pay the same kind of money to read on a screen what you could hear actors say out loud? Most historians say the break came when John P. Harris in McKeesport, Pennsylvania, in 1905 opened what he called a *nickelodeon.* At a nickel, who couldn't afford to go in and watch ocean waves threaten to wash right into your lap, or be a sort of voyeur as people with tremendous heads smooched, or witness a train robbery with astonishingly quick bandits tying up the station master? At a nickel, how could you lose? It was worth it.

The American people knew the value of *saving* the penny, but they had yet to learn (with Woolworth as one of the professors) the full value of *collecting* small change; how nickels, pennies, dimes can stack to millions. To the surprise of even canny ex-furriers, glove salesmen and amusement park operators who were now film producers, the nickelodeon was one of the most profitable small-scale enterprises ever devised. A cheap storefront would do. The equipment was simple: a sheet, a projector, some chairs. Film rents were not much. There were no union problems. Father could crank the machine, mother could sell the tickets, daughter could take the tickets, sister could play the piano (if you were running a first-class house). You started at one, maybe earlier, and ran the film over and over until you were sure you had collected the last nickel of the day. It paid O.K.

The idea was contagious. It seemed as though every man in

the country with a little will to risk wanted to try it. Within two years, there were three thousand nickelodeons being supplied by a hundred film exchanges in thirty-five key American cities, and in three more years there were ten thousand movie houses. Almost anything with a roof could be adequate—the first movie I ever saw was in a tent. The people who went to the Metropolitan Opera wasted few nickels on this "fad," but there were millions who did not go to the Metropolitan Opera and who paid eagerly to see the funny cops do the funny jump up in the air before they started to chase the other funny jumpers and who liked to see the pretty girls with the pretty legs.

Many things contributed to the success. At the time of the breakthrough, immigrants were coming or were being brought to America at ten dollars a head for the transportation. Here was entertainment they could enjoy without knowing a word of English. Here was a way to see what Americans did, how they did it. It was a good way for Americans to find out, too. It was a big country—the boy in Kentucky had never been to a city, the boy in Kansas had never seen an ocean, most girls everywhere had never seen people in evening clothes, most people in New York City or New Orleans or Springfield, Massachusetts, Illinois, or Ohio, had never seen a mountain, and how many anywhere had ever been hit in the face with a custard pie?

So this is how you ate on a train, how you drove an automobile, how people looked in a bathtub, what an Arab looked like, moving, a Chinaman, a Scot. This is how women flirt, how men seduce as seen close up, how fashionable girls do their hair, how the water goes over Niagara Falls. This wasn't pasteboard stuff, this isn't imitation ice on a stage, those are real cakes floating toward the brink 'way Down East. Marvelous! Even as you laughed till the tears came, you learned—when Charlie got hit with a coconut, you saw a real palm tree for the first time in your life. What a remarkable world to be seen!

The theatre actors chose not to worry. As they said, as they told each other—it would pass. They had learned their business, they were signed up for the season, ten dollars more a week than last year, so how could dumb *pictures* take the place of speaking people that you could clap for, who would come out to bow at the end? What, for instance, would Shakespeare be without *words?* Did anyone think all those opera houses, museums, academies of music, *theatres* that had been built all over the country were going to just close up? Nonsense, my boy, nonsense! Somebody has got to play *Hamlet!*

Then the word began to come about the money! More and more important people were succumbing until it was reported that Dustin Farnum, star of *The Virginian,* had been persuaded to do a film to launch a company called the Jesse L. Lasky Feature Play Company. The word was that Farnum had never been paid so well in his life. And he didn't have to travel. They wanted him to take stock in the company, but he was too smart for that.

The real jolt was the news about Bill Hart! W. S. Hart who played in *The Squaw Man, The Christian* and so on—$2,225,000 *from nine films in only two years!* You could play one-nighters until the end of your life and then send your corpse on tour and you still wouldn't get that kind of dough. And Chaplin! Even if you believed only half what they said, he was still getting more than the President of the United States!

The pictures were silent, but the money screamed. Actors were forsaking their pride to work in the golden sun of California. Writers were going, too, and directors. Also producers. It didn't seem as if the writers would be missed; if they wanted to jeopardize their careers by turning themselves into hacks, that was their misfortune. The theatre would survive; there would be others, they were beginning to teach playwriting at Harvard.

The theatre was like the consumptive who never looked better, who appeared to be getting well, just before submitting to ravage. For several more years, theatres were built in New York, play production *increased.* There might be six openings in a single evening. And the plays began to be literature. There was excitement and pride when the latest O'Neill came in or the Sherwood or the Howard, Behrman, Barry, Anderson or Rice. What gentle loveliness in *The Green Pastures,* what daring in *What Price Glory,* what great music from Gershwin!

How much more vital could a theatre be? That is why along Broadway there was small notice, few sighs, as the road "where the money was" shriveled. Out there live theatre had begun to die before World War I. The opera house found it could do better with Doug, Mary, Wally, Charlie Ray, during the week, and Pearl White and Tom Mix on Saturdays. *If* the opera house was still open, had not been vanquished by the Strand or the Bijou.

The road story was this:

Year	*Companies on Tour*
1900	339
1905	327
1910	236
1915	124
1920	39
1925	75
1930	56
1935	22

In my correspondence with drama editors about the situation now in towns and cities that once had full seasons of live theatre, their comments have been much the same:

—There is no such thing as a roadshow in Cheyenne and hasn't been for years. . . .

—Road shows in New Bedford are as rare as international good will. . . .

—Twenty years ago there was still an occasional road show in Cedar Rapids. But no more . . .

—Buffalo had seven shows for the year [and] the worst professional theatre hereabout [was] the touring shows. . . .

—Louisville had six attractions brought in for the season. . . .

—Troy had two roadshows for two nights. . . .

—Springfield [Ill.] has been without a community theatre since 1965 when the Orpheum was torn down. . . .

—Monterey and Carmel long ago ceased to be the mecca for road shows.

—Syracuse has four or five touring shows in the winter.

—The problem, as I see it, is that the Minneapolis audience is gun-shy. Roadshow productions, at best, have been second rate, shoddy, colorless and played out. . . .

—In Kansas City, perhaps eight or ten "legit" productions of runs averaging between three and six nights. *Hair* had an unusually good run, selling to the walls for three weeks—thanks in part to the hysterical moralists, who assumed our young would be forever stained by their encounter with such devil's handiwork. . . .

When you can find an authentic opera house still existing, you can stand on the stage and look into the house, and with concentration you may see the faces, rapt with attention, tense for the surprise, ready for the line that will want applause. Everyone out there is alone—alone in the audience—wives have forgotten the husbands they came with, sweethearts are unaware of one another, children are disembodied, all have left, have joined Lear or Rip or Isabel in their turbulent or enchanting worlds. All are watching the stage with head-still concentration, with silence, with heart-throbbing approval or with frowning disdain, for they are supporting the heroic, resisting the villainous—they are playing their parts, working for joy!

And if you go down into the house, sit back a bit, you may, if you can make the present be still, you may hear Lillian's high C, you may see that young girl entering center with the Barrymore voice and the manner that made it so difficult to watch anyone else. You may see staring at you, burning you, through the mind of Hamlet the eyes of Booth; you may see the puckish face of Jefferson, or you may be infuriated by that face at the window with the leering, grating voice asking Nellie why she fears.

You are in the town temple where ordinary people came to laugh and weep together, to vanquish difference and strangeness in shared experience, and, on the better nights, feel themselves so much more than they appeared to be in their ordinary days. There was awe in the sense of one's own greatness of heart and understanding when it was invoked by the artful actor, tragedian or comic, serving the inspired writer. The moment when it happened was hard to forget, and it was so sadly difficult to explain to a later generation what had happened.

Backstage the dust seems alive, a piano chord could make it dance, eagerly. There are voices as the stage door opens—"Any mail?"—anxious to hear from the world. Then the quick appraisal of the stage, the glance out front to see how much voice it will need, how close the audience will be, how high the balcony, where the eyes should sweep to gather response. Voices now right and left and below in the dressing rooms. Trunk locks snapping. A cheerful gabble—*that* is what sustained them until May and home, the sensible good cheer. What trooper doesn't give and accept support through the engagement, what trouper whines? If he does, let him be shot, let him walk home.

Then, wherever the opera house remains, everything fades as if snuffed like the last candle footlight, because other voices are coming, echoing in the lobby. They are discussing if it is best to tear it down and have just a parking lot or put up a taxpayer until the right offer. They say there is no sense in leaving it as it is, unused.

•

The Virginian *company, after the first twelve one-nighters, was settled for the 1905–6 season and was momentarily silent as the train approached Washington. Each could have been thinking ahead to the years of trouping, to the fame he and she might have in the theatre. With increasing need for plays and stars, any one of them might become as well known as Dustin Farnum, might have a night of triumph like his, then their names in lights in front of the thousands of theatres throughout the states for years to come:*

> Frank Campeau . . . Bennet Musson . . . Frank Nelson . . . Frank Vail . . . Charles Stanley . . . Charles Gilbert . . . Harry Holiday . . . John C. Hickey . . . George Morton . . . James Slevin . . . Otto Keim . . . George A. Weller . . . J. R. Furlong . . . Tony Mazzanovitch . . . Mary B. Conwell . . . Eleanor Wilton . . . Virginia Reeves . . . Ethel Powers . . . Wanda Wellington . . . Clara L. Chapman . . . Ada Morton . . . Gertrude Dalton . . .

Personal: In Confirmation

Advertisement, 1905

More members of
the Theatrical Profession
spent last Season in
Maine
at some point reached by
THE MAINE CENTRAL RAILROAD
than ever before. . . .
The Reason why
is Because it Offers More
in the way of Rest & Recreation
than any State in the Union.

I was born in the backwoods of Michigan beyond the railroad, electricity, gas, indoor plumbing, store bread, telephones and automobiles. When I emerged, it was something like Rip Van Winkle coming down from the mountain after twenty years' sleep to find a different world. Or, to give it dates, it was stepping from the nineteenth century into the twentieth. As a consequence, I have spent most of my life feeling older than everybody.

It was a regulation backwoods existence when I began. The horse-drawn stage brought the mail, including the Sears Roebuck catalogue so the women could catch up with the latest styles; everyone in the town knew too much about everyone else; there were six churches to service the three hundred population; there were endless repetitions of local sagas at the barbershop; most marriages were necessitated by pregnancy although everyone was supposed to be ignorant of sex; and there was one college graduate in the area: the doctor with his young beard to help people trust him.

It was a regulation village life with one great difference, and my grandfather, with whom I lived, was responsible for that. He ran a summer hotel. Long before I was born, he had beat his way back into this forest opening, had found a magnificent sand-bottomed lake, and had the lucky idea of making it a vacation place.

I still don't know how city people heard about it and I don't know why the actors came. I can only reason that the theatre had enough stability so that the actors had their fall contracts in the spring, and then it was a matter of their getting through the summer by rusticating as cheaply as possible. I don't remember much about the other resorters, but I vividly remember the actors. And this was the beginning of my understanding of what the theatre was like pre-movies, pre-Equity, in the days of triumph and glory plus hardship and stigma.

Of the actors who came to our hotel and the lakeside cottages, I remember particularly the Bennetts. It was my impression all the theatre people who came there had some connection with the Bennetts, and even if they did not they were brought under the domination of Mrs. Bennett when she (I am sure it was she) conceived the idea of amortizing some of their vacation expense by presenting shows in our opera house on Saturday nights. Since most of the actors were staying at our hotel, I was allowed to watch the rehearsals, sit in the men's dressing room as they made up, or stand in the wings during performance. Once I was even entrusted with lowering the curtain when the whole company was on for the last-act climax. The curtain was the usual one of that time—the canvas was rolled on a log, and it was raised and lowered like an inverted window shade—and no one had thought to ascertain which weighed most, the log and curtain or me. When on cue I rushed to loosen the ropes from the cleat, the weight pulled the ropes from my hands, giving the play a very fast curtain with a crash and cloud of dust to accent the tag.

So I lived in that remote world, and just as I know how to trim a lamp wick, prime a pump, and how to hitch a trace to a wagon and have more dated knowledge, I got insight into a theatre that was, in many respects, as old as Jefferson's in his childhood, or, for that matter, as old as supplicant theatre ever was, and I cannot resist giving you some of my impressions.

Mrs. Bennett (Catherine Marshall on stage in season) was formidable. I had no relatives like her and I knew of no female in the county to compare. I did not know if such exceptionality was to Mrs. Bennett's credit, but I could not have been more fascinated by her if she had worn pants, which at that time would have been as indecent as a bikini. Figuratively, she did wear pants and that was part of her uniqueness, for I had never known a woman who did not have to defer to the men. Actually, all the men, the actors, in this pick-up Saturday-nights-only aggregation deferred to *her* for she was inevitably the director. Whether there was any similarity or not, I think of her whenever I hear the name Modjeska—she was majestic and she was large; her tones could be basso, she could be regal and then again she could be fearfully bawdy just by letting laughter roll about in her bowels.

Now, today, I know these people were just actors typical of that time and earlier. I know they were not nearly so unique as they appeared to the boy me. But as I sat barefoot watching rehearsals, I found all of them as wonderfully unreal as characters in a book. For at that time, no book I had encountered had people as *I* knew people, my family and townsmen—repressed, monotonous "folks" with sagged expressions and judgments all alike—the books had *characters* like these actors.

I remember the second man of this company had a cigarette

dangling from his mouth always, even when he was acting, unless the part was a "man of the cloth." My people, because they thought such indulgence wasteful and because they owned a flammable summer hotel and lived in fear of fire, thought this habit was disgusting and this made me admire him for living such a reckless life. I waited expectantly for him to make an exciting conflagration that would include himself.

I remember all of them—the actress, the company's "second woman," who was constantly sewing. I think she made even her husband's clothes. Then suddenly, on cue, she could be so grand, so high society, so la-di-da you couldn't believe she knew which end of the needle had the point.

The leading woman, I remember, had the asset of frailty, she induced sympathy on sight, and young as I was I felt the urge to protect her until one day, during a rest at rehearsal, I saw her Indian-wrestling with one of the men. She didn't need me.

The leading man was squarely handsome, as clean-looking as a fresh brick of Ivory, and he was the only person in the troupe who received blank-faced, humorless patience from his fellows. I finally realized they felt he hardly had the intelligence to button himself up and that he should have put his life behind a counter, but folks in the audiences thought he was a real good hero, he looked so incapable of vice.

None of them, as I saw it, had Mrs. Bennett's aggregate ability. She could act *off* as well as on. She had *authority*, and it wasn't only because of her weight. She walked the streets of the village as if she were the queen in Holland, rusticating, willing to learn from the commoners and glad to teach them their own business. Her projection was such that a simple outdoor "Good morning" could be heard by every fisherman out on the still lake, and if something made her laugh, the leaves of the town seemed to rustle in response.

My memory of the performances they gave is grainy and broken, but I recall a bit of *Rip Van Winkle* and some of *The Squaw Man*; I remember Sol Cohen, a visiting concert pianist, suddenly going to the piano in front of the stage as Isabel was dying and playing Balfe's "Then You'll Remember Me." I have been told no one could play *East Lynne,* Isabel could never die, without that theme. It made everyone around me in the audience blubber, but for some reason I couldn't take it seriously and I was right because after the show I saw Sol Cohen laughing uproariously at his performance.

I remember Mrs. Bennett's "Next Week" spiels, and I was suspicious when she told the natives how important it was that they come see that "modern" drama, *Why Girls Leave Home.* How often since have I seen publishers' claims that *this* text will help parents understand their own, will bring peace to troubled homes, will help the family avoid disaster. Somehow, it all seemed too cautiously indirect for Mrs. Bennett. I didn't know what she was referring to, but I had the feeling that if she were being natural she'd *say* it.

I can see now that I was quite a student of Mrs. Bennett, and part of the reason I have not forgotten her was because one day at an August rehearsal, I saw one of her great performances—this one *off.* A young, redheaded, beaming, Windsor-tied itinerant reader of poetry somehow found the town and wandered in to watch the players getting up the show for Saturday night. I was aware of him, was even distracted from the rehearsal and watched him instead because his eyes danced, he instantly responded to the lines being read, he was so obviously eager for life and finding it startling, amusing, whichever way he turned—a man living perpetually in excitement. Dan Reed was his name.

At a break before resuming with the next act, Mrs. Bennett's autumn child by her last marriage, Isadora, a fifteen-year-old, came in to ask her mother's permission to go to the swamp to hunt for snakes. She was russet, quick, with movements like wind, obviously in love with summer and the adventure of being away from her world of trains, hotels and theatres. I saw the poetry reader watching her in wonder.

Permission granted, Isadora ran out in a ballet dash and Mrs. Bennett called everyone up for Act II, Scene 1. But they were interrupted—the young visitor who had been watching came forward and said to Mrs. Bennett, "Excuse me." She turned to him with the graciousness any manager would show someone who might want to buy a ticket.

"Was that your daughter?" he asked.

She acknowledged with a smile of immodest pride.

Then he announced, "I'm going to marry her!"

What might have been a simple or amusing surprise became a thunderclap silence of what consequence we could not imagine as Mrs. Bennett, mother of womankind, began to swell and increase in stature. Finally—at the precise second when tension, suspense, must break—she spoke.

"*IF*," she said, "IF you *ever* . . . so much as lay a finger . . . on that dear child, *I*—will cut out—your—*goddamned HEART!*"

I had never heard a woman say "goddamn"—even my grandfather gave the impression he might not know how to pronounce it. And her curse was not only verbal; she had a straight arm with a finger on the end of it pointing like a sword at the poetry reader's chin. All the people I had ever known just talked with their close-lipped mouths; they could hardly gesture to show you which way was east. I was thrilled enough when something like this happened in books and plays, but this was in *real life!*

It was a curtain line that made the next act inevitable. In those days, you knew you had something to come back for after intermission. In this instance, I had to wait some time to know how the play turned out. Nineteen years later I met Dan Reed in New York and he said, "You remember my wife, don't you—Isadora Bennett?"

The winters of my childhood were long. Living with my grandparents, often snowbound, I filled the boredom by reading what books about the theatre I could get and building my resolution to go someday and find that colorful world our summer actors came from. I wanted to be with them, with their kind; I wanted to feel as they did the excitement of the emotions of all the characters they played, of being loose enough to feel their own emotions like Mrs. Bennett, to laugh completely when amused, to blast and gesture when angered, to throw arms about friends because of joy, cheer any success or cry honestly over disappointment.

This I had seen them do, and I was young and old enough to make an irrevocable judgment: their life, whatever happened, had to be better than the one I had here in the village with my relatives and the people they approved, people who always avoided excess, kept themselves laced, eschewed any immoderation of speech and motion, people who, as they expressed it, "tried not to be common." I vowed I was going to be uncommon.

I held to my resolution after we moved away from there to a city of seven thousand. The school I attended was big enough for me to promote an inordinate amount of play production—so I could play the leads. I persuaded the English teachers that putting on a farce with a part I wanted to do was essential to their courses. They countered by proposing something "literary" by Sardou. We compromised and did both. Whenever I heard that my class or the school needed money for any reason, I convinced them they should back a play to raise it. This helped me be patient until I could get away and helped me to endure the dumb school casts I directed. No one but me had professional standards; the other kids had never been with actual actors!

My grandfather suddenly became old and indifferent to his authority, and that left only my mother to restrain me and keep me in school. Since she had to work to support us, she was usually too preoccupied or weary to notice how desperate I was in my ambition, and once when she went away on a rare vacation, merely telling me to be a good boy, I saw my chance and escaped. I took to the road to find my dream behind a stage door, I didn't care where it would be.

I hitchhiked and got as far as Cleveland, where, after washing dishes in a restaurant to get my bearings, I persuaded a bookstore to hire me as a clerk. They even advanced me enough so I could eat until payday. Although I lived at the YMCA, I could not seem to amass the cash for a proper assault on my goal, Broadway, and, realizing I might never get it, I gave up the nonsense of discretion and, with twelve dollars, took the streetcar as far as it would go and hitched from there to New York.

I arrived with exactly five dollars. I am explicit about this because money is the essence of the story. I arrived with that much cash and only one skill; I could run a typewriter. So evenings and nights I addressed envelopes for a company that addressed envelopes, being paid by the hundred and paid nightly, which was important. This gave me time to go the rounds of the theatrical offices in the daytime. Slowly but definitely I came to realize that Broadway had no desperate need for high school actors—there had been a full supply for years—and as I was getting exhausted running a piecework typewriter at night and underfeeding myself while I looked for an "engagement" by day, ending each week with just enough to survive over Sunday, I used an extra burst of energy and did enough envelopes to get the means to withdraw from New York to reorganize my attack. I went to Boston.

As I was studying the Yellow Pages to see what employment offices might be best for an experienced typist, I noted that Boston had a theatrical agency. It was a terribly seedy place and the man took my name without encouragement and mumbled something which I could understand only because I caught the words ". . . don't . . . us . . . you." By this time, with the benefit of my experience in New York, I had the sense to know I shouldn't be expectant, but when I returned to the place where I was staying with some of Boston's more prosperous derelicts, there was a message to return to the agency immediately.

There was a manager there who said he had a repertoire company that was doing three-day stands in New England, had been on the road all season and now suddenly needed a replacement for the leading man, would I be interested at seventy-five dollars a week? I said yes, I was definitely available. There was a silence as the manager and agent looked at me, looked at me the way a cat might regard a mouse who said he had washed and was ready for dinner. I was told to meet the company at the North Station the next morning at 11 o'clock.

I now stepped back to Jefferson's time when he and his family were hoping Galena, Illinois, might by the grace of God have enough of an audience to permit them to leave Galena and reach Springfield, where they would hope a merciful Christ might provide patronage to let them go on. I was joining the equivalent of every desperate barnstorming troupe of virtual beggars that the theatre had ever known. As I walked expectantly into the station, I saw the manager and around him his company, all staring eagerly my way as if they had been desperately watching to see if I would show. I almost faltered as I was introduced, they were so thin, so faded despite their feeble flair; one was almost toothless; they looked like mendicants who had been through a territory that barely had water. I was escorted to meet the star, who was the star because the company was called the Dora Deere Players and she was Dora Deere. She was the only one with extra flesh, even more than she needed, and I was soon to learn that the manager was devoted to her welfare, even to the extent of sharing her hotel room wherever we stopped, and that it was the purpose of his life to lift her from the burlesque house where he had discovered her to the drama, where a lady ought to be. Long after, when I met Mae West, I was struck by the resemblance between her and Dora Deere. Miss West undoubtedly had more intelligence, shrewdness, but as we were introduced and as Miss West was sipping Coca-Cola through a straw, I thought her belches sounded exactly like Dora's.

There in the station, I felt a cold urge to run, but I could not afford to withdraw from the Dora Deere company any more than they could afford to abandon me. As the train rolled along some branch line to the place where I would be briefly rehearsed and we would open, the character man sitting beside me, wizened and sharp-eyed as a monkey with empty stomach, filled me in on the history of the troupe I had joined. They had been playing the winter farther north, often in lumber camps, and on reaching Boston, the leading man had, true to his reputation, gone on a monumental binge. Though the manager had canvassed every whorehouse he could find, he had not traced the missing actor.

"It's lucky we found you," said the character man, and I felt like a life preserver with too many people hanging on.

I learned immediately not to expect salary. The audiences we got were as small as committees, and they viewed us as if sent to see if we were infectious. By the time we reached the second stand, I saw that it was the players' custom to ask the manager for fifty cents or a quarter or a dime as the need might be. He paid everyone's hotel expenses, room and food, at places he selected, but there were other needs, and once when I asked him for a quarter he looked pained and asked what for. I said I needed shoelaces and wanted to write to my mother.

The fifth week, in Walden, New York, the small luck of the Dora Deere Players ran out. The manager did not have the means to lift us to the next town. We were stranded. I had read about this, about actors walking the ties to get home, but I thought tales like these were only reminiscent jokes and I was terribly shocked by the reality when the sheriff began tailing our every move. He was making sure we didn't skip before all bills were paid, and I soon sensed that every person in town was his deputy. We did not go hungry because a restaurant owner took pity and said he would feed us, the actors, but not *him*, the manager.

I felt desperately humiliated. The glowering sheriff and the magnanimous restaurateur made me feel criminal and, by the standards of the people who raised me, something equally inexcusable, a mendicant, a pauper. I wanted to make them understand that I *did not mean to DO it!* I had no intention of defrauding anybody or of being a public charge; it would be an incredible mistake to lock me up!

Long, long after, when I saw *A Long Day's Journey into Night*, I felt like railing at those snotty O'Neill sons who were ridiculing their father's niggardliness simply because he had been poor and stranded in his youth. I wanted to write to both those ingrate sons—even though they were dead—to say, you don't understand, you don't realize how your old man was frightened, how his pride was mortified, so why don't you leave the poor old bastard alone!

It took me time to subside and see this was how Eugene *wanted* me to feel, to understand that in his last and too-late years he had begun to understand.

There came a rescue as improbable as the turn of the plot in *The Woman in Red,* one of the dramas in our three-play rep. In Walden, New York, there was a vaudeville couple in temporary retirement while the wife had a baby. I had actually seen their act in Cleveland, although I did not see much of them. They played and did cute gymnastics in catskins, they were a pair of large cats, and though they removed their feline masks for the bow, I could not recall their faces.

They were sympathetic and wanted to help us and said they would wire an organization called NVA, National Vaudeville Artists, to see if they would send some money to allow us to escape from Walden. I could not understand why NVA in New York should be interested in our plight, and it was only years later that I learned that NVA was a sort of Keith-Albee company union distributing minor largess so as to promote contentment and loyalty among comics, jugglers, singers and cat acts.

I had told my friend the character man the story of my life, including my unsuccessful assault on Broadway, and he had said, what you ought to do, kid, is get to Chicago, you got a better chance if you go there. When the money unexpectedly came from NVA, we were summoned to the office of a local lawyer at 10 o'clock at night to receive it. There the bemused attorney asked how much each of us would need to absent ourselves from Walden. The others meekly requested enough to get, at most, as far as Boston, but I brazenly asked for enough to get to Chicago. Much to the obvious irritation of the others, the lawyer counted out and gave me fifty dollars. I left immediately, got my bag, went to the station and took the first train, a 1 A.M. milk train, to escape the disgrace I thought I would never mention to anyone for the rest of my life.

In Chicago, I went to the office of the A. Milo Bennett Dramatic Exchange (no relation to *my* Mrs. Bennett). Unwittingly, I said the words that were magic in Chicago. I said I had been in "New York" and I had just closed with a show. Mr. Bennett said it happened he had a place for me. Miss Ross of the Mertie Ross Players in Lafayette, Indiana, had sent a request for a New York actor to play juveniles. We had no trouble agreeing on terms; he got me a ticket; and I arrived in Lafayette that midnight.

Early the next morning I went around to the theatre, went back and discovered a small, middle-aged woman down on her knees nailing flats. When she looked up, I asked if she could help me find Miss Mertie Ross. She said, spitting tacks out of her mouth, "I'm Mertie Ross, what can I do for you?" I explained that I was her new juvenile sent by A. Milo Bennett. She stared at me and then said distinctly, "That fucking sonofabitch, I told him I wanted *a character man!*" And so I borrowed wigs and played characters and, in the manner of juveniles playing characters, I succeeded in making every fifty-year-old man I acted no less than ninety and sometimes older. And I hung on until the close six weeks later.

There was a comedian with Mertie's company blessed with the name of Roscoe Patch. He asked me what I was going to do. I said I didn't know. He glanced sympathetically at my loose-soled shoes and said, kindly, "It's going to be summer, there won't be much stock in the summertime, what you ought to do is get with a tent show, they play such small towns you can't spend any money and you can get yourself some wardrobe, understand?" I asked, "What's a tent show?"

I joined the Hank Martin Tent Show in Princeton, Iowa, a town so German I never heard a native speak English even on the telephone. The Hank Martin Company, I was to learn, played country towns, one each week, with seven plays, one for each night. There were no Sundays off, for although the "enlightened" East continued to be resistant to almost any public amusement on Sunday, the "wholesome" Middle West permitted Sunday shows. The towns were very small; I checked one town when I could get to an atlas and found it was granted seventy-six inhabitants. Our audiences came mainly from the farms. So it was that I gained further insight into the kind of trouping—Tom shows and the like—that had once been common.

Hank Martin was an entrepreneur of uncertain past. A portly gent, he was active on Saturday nights directing the roustabouts in taking down and Sunday nights in putting up at the next stand; otherwise he left things pretty much to the direction of his sad wife, who always looked as if she would prefer to be decently attached to a kitchen range in one unmovable place. She was, or had been, the "comfortably-well-off" widow of a saloonkeeper before she married Hank. Now he had her tied down selling tickets so he could get away to return some of her late husband's money to a local bar or blind pig. If there was no such place, he always found a bottle and companions. I had only one conversation with Hank about things theatrical, when I asked him what was the best show he had ever seen. He thought and then said it was Richard Mansfield "in Shakespeare's *Midnight's Summer Dream.*"

The tent show actors were a breed I had never met and could not have imagined. Of this particular lot, not one had ever spoken a line under a roof that wasn't canvas. For the most part, they worked out of Kansas City. They knew their business, which was to observe the traditions—meaning that all their characterizations were as set, as passed on, as the playing of Shakespearean or Greek roles may once have been. I watched the director pass out the parts, and he would indicate all that his actors needed to know. He would say, "It's a Banker Beans part [the mortgage forecloser]"; "It's an Aunt Samanthy part [village gossip]"; "It's an Elviry [comedy hired girl]." When he came to me, he simply said "It's a blue-shirt lead," and after I had rehearsed all seven of my blue-shirt leads, I knew the character was undeviatingly honest, simple, sincere, and a schnook who permitted himself to be falsely accused of something or in some other foolish way gave his trusting mother and sweetheart cause to worry until circumstance sprang him from suspicion.

When the director handed the comedian his parts, there was

no need to comment because they would all be Toby. Hank Martin's was what was known as a Toby show, so called for a character invented many years before and loved for decades by the patrons of rural drama. He was always the same in every play: a red-wigged, freckled, gap-toothed, excited and breathless ("a-huh, a-huh, a-huh") rube hired-man. The hired girl was always showing her affection by chasing him with a broom, and Toby, in his ridiculous way, usually solved the plot just before the final curtain so that son and mother, son and sweetheart, Toby and Elviry could fall into each other's arms. "Aw, shucks!" was the tag.

Of the seven plays we did with Hank Martin, all were written by Robert L. Sherman, using practically the same stencil for each. In five of them, at climax, Toby dashed in to announce a discovery somewhere on the property that would make everyone who was virtuous enormously rich. Rushing in, pointing a wagging finger off, panting long enough for everyone to build it by saying, "What is it, Toby!" "What do you want? *Say* something!," he gulped and choked and finally said, "A-huh, a-huh, a-huh, they've *found it!*" "What, Toby, what? For heaven's sake, tell us!" "Gold!" he shouted (Monday night) . . . "Silver!" (Tuesday night) . . . "Oil!" (Thursday night) . . . "Coal!" (Friday night) . . . and "Zinc!" (Saturday night).

It was the first time I had been required to learn seven parts in one week while playing a new and different role each night. I learned fast how it was done. I learned to wing, coming off after each scene, grabbing my part secreted on the back of a flat, madly thumbing the pages to find what I was supposed to say and do next. With these veterans I was reasonably secure for they were wonderfully adept in covering lapses. I learned to be, too. You got so you could tell when someone was going up, was groping for the next line, you could see it by their out-of-focus expression, and so you made their cue more practical than it was in the script: "Which reminds me, don't you want to tell me where you've been?" The Person Opposite (as he/she got it): "Oh, yes, I was going to do that. I was down at the store just now talking to—" Or: "You know, I was sitting here thinking. I was wondering if you remember the time we went to the social—" The Opposite (picking it up): "Oh, yes, I do! I was going to ask if you remembered that time we went to the social and—" Or (quarrel scene): "And now I suppose you're going to blame me for the time I was late and—" "Well, I sure am! I came all dressed up to get you and where were you! You were out in the yard talking to that ridiculous—" It usually worked. When it didn't, you could get into fascinating improvised subplots until someone offstage found the right script, found the right place, and threw you the line so you could go straight.

The first day after rehearsal, Hank Martin came to me and said, "We sell candy." I looked blank, so he said, "Between the acts. The men go in the audience and sell candy. They get a commission. You don't have to if you don't want to." Feeling my status as leading man, I thought it could be demeaning, possibly disillusioning to the audience, to be a candy butcher, and I declined as tactfully as I could. The other men didn't mind, so much more for them, and it helps explain why I have never been "comfortably-well-off."

One of the men would make the spiel. "Frozen Sweets, ladies and gentlemen, a prize in every package. And I call your attention to this grand prize for the lucky person who gets the winning numba. This lovely genuine fabric and colorful bed blanket that will keep someone nice and cozy warm this winter. A beautiful twelve-dollar item given absolutely free . . ."

The packages were coded. A salesman spotting the right kind of customer—a sporty-looking gent, perhaps—would slip him the package with the ladies' panties in it. When the customer opened it, the salesman would grab the drawers and shake them out for the audience to see. "Look at this lovely prize this lucky gentleman just won!" Hysterical laughter. As for the grand prize, there was one for every 250 packages of candy. If sales were slow—say, only 150 packages—the prize could naturally not be awarded because then there would be no bait for tomorrow night. "We're very sorry, ladies and gentlemen, I guess nobody got the lucky numba. Tomorrow night they'll get it sure, so be sure to . . ." If the prize was to be given, the head butcher would look for some poor poor-widow type, someone the audience would be pleased to have receive it, and he would give her the package with the right number. Humor, excitement and goodhearted cheating between the acts.

The salaries we received were pitiful. Though our expenses were minimal, some of these people would not work again until next summer, and many of them had kids; they clutched the coins like the gypsies they were. They never complained, were good-natured and, what impressed me, they were very moral people. They were carry-overs from the time when actors were watched with suspicion and considered libertines, and they recognized their obligation to be more circumspect than missionaries. One night, packing up, I slammed my trunk shut on my hand and yelled "Jesus!" The men with me in the dressing room turned to look at me, and one of them said, "Be careful! The ladies will hear you!"

I cannot remember that we stayed in a hotel any time that summer. On arriving in a village, we would quickly go from house to house knocking on doors, explaining ourselves and asking with desexed charm if they could possibly rent a room for sleeping while we were here with the show. The women usually reacted as if they had never received a more startling proposition, some said they'd have to ask their husbands, and if they did assent they didn't know what to charge. If I was feeling soft or generous, I would say the usual charge is $4, but if the house depressed me, I'd explain we didn't like to pay over $2.50 for the week. The deal made, I invariably found myself in the spare room, spending the breathlessly hot Iowa nights deep down in feather mattresses, with departed spade-bearded grandfathers and black-gowned grandmothers watching with disapproval from their photographs on the wall. I will have to die to sleep with so many deceased again.

I was the only unmarried person in the troupe. By the time I got my makeup off, everyone who had been to the show had vanished into their homes in the village or out to the farms. As I walked about wishing there were at least the sociability of a cup of coffee, the noisiest thing in the nights was the stars or possibly a street lamp. I was learning what I was to learn too well in the following years when I traveled with shows: to be close to, to entertain, a thousand, two thousand, share their thoughts, laughter, vibrations, then to be alone while everyone else went to the comfort of homes, lay with each other, was a lonesomeness much sharper than any life in solitary. I had given to these people! They liked me, applauded me! Why doesn't someone want me after the show? I have entertained you, why can't we *talk?* I once thought that this lonely pain was due to some abnormal sensitivity on my part, some pathological self-pity, but then I read in a *New Yorker* profile how Artie Shaw had cracked up after years of such public loneliness when trouping with dance orchestras.

The season ended, and I still didn't have enough money to make a stand for it in New York. Someone told me about rep shows. By answering an ad, sending my pictures, corresponding, I got a job to play the leads with Clint and Bessie Robbins. When I got to their world of northern Iowa, the Dakotas and Minnesota, I seemed like a freak, never having heard of Clint and Bessie Robbins. The people there knew them like cousins.

They had been playing that territory for thirty-six years. All they did was put up their billing. It consisted only of the name, "CLINT & BESSIE ROBBINS," with date and place, and that did it. I never saw an empty seat in the house in the four months I was with them; in fact, the aisles were usually full. Again it was like the past: those shows and players that were welcomed year after year. Announce the return: the people were waiting.

The past, in fact, was with us, because the opera houses often held reminders of shows that had played there when those houses were open through the seasons. Faded cards, posters, other remnants spoke of old excitement: "ROBERT MANTELL, THE BOY TRAGEDIAN." Once, looking for a broom to sweep out my dressing room, I opened a closet door and saw on the back of the door the ancient announcement that Sarah Bernhardt was coming. So, as I have said, it was like playing in another era; sometimes, too, we were the last voices heard before the final curtain.

The Robbins show brought plays—six of them for the week's stand, with Sunday off—that were fresh from Broadway. Since they were the only company in that part of the earth that would ever present them, they were often granted rights to plays still running in New York. They were comedies or plays with mild personal social problems (*Dancing Mothers*)—all social problems were then mild; after Oswald Alving got his syphilis, it was fifty years before playwrights tried to top that.

I was the leading man and played opposite Bessie. She was literally old enough to be my grandmother. She had a face that had become dry leather, but her figure was better than any sixteen-year-old female's in North or South Dakota, Minnesota or Iowa. Whatever incongruity there was in my making baby-faced love to her wrinkles did not seem to trouble the audiences in the least. I don't think they took our acting seriously, or we were back in a less literal time when audiences accepted Booth's gray-haired Hamlet.

I joined the Robbinses in August in Atlantic, Iowa. We rehearsed the six-play rep for one week in heat that would make an infidel go to his knees praying for winter. In the stale air of the opera house, I would read my sides with my eyeballs sweating and would collapse when I was out of scene and watch, in disbelief, as John and Anna MacFarlane, looking cool as cucumbers, would cheerfully rehearse.

They were the character people, both snow-white, and they had retained enough beauty, each of them, to tell you how striking they must have been when they began. Someone who knew them told me later that they might have had better careers than this trouping in obscurity if they had not decided always to work together. Perhaps the explanation for this lay in another story I heard about this gentle pair. They had one child, a son, and when he was fifteen, they left him for a season with friends in San Francisco while they toured to make their living. The boy disappeared, and for years John and Anna had written letters to all parts of the world seeking some trace (someone had heard he was taken aboard a ship), only to find that each lead was a cruel rumor. He was never found.

I realized then, as I do now, that they were the embodiment of the term "trouper." There was never a complaint from either, and I remember in particular the miserable test of one jump and one night. We had played Detroit Lakes, Minnesota, and the company (Clint and Bessie went by car and were not with us) was moving to McLeod, North Dakota. The first leg of the journey was to Fargo, aboard a fast and luxurious Chicago-Seattle train of the Northern Pacific, so we began in elegant comfort.

We arrived in Fargo at 9 in the evening and had a two-hour wait for the next connection. As there was no place to eat at the station, we had to find something in the town. It was only a matter of three blocks to a diner but, as I remember it, it was as challenging as Eliza's crossing. The wind was from somewhere back of Alaska, and that night there could not have been a blood-red trace in any Fargo thermometer. There was a young musician in the company's four-piece orchestra, and she and I ran to see if we could make it before our fluids froze. We stumbled into the diner, too numb to comment, and we waited, speechless, eyes and noses running, until John and Anna MacFarlane entered as if pleasantly invigorated by the crispness of the evening. As I sat steaming my face in coffee, I wondered how unusual this night could be to them. How many similar experiences had they known in their lifetime of trouping across America? The luxuriousness of the Northern Pacific must have been a solacing contrast to the stagecoaches they had actually ridden. Once Mr. Mac mentioned playing the mining camps, which could have been an incommodious life, to say the least, but his only criticism was his comment that they were sometimes rather vulgar.

When it was time, we returned to the Fargo station to shiver and wait, and, half an hour after it was due, we heard a train. But it sauntered in and was only a freight. A long procession of sixty or seventy cars crawled tediously past the station windows and then, as a day coach came into view at the end, the train stopped.

This, we were informed, was ours, and, breathing the odor from the sixty or seventy cars—for the freight that night was cattle—we stepped aboard. It hurt to draw breath; the blazing coal stove and the kerosene lamps in the coach had burned everything usable out of the air. Breathing was like swallowing the dust from hot ashes.

The freight ambled through the frozen night while the stove emitted gas to blend with the stink of the lamps. Once we opened the door to freshen the air, but this made us beneficiaries of the stench from the stock traveling ahead of us. At 4 A.M., the train stopped and the conductor-brakeman grumpily told us to get off. We stepped down and sank into snow. There was no platform and no station that we could see. As we stood there congealing, we concluded that the station must be on the other side, we would see it as soon as the train moved on. When it did, there was no building; all we saw was a coach with a dim light on a siding some distance away, and, hauling our luggage, we stumbled toward it through the deep snow. I was concerned about Mrs. Mac and stayed close in case she needed help, but I had now trouped long enough to know that it might be considered professionally gauche if I offered aid. She made it, smiling as if she'd been to the garden and was lifted by the scent of roses.

Our waiting room, the coach, was about a hundred degrees warm. There was a blazing fire in the stove, left by some mysterious, vanished attendant. I was positive the coach had hauled celebrants to the ceremony of the golden spike. The seats had accumulated decades of dust; we dared not disturb it, we would all have had asthma. There was no choice but to cover the gray-on-maroon seats with our overcoats before we sat down.

We thought—and were right—that we had seen a building somewhere in the starlight. The men of the company wallowed their way there, and we pounded to wake people up and then politely asked the lady if she could make some coffee to take to our ladies. We assured her we would pay. Wordlessly, the woman made the brew. When we returned to the coach and tasted it, we might have thought she meant to poison us as troublesome varmints if we had not tasted worse in that land of everything-fried, with the choice of iodine tea or Argyrol coffee.

Now we sat silent in the stillness of that vast prairie night. The light from the one lamp was too dim for reading, we were anyhow too dazed with tiredness, but we could not bring ourselves to lie down in the dust to sleep. We sat in that ancient coach as if we were becalmed on a raft in mid-ocean, helpless, waiting for rescue. After an hour or so I discerned light at the horizon, and with cold deliberation the dawn came to the Dakota snow desert. To my amazement I saw we were surrounded by busy life. There seemed to be millions of jackrabbits happily going about their morning business; I was positive I could hear them saying "Good morning! Sleep well? Isn't this a pleasant day, only twenty below!"

The sun climbed to near noon, the fire went down in the stove, no one came. When I was convinced that those responsible had forgotten us, a four-coach train rambled in, we forded the snow distance and got aboard. At 5 in the afternoon, we arrived at McLeod, where we were to open at 8 o'clock.

There was, God be thanked, a hotel. The lobby was hot, again with a full-blast stove, but when I was given my key and told where the stairs were, "through that door," I found the rest of the inn was sealed off from the heat and never had that benefit through the long below-freezing winter. In my room, there was no water to shave with—of course not, it would freeze; I would have to get some from the kitchen. I was too weary. I partly undressed, pulled back the covers of the bed to get some sleep before going to work and observed that many guests had been here before me: the sheets were obviously changed only when the climate was clement for the maid. I crawled in; my teeth and muscles chattered as if I were between plates of ice on steel; I could not believe I would ever sleep. But I did. And that night at the theatre, Mr. and Mrs. Mac talked about everything except the ordeal of the night. I began to wonder if they had been with us until I reminded myself that they were, after all, *troupers!* Given another fifty years, I might be one too.

Did I learn much in those years of rep and, later, stock in Winnipeg, Sioux Falls, Omaha, Des Moines, Battle Creek, Williamsport and more? Did I learn anything in the weekly rush through different parts with directors who hardly had time to say more than, "You enter down right"; "Step a little more to the left, you're covering Joe"; "Come in on that a little faster"; "Be sure they hear that cue so she can get her laugh"; "Take your time"; "Everybody turn and look at Marie"? I thought I was learning, actors can teach one another and audiences teach more, but I was never sure how much of it was right—audiences can mislead, often you have to fight them. I could only think of all the good people who had come from such training—Jeanne Eagles from a Kansas tent show; Laurette Taylor, as they always said, not only played the leads in her husband's stock company, she swept out the theatre—in those days what good person had not learned his business in stock? Still I wanted more, and I yearned to have the benefit of the directors on Broadway.

Later, I found myself there, and I have kept a total memory of my final stint as an actor. It was a Theatre Guild production. I had been in one of their presentations before. That one had been a preposterous spectacle hacked from Biblical legend, with a cast of forty, twenty-five of whom wore faces stiff with false beards. But I still had the hopeful nature of the actor and *this* new opus was not only carpentered by a famous novelist, it was to be directed by Max Pingloss. (In order not to distract from the point of the story, I am using fictitious names . . . beginning with this one.)

Max Pingloss was not necessarily famous as a director, but he had been associated with others who had pioneered a new kind of realistic theatre which had produced playwrights with fresh themes and novel ethnic characters. Now he was to direct a sprawling testament to the horrors of war when the good men lose. He had heard me read for my part, expressing doubt only about the foreign accent I used. When I heard others speaking with an accent he commended, I got the point, shifted to Brooklynese and received Pingloss' approval of my Spanish.

I was looking forward to the rehearsals because Pingloss was reported to be a profound exponent of a new imported method that could help the disciples be absolutely actual in their parts. An actor had explained it to me in a voice of enthusiastic awe. He said it involved affective memory, which meant that if you were playing a millionaire, you thought back until you recalled an experience that reminded you, told you what it was like to be very rich, even if all your life you had been afraid to take your shoes off in public because of the holes in your socks. I think all of us were anxious to learn the system, especially as none of us was Spanish nor had we been in the war there, and we were eager to be instructed in remembering so as to be authentic.

Pingloss was a small man with the theatrical handicap of looking as undistinguished, ordinary, as a dull penny. He seemed so misplaced that it provoked a foolish sympathy in me, and I was prepared to respond as I had long ago to a wild-haired stuttering boy at a school I once mistakenly attended. This was a Presbyterian academy founded primarily to produce preachers for that denomination, and the lad I speak of was the only Jewish scholar in attendance. I was attracted to him because he was infinitely more cerebral than most of the Protestants, especially the tobacco-chewing monster I roomed with for a time, who had been bribed to enroll and then endowed, in order to help the Presbyterians keep their rank in football against teams from Baptist, Congregational, Lutheran and other institutions of misguided faith.

The name of my friend was Morrie Wertz. I felt sympathy for his minority of one, and thus found myself learning an important lesson: a well-meaning heart does not inevitably provoke affection for the odd one, nor does it always close your mind to the fact that accumulated learning can induce stupidity. If you said "Good morning" to Morrie, he would stop dead and want you to stop dead too, while he told you that "Good morning" in Norwegian was "*Farvel*" and in Danish it was "*Farvel,*" while in Swedish it was "*God dag,*" which he found significant in view of the animosities among the Scandinavians. At such times, hoping to deflect him with a challenge, I would ask, "How do you know so much, have you been there?" "No." "Then how do you know there are these animosities you're talking about?" His answer would be he'd heard it, he'd read it, and when I said "Good morning" he'd just happened to think what it meant to them. But what, I'd insist, did "Good morning" have to do with it even if they did hate each other? Which only bogged me further in the rich swamp of Morrie's mind as he launched into an etymological explanation of international antipathies past and present which he had just happened to think about and some of which he just happened to create to fit the argument.

Eventually, when I had been forced to know him too well, when I saw that his headpiece operated like a kitten unwinding a ball of yarn but incapable of winding it back up, when I saw he would never be able to make anything of his job-lot erudition, could not write a simple statement with a single subject any more than he could say a simple "Good morning," I, too, did some thinking and concluded that obsessive intellectualization is the refuge of the uncreative.

Unfortunately, I had forgotten this lesson when I met Max Pingloss. He began the first rehearsal with an address to the cast that was half throat-clearings, in which he said that the play had many interesting connotations. He explained these in terms needing exegesis. I watched the cast. By the way they smiled and batted their eyes as if never in their lives had they heard anything so fascinatingly profound, I could tell that not one of the twenty-eight understood what he said any more than I did. According to the Equity contract, you have to get through the first three days to hold your job; after the third day they can't fire you without at least paying you off. After the third day, I noticed that the actors stopped smiling with amazement at Pingloss' profundity.

But I'm getting ahead. That first rehearsal, he began with the first page of the script, a scene involving three players, and he got through that and well into the second page that first day. As he made this intricate progress, the other twenty-five actors gave him audience, watched closely the master. They were as eager for insight as I was, for any hint from Pingloss that could give the key to the mystery of affective creation and could make them methodically infallible, give them the edge in a crazy business where some girl from Kansas who isn't sure how to spell "Ohio" or some kid from the Bronx who was almost too stupid to pass his bar mitzvah may walk on a stage and excite an audience more than someone who has *thought* about what he's doing! This has always been exasperating to the scholars.

So the actors were patient. But after about the sixth day, they seemed suddenly to decide the message wasn't going to arrive and, when not rehearsing, they began reading racing forms, writing letters, or playing poker in a dressing room with a lookout. I continued to listen in order to catch any casual wisdom Pingloss might drop, especially as the three stars appeared to follow him and I thought, up to a point, that what was good enough for them ought to be superb for me. One star was a rich movie name with a natural grace that made him attractive whatever he did. The other man reminded me of what I had read about Forrest; he was formidable in his projection of physical strength and emotional power. The female star was an actress who had scored with a note of pathos in a part the season before. She was now about to parlay that note into a whine and she would never star again.

I had one scene with the three of them and I got quite tense when we began to rehearse. I feared it might be my fault when I did not understand the directions Pingloss gave any of us, for the others looked at his chest as they listened, then nodded as if they of course comprehended and agreed. Pingloss had announced, "Now in this scene I wish to see three colors." Period. I did not feel it was my place to speak in the presence of the much-better-paid stars, but I thought it might help if one of them would ask which colors he preferred. Because Pingloss didn't say. I was especially fussed when he stopped me once and said, "No, no, you have only *two* colors!" I said I would try it again. I did and he said it was right. I had added a dash of vermilion.

It was not until the beginning of the third week that the other lesser actors began to jerk and grumble out loud. A character woman suddenly turned to me as we were standing offstage and said, "May I ask, have you the remotest idea what that colorful sonofabitch means?" The snarling began to sound mutinous because the whole production was starting to disintegrate just when it should have been cohering, and the actors felt panic. As for the three stars, they continued to mask any doubts; as stars, they may have felt they were supposed to understand what others didn't, that they were supposed to show confidence—but I noticed their eyes were getting glazed.

Actors are usually forbearing, generous, and this was the only time I ever watched a cast grow more embittered by the hour until their collective disgust was dangerous. Max Pingloss, if he felt it, was never perturbed. I thought again of Morrie Wertz; I was sure Morrie didn't mind being in an alien land among all those self-chosen Presbyterians as long as he could know what they didn't. "D-d-did you know-know the leaves of the true laurel, *Laurus nobilis*, are sold for b-b-bayleaves? Did you know that? While the leaves of the American laurel are poisonous. It occurs to m-m-me there is something significant because I just happened to think—"

Once at a rehearsal break, Pingloss crossed the stage to speak to me. With his head tilted back professorially, he stared at my Adam's apple. I had noticed that he never looked at people, he stared at parts of them as if his glasses had crooked focus. It bothered me, and I always wished he would make himself recall some time when he had looked at a whole person. Clearing his throat three times, he said he had observed that in my scene with the Captain, when he handed me the dispatch from his desk, I did not look at it. What was my reason?

The question confused me, and I hesitated to give the simple answer for fear it would not be consonant with his concept of dramatic reality. I countered. I said, "Am I supposed to look at the paper?"

He said, clearing his throat, it depended on what I was feeling. He asked what I was feeling.

"Feeling?"

Hadn't I thought about it? Hadn't I thought what I was supposed to feel?

I stared at him. I had been so eager to learn, to apply what I *had* learned, and now I stood at the end of the road, on a Broadway stage, with no idea what the director was getting at. Was the extent of my ability a blue-shirt lead? I felt sweat.

He was talking, discoursing. I must have been in a similar situation, he said, I must have had an emotional experience that would guide me, tell me what I should do when I picked up the paper, and he talked on until I suddenly remembered a thought I once had about Morrie Wertz: the man could intellectualize a plate of grits!

I waited for Pingloss to run down, which he did in his usual way, suddenly stopping as if he'd forgotten the subject. Then I spoke. "I don't look at the paper, the dispatch, when I pick it up for two reasons."

He looked now as if trying to think what paper I was talking about.

"The paper the Captain hands me. I don't look at it because he is talking to me, the Captain is, and he outranks me and I think I'd better give him attention. The second reason I don't look at the paper he hands me is because he is talking to me and he is the star of the show and I think I'd better give him attention. At the same time, I am thinking—I'm thinking that I've been directed to stand in front of him so that half the audience can't see his piece of business handing me the paper and my affective memory is making me wonder how long he's going to accept that."

A pause and then Pingloss walked away as if he had just remembered a Russian footnote to the effect that tea from a brass samovar can be drunk from a glass or a cup and it made him wonder why samovars were made of brass.

Equity allows four weeks to rehearse a new play. We were in the fourth week and had hardly touched the last act. The actors were tense; *they* would be the ones on stage when we opened, not Max Pingloss. We went to New Haven Sunday morning to open Monday night. The show was a heavy one with its seven scenes on wagons that were supposed to move right and left, upstage and down. At 3:30 in the morning, Monday, with the waiting actors cold and bleary, the first scene of the first act was still not in place. Pingloss was giving futile, incoherent instructions to the stagehands, who, on overtime, were patient, unperturbed by the lack of progress.

Suddenly from the dark in the auditorium we heard a shout, a snarl. "Get out of the way! I'll take care of this!" We recognized the man running down the aisle. It was the Broadway operator, Teddy Garlick. He had staged everything from carnivals to striptease extravaganzas and had made fortunes. We had heard the rumor that in a thrust for culture, Teddy Garlick had invested in this show. He had come to New Haven in the night to check how his culture was doing and he was now about to protect his investment. It was wonderful to behold—like an experienced driver with a voice of incontrovertible authority, he yelled "Mush!" and the stagehand huskies fell into line and the sets were soon gliding like swans called to a feeding. Pingloss sat and watched, just the scholar observing.

I think the cast might have overlooked some of this ineptness if we had not become aware of his small-man's sadism. There was a featured player in the cast, Lorelei Unger, who in years past had been, for a dozen seasons or so, the hottest ticket on Broadway. She had a purring style that stirred lust and humor at the same time. Now she sat day after day with impressive dignity, patient, obedient, willing to serve. We became aware that Pingloss called her to *all* rehearsals, with never an exception such as he granted others, whether she would be needed or not, and we began to see his contempt for Lorelei Unger.

I thought I knew why. She was old-school, she had succeeded even before the book was written and he was sure that of all the cast she was the only one who had probably never even heard of the book and would not be interested, and he was punishing her presumption in still trying to act. If this was right, I resented it, but then I thought it didn't matter, I didn't see how he could win against her dignity. Later, however, when I read her obit and learned she had died in an insane asylum, I wondered if this might have unsettled her, the fact that her wonderful world had come to Max Pingloss and his colors—three shades of flux.

We were playing Baltimore, the second week on the road, and one night I came to the theatre early and found a boy who had a small part with his head down on the dressing-room shelf, crying. He had just had word his brother had died in New York. I took the telegram out of his hand and read it. It was from his sister saying their mother would like him to come home.

I went to the stage manager and asked if it was possible for the boy to be released to go home to comfort his mother; I knew his part could be easily covered.

Pingloss came in as we were talking, and the stage manager turned to him, explaining the situation and asked if the lad could go. "No," Pingloss calmly answered, "I think not. I think tonight I will hear him read some other part."

The stage manager looked at him as if Pingloss had uttered the greatest obscenity he had yet heard. An accumulated wrath exploded as he yelled, "You goddamn wormy bastard, *LET THAT KID GO!!*"

The stagehands stopped to watch. Pingloss' second reaction shocked me as much as his first. Imperturbably, lightly, indifferently, he said, "All right," and walked away.

A few months later I was doing a stint in Hollywood and met Pingloss in the front office of the studio where I was working. Before I could check myself, I blurted, "What are *you* doing here?" He said he was under contract, was going to direct a picture. Only four days later, a writer asked me at lunch if I had heard what happened to Pingloss. He had been fired his second day.

When the head of the studio reviewed the rushes to see what Pingloss had done in his first day directing a moving picture, he saw that Pingloss had chosen the most static scene in the script, had sat the two actors in the scene on a garden bench and had shot an inordinate amount of footage of their thoughtfully dull conversation.

Hollywood was less tolerant than Broadway, although the fact is that Max Pingloss was never given another Broadway play to direct. Nevertheless he has done well. He became an actors' guru, the teacher of the true histrionic art, and there are those who say they owe what they are to him. Which may be true.

And still audiences stand up and cheer for the girl from Kansas and the boy from the Bronx who don't know where they got it and have no theories. This does not, and of course should not, deter those who hope to improve, whether by codification or otherwise, the techniques and styles of theatre acting, even though in this age of hypothetical conviction part of the result has been to question the very purpose of the stage, as Mr. Lee Strasberg, director of a student theatre, recently has in an interview in the *New York Times*.

Mr. Strasberg would appear to speak with authority for, the *Times* said, "The Actors Studio is not at all unsure of its place in the modern history of the American theatre." The *Times* then reported that Mr. Strasberg "drew a distinction between what he called 'the entertainment part of the theatre and . . . the theatre as it remains in the history books.' " Mr. Strasberg said, "The entertainment part . . . can be better taken over by the mass media . . . therefore the theatre can center on . . . the great plays of the past, of the present, of the future."

There may be some who will maintain that such plays as *Agamemnon* and *Medea, Macbeth* and *Lear, Le Bourgeois Gentilhomme* and *Uncle Vanya* were designed to entertain, and they might question which great plays of the past Mr. Strasberg has in mind. For the answer we can only watch to see what Mr. Strasberg's theatre offers, having been assured it will not be entertaining.

All of which leaves the suspicion that it may have been easier to be a spectator, to respond and enjoy, when writers and actors believed they must first entrance, fascinate, communicate—in short, entertain—whether in Shakespeare or such simple-minded sludge as *O'Flynn from Mexico.* They entertained *us* as we really were every day, here in our home town—down at the opera house—tonight. If lucky, we saw them on the street, saw them eat—often restaurant owners who enjoyed the custom of the actors would advertise: "COME AND WATCH THE ACTORS EAT"—saw them on in-person display in front of the theatre before the show, willing to let us believe that men and women can carry magic and gifts as beautiful and potent as the voice of Edwin Booth.

All a pleasure as explicit as

Our revels now are ended. These our actors,
As I foretold you, were all spirits, and
Are melted into air, into thin air;
And, like the baseless fabric of this vision,
The cloud-capp'd towers, the gorgeous palaces,
The solemn temples, the great globe itself,
Yea, all which it inherit, shall dissolve,
And like this insubstantial pageant faded
Leave not a rack behind. We are such stuff
As dreams are made on, and our little life
Is rounded with a sleep.

☛ 13

Curtain Call in Silence

It would seem to be forgotten. The road—meaning regular entertainment for the whole town as given by actors accustomed to trouping—has retired into scrapbooks. There is now a college circuit which books concerts, poetry readers, lecturers and occasionally a play of special literary merit and student interest.

Otherwise the attractions that are booked for general road-showing are either inexpensive, one-set, small-cast plays or larger shows of broad appeal because of a star with a reputation beyond the theatre and/or the fame of the show itself, which may have been acquired in any number of ways.

Yet, despite the decline, the road may still be "where the money is" when the attractions are wanted and when they play huge auditoriums, which is possible now that actors are electrically amplified like guitars. *Hello, Dolly!* with Carol Channing grossed $208,232 in Richmond for one week, eight performances (after the country had heard Louis Armstrong singing the song), and in one week, ten performances, took in $295,120 in Oklahoma City. But all this is obviously a far cry from the era when there was something at the local theatre every night and that something was live, played by actors who brought it in person. Now that most shows do not even go out of town for tryout, it is possible for an actor to have a career without ever packing a suitcase.

Can it mean that all actors soon will be material only for the scissors of editors, that the fabulous invalid may actually be inhumed in a shroud of tape? As ever, it is too soon for crape. Where the road was there is new theatre, "regional theatre," and tonight live actors speak to live audiences in Minneapolis, Dallas, San Francisco, Princeton, Pittsburgh, Cincinnati—a list of places that is beginning to look like a road sheet of the past. Equity reports that once again there are more actors working outside New York than there.

New theatres are being built—some as simple as modern box architecture, some as grandiose as the Kennedy—and they often seem as far from tradition as the smell of their chilled filtered air is from the scent of Stein's greasepaint. Yet—if we pause, stop the rehearsal to think—we know we are here, we know it all exists, because they kept the curtain up.

Up because that player of the forgotten name was so damned funny that very first performance of *Lysistrata*, because they turned them away at the Globe with *Richard*, because he was such an amusing Lord High Executioner, because she put her elegant legs in tights, because he lost his shirt playing *The Wild Duck*, she skipped their hearts taking off her wig to reveal Willie's Mother, he made them want to go to war by threatening to throw Uncle Tom to the hogs, and she could make them believe she saw the dagger before her—because they filled a need of contact that films, religion, encountering, even easy sex can't seem to satisfy as well.

At the curtain tonight, answering the call, they are present. They came through blizzard, from a dinner of grease at the hotel, made themselves up immaculately in dressing rooms fit for rats, earning applause from commoners clinging to their sense of moral primacy; packing, snapping their trunks to make the jump to—what difference the place?—to an *audience* waiting, hoping for a few hours of forgetfulness or enlightenment as to who they are, why this way, what they might be even though human. It was wearisome, took stamina with a trace of madness, but they are here for the call, having arrived via the Aspiration and Tradition.

The curtain is still up even though there hasn't been a road show in Cheyenne in years. Something is the same despite the contrivances of change.

•

The new theatrical season is opening with a rush. . . . A glance at the annual Roster of Theatrical Companies suggests that this season will perhaps be the most active the American theatre has ever known. General conditions outside the theatre are favorable for a very good season.

—New York Dramatic Mirror, September 9, 1905

RICHARD MANSFIELD'S PLANS

Rehearsals of Don Carlos *began last Thursday, and the preparations indicate a performance and spectacle beyond anything this artist has done. . . . A company of 117 has been engaged. . . . In addition to* Don Carlos, *Mr. Mansfield will make productions of Shakespeare's* King Richard III *and* The Merchant of Venice, A Parisian Romance, Beau Brummel *and Stevenson's* Dr. Jekyll and Mr. Hyde. *Following three weeks at the Grand in Chicago, Mr. Mansfield will dedicate two new theatres in Anderson and Goshen, Indiana. Thence he goes directly west to Omaha, Denver and San Francisco. . . . The tour will continue to Los Angeles, New Orleans, Baltimore, Philadelphia, Pittsburgh, Cincinnati, Saint Louis, Detroit, Toronto, Buffalo and Boston into New York for his annual four weeks in April.*

—New York Dramatic Mirror, September 23, 1905

A New Méliés *Film*

AN ADVENTUROUS AUTOMOBILE TRIP

Paris to Monte Carlo

A Farce Comedy in Moving Pictures

Length 660 feet *Price $100.*

This film has been shown during the past summer at Klaw & Erlanger's Aerial Gardens, New York, with Enormous Success. Their rights expire Sept. 1, when the film will be Ready for Open Sale. We anticipate a heavy demand.

Kleine Optical Co.

—New York Clipper, September 2, 1905

Page

13 Since the producer was not likely to pay: Alfred Harding, *Revolt of the Actors* (New York: Morrow, 1929), p. 7; *American Magazine*, June 1910, p. 209.

A small self-selected group of producers: Stagg, *op. cit., p.* 17; Poggi, *op. cit.*, p. 11.

14 Syndicate had signed up a thousand choice theatres: Poggi, *op. cit.*, p. 13.

As Frohman explained to a reporter: Lloyd Morris, *Curtain Time* (New York: Random House, 1953), p. 285.

The new efficiency and the appetite for entertainment: George D. Ford, *These Were Actors* (New York: Library Publishers, 1955), p. 134.

"Sisterville [W.Va.]—New Auditorium: *Cahn's Official Theatrical Guide*, p. 122.

What changes and improvements since that night: George Sands Bryan, *Edison* (New York: Knopf, 1926), p. 130.

16 The leading actor, Dustin Farnum: Owen Wister, *The Virginian* (New York: Macmillan, 1902), Foreword.

Foreign patents on the "toy": Arthur Mayer, *Merely Colossal* (New York: Simon and Schuster, 1953), p. 3.

18 In 1880 . . . fewer than 5,000 actors: *U.S. Census: Population Engaged in Specific Occupations* 1910/1880.

2. A Different Illegitimate Birth

19 "To prevent and avoid the many mischiefs": Richard Moody, *America Takes the Stage* (Bloomington, Ind.: University Press, 1955), p. 201.

20 If New Englanders could have treated their emotions: Mary C. Crawford, *Romance of the American Theatre* (Boston: Little, Brown, 1913), p. 36.

21 "I have been to one play": *Ibid.*, p. 104.

We know that the first professional troupe: *Ibid.*, p. 23; Howard Taubman, *The Making of the American Theatre* (New York: Coward, 1967), p. 35.

22 Governor Dinwiddie presented them: Margaret Mayorga, *A Short History of American Drama* (New York: Dodd, Mead, 1932), p. 35.

Attitude of the Puritans in the Mother Country: Oral S. Coad, *The American Stage* (New Haven: Yale University Press, 1909), p. 9.

Newport was tried, but there were laws: Moody, *op. cit.*, pp. 39, 41.

23 There were those who supported the actors: Taubman, *op. cit.*, p. 51.

In Philadelphia, the people who wanted amusement: John B. McMaster, *History of the People of the United States* (New York: Farrar, Strauss & Giroux, 1964), v. 1; Barnard Hewitt, *Theatre U.S.A.* (New York: McGraw-Hill, 1959), p. 43.

24 A remarkable subterfuge: *Ibid.*, p. 26; Taubman, *op. cit.*, p. 28.

Notes

1. Tonight: All's Well

Page

2 "The handsome coat is of pale mauve cloth": *The Theatre: Illustrated Magazine*, January 1905.

3 310 other troupes leaving New York: New York *Dramatic Mirror*, August 1905.

5 "If you're not going up, get out of the way": Allan Keller, *The Spanish-American War* (New York: Hawthorne Books, 1969), p. 160.

7 228 different shows through the winter: New York *Dramatic Mirror*, September 1905.

The theatre symbolized the new release from drudgery: Foster R. Dulles, *A History of Recreation: America Learns to Play* (New York: Appleton, 1940), p. 67.

In Springfield (2 nights): New York *Dramatic Mirror*, Nov. 11, 1905.

"Direct from New York" was the clincher: Jerry Stagg, *The Brothers Shubert* (New York: Ballantine, 1969), p. 101.

9 This *was* the business, touring: Jack Poggi, *Theatre in America* (Ithaca, N.Y.: Cornell University Press, 1969), p. 45.

Charles Frohman, had ten thousand employees: Glenn Hughes, *A History of the American Theatre* (New York: Samuel French, 1951), p. 239.

Some three thousand theatres in America: *Julius Cahn's Official Theatrical Guide*.

"FIRST CLASS HOUSE to open April 25th": New York *Dramatic Mirror*, April 8, 1905, p. 3.

10 "AMERICUS [Ga.]—Pop. 10,000": *Cahn's Official Theatrical Guide*, p, 275.

11 This was called wildcatting: H. R. Hoyt, *Town Hall Tonight* (Englewood Cliffs, N.J.: Prentice-Hall, 1955), p. 3.

Page

25 Douglass felt so encouraged: *Ibid.*, p. 28; Arthur Hornblow, *History of the Theatre in America* (Philadelphia: J. B. Lippincott, 1919), p. 101.

26 John Hodgkinson arrived: *Ibid.*, p. 190.

27 "Hodgkinson was a wonder": *Ibid.*

"To indulge a taste for playgoing": Crawford, *op. cit.*, p. 24.

"His ignorance of all": Hornblow, *op. cit.*, p. 190.

28 Edwin Booth had built: Edward Wagenknecht, *Merely Players* (Norman: University of Oklahoma Press, 1966), p. 150.

"Joseph Jefferson was also": *Ibid.*, p. 191.

"Edwin Booth, Dec. 23, 1886"; *Edwin Booth's Route Book* (Players Club).

"Albany, N.Y.": New York *Dramatic Mirror*, Sept. 2, 1905.

31 "In the year 1838": Joseph Jefferson, *Autobiography* (New York: Century, 1890), pp. 164–167.

3. You Should Have Been Here in the Old Days

33 "THEATRICAL MANAGEMENT": Sol Smith, *Theatrical Management* (New York: Harper & Brothers, 1868).

37 The camp meetings had become: C. A. Johnson, "Frontier Camp Meeting" (*Mississippi Valley Review*, June 1950); Alice Tyler, *Freedom's Ferment* (Minneapolis: University of Minnesota Press, 1944); John Kennedy, *Camp Meetings* (Newburgh: Paremeter and Spalding, 1826), p. 8. "Camp Meeting Hymnody" (Minneapolis, *American Quarterly*, v. 4, Summer 1952), p. 112.

38 "Springfield being the capital": Jefferson, *op. cit.*

39 Mobile and New Orleans where yellow fever: Hewitt, *op. cit.*, p. 43.

His talent was such: Taubman, *op. cit.*, p. 84.

Actors who played with him: Eleanor Ruggles, *Prince of Players* (New York: Norton, 1953), p. 19.

Tyrone Power: Crawford, *op. cit.*, p. 250.

40 "[We were] anticipating": Tyrone Power, *Impressions of America* (London: Bentley, 1836).

43 Despite the still strong feeling: Edgar Johnson, *Charles Dickens* (Boston: Little, Brown, 1952), p. 445.

However, in keeping with the nature of drama: William R. Alger, *Life of Edwin Forrest* (Philadelphia: J. B. Lippincott, 1877), p. 241; Richard Moody, *Edwin Forrest* (New York: Knopf, 1960), p. 80.

"Late in the winter of 1823": Smith, *op. cit.*, p. 26.

44 He had a magnificent body: Wagenknecht, *op. cit.*, p. 97.

"I never heard anything": *Ibid.*

45 Walt Whitman thought he was phenomenal: Hoyt, *op. cit.*, p. 93.

There was a question: Hornblow, *op. cit.*, p. 57.

Forrest announced he would give: Morris, *op. cit.*, p. 89.

"With a slow and heavy step": Alger, *op. cit.*, p. 241.

50 "ELEGANT THEATRICAL CRITICISM": Moody, *Edwin Forrest*, p. 168.

Page

50 "Forrest's critics: Morris, *op. cit.*, p. 99; Wagenknecht, *op. cit.*, p. 107.
Whenever he acted in *Damon*: Morris, *op. cit.*, p. 197.

4. The Saints Enter the House of Satan

53 The men who laid out the towns: Arthur M. Schlesinger, *Rise of the City* (New York: Quadrangle, 1971), p. 63.
By that time the thrill of pioneering: Dulles, *op. cit.*, p. 68; Schlesinger, *op. cit.*, p. 50.
55 A Reverend W. G. Elliott gave a "Lecture . . .": Smith, *op. cit.*, p. 208.
56 as the Howard family was aware: Edward B. Marks, *They All Had Glamour* (New York: Julian Messner, 1944), p. 70.
60 "I have considered your application": Hoyt, *op. cit.*, p. 70.
61 The ad, except perhaps: Hewitt, *op. cit.*, p. 174.
62 "Among the audience": Hewitt, *op. cit.*, p. 174.
70 In the succeeding years: Crawford, *op. cit.*, p. 381.
74 "GRAND [New York City]—*Uncle Tom's Cabin*": New York *Dramatic Mirror*, Sept. 23, 1905.

5. Hits! Palpable Hits!

76 While the actors took their bows: Morris, *op. cit.*, p. 273.
The Civil War ended: Ward Morehouse, *Matinee Tomorrow* (New York: Whittlesey House, 1949), p. 87.
The only thing that relieved: Harding, *op. cit.*, p. 110.
77 William Penn started breweries: Edward B. Dunford, *A History of the Temperance Movement* (New Haven: Lecture at Yale School of Alcohol Studies, 1943), p. 143.
George Washington would fight: Herbert Asbury, *The Great Illusion* (New York: Doubleday, 1950), p. 14.
Grandmother Brown: Harriet C. Brown, *Grandmother Brown's Hundred Years* (Boston: Little, Brown, 1929), p. 21; John A. Krout, *Origin of Prohibition* (New York: Russell and Russell, 1967), p. 74.
"No child was properly christened": Krout, *op. cit.*, p. 38.
78 The Rev. Leonard Woods: Asbury, *op. cit.*, p. 13.
John and Abigail Adams worried: Page Smith, *John Adams* (Garden City, N.Y.: Doubleday, 1962), p. 668.
130 performances, breaking the custom: Dulles, *op. cit.*, p. 113.
81 Watkins ruined his health: *Ibid.*, p. 113.
82 "Father, dear father": Sigmund Spaeth, *Read 'Em and Weep* (New York: Doubleday, 1927), p. 149.
83 era of "combinations": Poggi, *op. cit.*, p. 4.
a stock company—so called because: Edmund Fuller, *A Pageant of Theatre* (New York: Crowell, 1965), p. 225; Dulles, *op. cit.*, p. 108.

Page

83 "a sweatshop life": Gladys Hurlbut, *Next Week East Lynne* (New York: Dutton, 1950), p. 25.
we are told by a diarist: Maud Skinner, *One Man In His Time: H. Watkins, 1845–1863, From His Journal* (Philadelphia: University of Pennsylvania Press, 1938), p. 67.
After this original stock company era: Poggi, *op. cit.*, p. 4.
84 a member of the audience in Philadelphia: Dulles, *op. cit.*, p. 109.
Walt Whitman: Poggi, *op. cit.*, p. 7.
Even in remote places: Schlesinger, *op. cit.*, p. 292; Poggi, *op. cit.*, p. 7.
85 had begun a union in 1886: Hewitt, *op. cit.*, p. 237.
ELYRIA [Ohio]: New York *Dramatic Mirror*, January 1905.
in the case of *The Old Homestead*: Hoyt, *op. cit.*, p. 92.
86 As a biographer said: James Jay Brady, *Life of Denman Thompson* (New York: E. A. McFarland and A. Comstock, 1888).
87 "*Old Homestead* in Keene, New Hampshire": Moody, *op. cit.*, p. 113.
Country people were becoming aware: Frederic E. McKay, *Famous American Actors of Today* (New York: T. Y. Crowell and Co., 1896), p. 391.
94 With almost no education: *Ibid.*, p. 300.
95 "His face is beautiful": *Ibid.*, p. 307.
The Gelbs in their superb biography: Arthur and Barbara Gelb, *O'Neill* (New York: Harper & Row, 1962).
97 "In the role of Dantès": McKay, *op. cit.*
98 "1905–6": New York *Dramatic Mirror*.
99 "There is scarce a new word": New York *Dramatic Mirror*, Nov. 3, 1900.
100 Yet the audience there could be sharp: Morris, *op. cit.*, p. 174.
Mother and her about-to-be: Constance Rourke, *Troupers of the Gold Coast* (New York: Harcourt, 1928), p. 125.
102 "She can dance a regular breakdown": *Ibid.*, p. 192.
103 "Yes, we started out quite fresh": *Ibid.*
When she played San Francisco: McKay, *op. cit.*, p. 323.
104 Charles Frohman, 1905": Morris, *op. cit.*, p. 272.
A boy from Sandusky: Hewitt, *op. cit.*, p. 253; Schlesinger, *op. cit.*, p. 294.
105 There were complaints: William Winter, *Other Days* (New York: Moffat, Yard and Co., 1908), p. 307.

6. Life on the Road

110 In the slow trains: Hoyt, *op. cit.*, p. 11.
111 It was an era of the "junctions": *American Magazine*, June 1910.
115 "The new theatre at Natchez": Smith, *op. cit.*, p. 52.
117 The players were briefly the best-known: Ruggles, *op. cit.*, p. 32.
120 When the all-male theatre: New York *Dramatic Mirror*, May 15, 1905.

Page

121 For there, in the year before: Mark Sullivan, *Our Times,* v. 2 (New York: Scribner's, 1927), p. 622.

7. Gentility in Makeup

123 American actors was Mr. John Drew: Ward Morehouse, *op. cit.,* p. 77; William Winter, *Shadows of the Stage,* v. 1 (New York: Macmillan, 1892), p. 28.
Drew came from a line: Schlesinger, *op. cit.,* p. 292.
124 There were actors of such genius: Crawford, *op. cit.,* p. 327; Hewitt, *op. cit.,* p. 201.
No American actor has been: Wagenknecht, *op. cit.,* p. 186.
"Business was bad": Jefferson, *op. cit.*
125 Several people were trying to dramatize *Rip*: Wagenknecht, *op. cit.,* p. 190.
"He [Jefferson] was anxious": Crawford, *op. cit.,* p. 330.
126 going to see Jefferson, year after year: Moody, *op. cit.,* p. 172.
128 no other actor but Joe Jefferson: Wagenknecht, *op. cit.,* pp. 186, 192.
130 "The most remarkable thing about Jefferson": *Ibid.,* p. 186.
"He was the most lovable person": *Ibid.,* p. 187.
a photographer placed his picture: New York *Dramatic Mirror,* Mar. 29, 1905.
131 It is impossible to leave: Crawford, *op. cit.,* p. 140.
"I called at the house": Jefferson, *op. cit.*
132 Edwin Booth was the theatrical equivalent: Taubman, *op. cit.,* p. 119; Moody, *op. cit.,* p. 202.
133 "In Boston, the opening night": Crawford, *op. cit.,* p. 311; Ruggles, *op. cit.,* p. 40.
134 When Edwin was eighteen: Moody, *op. cit.,* p. 202.
In San Francisco, Edwin: Lloyd Morris, *op. cit.,* p. 169.
a melodrama, *The American Fireman: Ibid.,* p. 169.
"MRS. JEROME: [*Sighing*]": Ruggles, *op. cit.,* p. 66.
136 Edwin . . . blamed himself bitterly: Wagenknecht, *op. cit.,* p. 126.
"If he will but apply": Ruggles, *op. cit.,* p. 72.
"It was palpable that the part": *Ibid.,* p. 72.
McCloskey . . . years later told reporters: Ruggles, *op. cit.*
139 *Hamlet* for one hundred nights: Morris, *op. cit.,* p. 201.
The repertoire of parts: Winter, *Shadows of the Stage, op. cit.,* p. 287.
Not long after, he was playing: Wagenknecht, *op. cit.,* p. 143.
145 There is also the recorded opinion: *Ibid.,* p. 129.
J. J. McCullough, a proud actor: Morris, *op. cit.,* p. 226.
146 Ellen Terry felt hostile: Wagenknecht, *op. cit.,* p. 130.
"Its sweetness and strength": *Ibid.*
147 "he approached his task reverently": Moody, *op. cit.,* p. 202.
"He had just finished": Winter, *Shadows of the Stage, op. cit.,* p. 181.

Page

148 "He knew that he always acted": Wagenknecht, *op. cit.*, p. 193.

8. Moist Eyes and Wet Pants

152 The list of great actresses: Hornblow, *op. cit.*, p. 230.
153 It opened in New York: Hewitt, *op. cit.*, p. 187.
the snarls of disapproval: *Ibid.*, p. 187.
157 America was learning: Charles A. and Mary R. Beard, *Rise of American Civilization* (New York: Macmillan, 1933), p. 805.
"But," says a biographer, "his pride": Morehouse, *op. cit.*, p. 18.
The emphasis was on effects: Dulles, *op. cit.*, p. 215.
159 The Metropolitan Printing Co.: *Cahn's Official Theatrical Guide*, p. 116.
160 Another sample of melodrama: Dulles, *op. cit.*, p. 215.
Under the Gaslight: Maurice W. Disher, *Melodrama* (London: Rockliff, 1954), p. 13.

9. Expressive Music

167 The origin involves a comedian: W. T. Marrocco and Harold Gleason, *Music in America* (New York: Norton, 1964), p. 261.
168 "*O Ladies and Gentlemen*": Jefferson, *op. cit.*, p. 6.
172 What did the minstrels in: Moody, *op. cit.*, p. 88.
173 He was given four days: Marrocco and Gleason, *op. cit.*, p. 276.
"I have concluded . . . to pursue": Gilbert Chase, *America's Music* (New York: McGraw-Hill, 1955), p. 283.
Born in a town called Lawrenceville: David Ewen, *Popular American Composers* (New York: H. W. Wilson and Co., 1962), p. 62.
174 They heard that William Wheatley: Cecil M. Smith, *Musical Comedy in America* (New York: Theatre Arts Books, 1950), p. 14.
176 The *Tribune* said: Hughes, *op. cit.*, p. 199.
177 On November 25 . . . *Pinafore*: Cecil M. Smith, *op. cit.*, p. 71; Lloyd Morris, *op. cit.*, p. 237; Dulles, *op. cit.*, p. 237.
178 A people long depressed: Edward B. Marks, *They All Sang* (New York: Viking Press, 1934).
He was an Irishman: Ewen, *op. cit.*, p. 87.
180 There was still a market: *Spaeth, History of Popular Music in America* (New York: Random House, 1948), p. 219.
181 Longfellow had given: Cecil M. Smith, *op. cit.*, p. 40.
The most successful was Chauncey Olcott: Morris, *op. cit.*, p. 277.
182 In the old days": New York *Dramatic Mirror*, Oct. 2, 1905.

10. Dirt: Imitation and Real

187 The first person in America: Crawford, *op. cit.*, p. 442.
188 account of her first rehearsal: Edward B. Marks, *They All Sang*, *op. cit.*, p. 251.
described as "exquisite": Crawford, *op. cit.*, p. 443.

Page

190 Her third marriage: Bernard Falk, *The Naked Lady* (London: Hutchinson and Co., 1934), p. 25.
One historian-investigator: Marks, *They All Sang, op. cit.*, p. 243.
especially in Virginia City: Moody, *op. cit.*, p. 175; Dulles, *op. cit.*, p. 173.
Mazeppa in Paris: Crawford, *op. cit.*, p. 442.
191 "without a vestige": Cecil M. Smith, *op. cit.*, p. 13.
192 "the immodest dress": *Ibid.*, p. 15.
A Miss Olive Logan: Coad, *op. cit.*, p. 230.
193 Olga Nethersole was an actress: Morehouse, *op. cit.*, p. 18.
when *Man and Superman* was published: Edward B. Marks, *They All Sang, op. cit.*, p. 54.

11. Climax with a Wrong Ending

196 Uniontown . . . where *Ninety and Nine:* New York *Dramatic Mirror,* September, 1905.
The *Digest* said: Mark Sullivan, *Our Times, op. cit.*, v. 1, p. 365.
198 WILLIAM S. HART: New York *Dramatic Mirror,* Feb. 11, 1899; Jan. 7, 1905.
W. C. FIELDS: New York *Dramatic Mirror,* Dec. 23, 1905.
MARY PICKFORD: New York *Dramatic Mirror,* April 15, 1905.
202 DOUGLAS FAIRBANKS: New York *Dramatic Mirror,* Jan. 21, 1905.
BUSTER KEATON: New York *Dramatic Mirror,* Jan. 7, 1905.
Out on Long Island: New York *Dramatic Mirror,* Mar. 18, 1905.
Charles Chaplin, when he: Kenneth Macgowan, *Behind the Screen* (New York: Delacorte Press, 1965), p. 208.
And when there began to be: Richard Schickel, *Movies* (New York: Basic Books, 1964), p. 30.
205 Dustin Farnum, star of *The Virginian:* Deems Taylor, *Pictorial History of the Movies* (New York: Simon and Schuster, 1943), p. 26.
206 The road story: Poggi, *op. cit.*, p. 30.
"a roadshow in Cheyenne": Kirk Knox, *Wyoming State Tribune,* Cheyenne.
"Road shows in New Bedford": Earl J. Dias, New Bedford.
"road show in Cedar Rapids": Nadine Subotnik, Cedar Rapids *Gazette,* Cedar Rapids.
"Buffalo had seven shows": Terry Doren, Buffalo *Evening News,* Buffalo.
"Louisville had six attractions": William Mootz, Louisville *Courier-Journal,* Louisville.
"Troy had two roadshows": Joseph A. Parker, *The Record Newspapers,* Troy.
207 "Springfield [Ill] has been without": Wayne Allen, *Illinois State Journal,* Springfield.
"Monterey and Carmel": Irene Alexander, *Monterey Peninsula Herald,* Carmel.

Page

207 "Syracuse has four or five": Nevart Apikian, *Herald-Journal*, Syracuse.
"Minneapolis audience is gun-shy": Mike Steele, Minneapolis *Tribune*, Minneapolis.
"In Kansas City": Giles M. Fowler, Kansas City *Star*, Kansas City.

12. Personal: In Confirmation

226 I read in a *New Yorker* profile: *The New Yorker,* May 19, 1962.

Acknowledgments

Obviously the writer of a book such as this must be grateful to many, present and past. I have cited the majority of them in the text and in the list of references. In addition, of those present to receive my thanks I would like particularly to mention Mr. Paul Myers, Curator of the New York Public Library Theatre Collection at Lincoln Center and his staff; Mr. Louis A. Rachow, Librarian, The Walter Hampden Memorial Library at The Players Club; and Miss Maggie Blackmon, Assistant Curator of the Theatre Collection, Museum of the City of New York. No less obliging have been the people at three regional libraries, in Tenafly, Englewood and Teaneck, New Jersey. Also many correspondents, including entertainment editors of various newspapers and the people at a number of state historical societies and libraries. I invite them all, if they wish, to take a brief bow.

Index of Towns and Cities

Index of Plays and Musicals

Index of Songs

General Index

73 74 75 76 77 10 9 8 7 6 5 4 3 2 1